Praise for

My Eyes Looking
Insight Into a Surv

"The rich details of each character and the ....e, mark the reader forever. Menucha Meinstein's prolific writing style transforms Leah's life's journey into a work of art and a textbook on this period."

— **Rabbi Shabsi Alpern**, Chabad - San Paulo, Brazil

"This is the enormous dedication, energy and the giftedness of a brilliant, soulful writer, telling the story of a woman who survived and defied all of her experiences by sharing her story, her message through the living eyes of a beautiful human. Thank you Leah and Menucha for so enriching the world."

— **Miriam Jaskierowicz Arman**, Vocal Pedagogue, Author, Poet and Fine Artist - Tiberius, Israel

"... told with depth and painful honesty. ... a tribute to a friendship between two women, who had the courage to look back on the past together and the skill to tell of that past so compellingly."

— **Michael Berenbaum, Ph.D.**, Professor of Jewish Studies, Sigi Zieirng Institute - American Jewish University, Los Angeles; Former Project Director, US Holocaust Memorial Museum; Former President and CEO of Survivors of the Shoah Visual History Foundation

"I have been given a chance to promise that we will do everything to lead our children into a world where all the atrocities she suffered will no longer be possible ... We both know that education is paramount. ... her story matters to history."

— **Jürgen Borsch**, Consulate General of the Federal Republic of Germany - Miami, FL

"This book is a "must read" for the younger generations who may not realize how much evil man is capable of, and may not understand why it is so important for all of us to stand, together, against the apostles of hate."

— **Ranley Desir, MD**, Haitian Born Cardiologist - Aventura, FL

"The Holocaust only acts as a backdrop...Her eyes may be looking back, but they always revert to a future of hope. It will impact and imprint itself on every reader's heart. Leah Roth's struggle and survival interpreted by this new writer, to be watched in the future, produces a prize-winning portrait not to be missed."

— **Hindi Diamond, z"l** (1924-2014), Former Latin American Foreign Correspondent - TIME/Life, Newsweek, United Press, McGraw Hill, NBC; Former VP South Florida Int'l Press Club

"It has a Bashevis Singer or even Dylan Thomas-like quality to it. This is an essential read to comprehend those times so that it can be passed on from generation to generation."

— **Alan Freeman**, Vice President, Jerusalem Foundation - Jerusalem, Israel

"Luckily for humanity, Leah Cik Roth met Menucha Meinstein, who was able to elicit and express the extraordinary courage and perseverance in one Survivor's tale, as an example to the world of the meaning of LIFE! Remember Forever!!!"

— **Avi Hoffman**, Entertainer, child of Survivors and Director of the Dachau Album Project - Coral Springs, FL

"I will be recommending this memoir to all students of the Nazi Holocaust of 1933-1945 as a primary resource, whether they be high school students, college students, or scholars and professors. It must be read and reread and retold for future generations."

— **Miriam Klein Kassenoff, Ph.D.,** University of Miami – Coral Gables, FL, Director, Holocaust Studies Summer Institute/ School of Education, District Education Specialist/Holocaust Education, Miami-Dade County Public Schools/Miami Beach Holocaust Memorial

"At the age of nineteen — the same age Leah was when she fought for her life in Auschwitz — I was denouncing the atrocities of the Holocaust. I denied that Survivors like Leah existed....Menucha's beautiful prose combined with Leah's raw account of being a Holocaust Survivor make this work a compelling personal narrative ... It has freed me from the prison in my soul."

— **Angela King, M.A.**, Former Skinhead; Editor-In-Chief, *Life After Hate*, Specialist: Violent Extremism - Miami, FL

"... told beautifully and with great compassion ... unique in the galaxy of holocaust memoirs ... the portrait of an era ...an invaluable tool in a renewed approach to education for our time."

— **Joyce Klein**, Educator, Storyteller, & Playwright - Jerusalem, Israel

"... a page-turner, a tear jerker; a true Kafka-like story so true that it couldn't be written as fiction."

— **Joseph Lebovic, Ph.D.** (h.c.) Humanitarian and Philanthropist, President, Lebovic Enterprises, Ltd., BILD Lifetime Achievement Award; Joseph and Wolf Lebovic Jewish Community Campus - Toronto, Canada

"To those who care and those who need to care. Together they have created a manuscript that is truly Theater of the Mind."

— **Arnold Mittelman**, President/Producing Artistic Director, National Jewish Theater Foundation - Coral Gables, FL

"...a must-read, for to be moved to action one needs to be moved emotionally.... eye opening, sometimes heartbreaking and other times inspiring. ...alive with the colour of emotion. From Survivors of the Holocaust and also from Survivors of genocides from Rwanda and Cambodia, I am struck by the similarities in their experiences as they are from different times, continents and cultures ...message of hope and the importance of understanding and tolerance... the power of positivity."

— **Maurice Ostro, OBE, KFO**, Prime Minister's Holocaust Commission, Vice-Chairman, Council of Christians and Jews - United Kingdom

"Leah and her progeny are the victors, not the vanquished...a testimony of historical and personal endurance that must be told again and again."

— **Wendy Reiss Rothfield, MSW, LCSW** - Aventura, FL

"... an act of love, combined with exquisite writing... Menucha turned Leah's rough-hewn, untold story into a powerful work of art ... At times it reminds me of Isaac Bashevis Singer, the Yiddish Nobel Prize winner, at times of the beautiful prose of Elie Wiesel ... stands out, not only for the beauty and clarity of the writing, but for how it finds an indelible mark on the reader's heart."

— **Roberta Shapiro, M.ED., LCSW, NBCCH**, Creator and author, "The Calming Collection" - Miami Beach, FL

"Your visit to the Memorial...is well written, moving, poignant and sad....I will remember it, for it reinforces my original commitment to make the Memorial a sacred place."

— **Kenneth Treister**, Architect, Sculptor, and Author, "A Sculpture of Love and Anguish," Miami Beach Holocaust Memorial - Winterhaven, FL.

"Permit me to express my words of appreciation for the 'mitzvah' you have performed by producing this manuscript. As Rabbi Klein writes in his eloquent introduction, so many survivors will soon disappear without having left their stories recorded. You have made sure that Leah is not among them. For that, I feel that I, and the Jewish people, owe you a debt of gratitude. 'Yasher Koach.'"

— **Peter Weisz** , Peter Weisz Publishing - Boca Raton, FL

"...she enables others to enter into the pain and ongoing history of her family during the Holocaust within the wider context of the world and a unique biblical people going back millennia....helped teach the world a lesson about what can happen when we do not remain vigilant and true to our highest and best selves as all children of God."

— **The Reverend Dr. Priscilla Felisky Whitehead**, Minister Emerita, The Church by the Sea (United Church of Christ) - Bal Harbour, FL

My Eyes Looking Back at Me

Menucha Meinstein

Insight Into a Survivor's Soul

As Told By
Leah Cik Roth

ISBN: 978-0-9861293-0-8
Library of Congress Control Number: 2015901707

Printed in the United States of America February 2015

Permission from Kenneth Treister to use photos from his book, "A Sculpture of Love
and Anguish" - Copyright © 1993

Editor: Marcia Cohen, Esq.
Book Cover, Design and Layout: Peggy Swanson

10 9 8 7 6 5 4 3 2 1

1. Memoir – Historical. 2. Holocaust survivors – Florida– Interviews.
3. History – Holocaust. 4. Holocaust, Jewish (1939-1945) – Czechoslovakia – Personal
narrative. 5. Auschwitz (Concentration camp) – History. 6. Holocaust, Jewish (1939-
1945) – Poland. 7. Germany. 8. Roth, Leah Cik.

Key words:

Adolph Eichmann Trial; Anti-Semitism; Auschwitz, Poland; Bat Yam, Israel; Birkenau,
Poland; Brano; Poland; British Mandate; Brustury, Czechoslovakia; Brusturyanka
River, Czechoslovakia; Brutality; Budapest, Hungary; Bucharest, Roumania; Bologna,
Italy; Carpathian Mountains, Slovakia; Chust, Czechoslovakia; Concentration
Camps; Crematoria; Gas chambers; Death; Death March; Dr. Mengele; Faith; Final
Solution; Forgiveness; Ghettos; Graz, Austria; God; Haifa, Israel; Hadera, Israel;
HaTikva; Hope; Humenné, Slovakia; Inhumanity; Jewish Weddings; Kibbutz Gesher;
Kibbutz Life; Koshalie, Czechoslovakia; Krakow, Poland; Logging; Loneliness;
Nonantola, Italy; Nazi; Nazi Bomb Factories; Nazi Slave Labor; Nuremberg Trials;
Padova, Italy; Palestine, Israel; President Masaryk, Czechoslovakia; Pre-WWII
Czechoslovakian History; Resilience; Righteous Gentiles; Satmar, Roumania;
Sekernice, Czechoslovakia; Sighet, Roumania; Soul Writing; Starvation; Stettin,
Poland; Stutthof, Poland; Tattoo; Temeswar, Roumania; Torture; Vienna, Austria;
Village Life; Wallenberg; Wig Making; Yellow Star of David; Zion; Zionist.

We acknowledge the very generous gift of our friend, Tzippy Faye Rapaport Holand, which will enable Leah's story to reach many more readers around the world, and to open hearts to Holocaust awareness. With gratitude, Menucha Meinstein and Leah Cik Roth.

"In memory of my dear parents,

Tzvi Rapaport, z"l
and
Tova Abromowitz Rapaport, z"l

and my beloved husband,
Joshua Holand, z"l.

I support this worthy Holocaust educational project as my legacy for my children, Sharon, Adina and Jeff, and grandchildren, Evan, Zachary, Nicole, Justin and Tyler.

Leah's story is OUR *story. We must* REMEMBER *to tell our children so that they will pass it on to their children, strengthening our link for future generations to* NEVER FORGET.

With gratitude for my beautiful life and all who have helped me to become who I am today."

Tzippy Faye Rapaport Holand
Holocaust Survivor

With recognition and gratitude to

הקרן לירושלים
THE JERUSALEM FOUNDATION
مؤسسة صندوق القدس

for launching our book

My Eyes Looking Back at Me
Insight Into a Survivor's Soul

In Concert with the

מרכז למוסיקה ירושלים
JERUSALEM MUSIC CENTRE
President: Murray Perahia

on Yom Hashoah April 16, 2015

Published for the

triumph of light over darkness.

Commemorating the

70th Anniversary of the end of

World War II

May 8, 2015

Victory in Europe Day

Donations for this educational project may be made to the One to One Foundation,
2000 Island Boulevard, Tower Suite 3004, Aventura, Florida 33160
myeyes@meinstein.net

Leah's Dedication

With sad and loving memory of my
dear Father and Mother:
Shlomo Cik and Elka Adler Cik

And Siblings:
Brothers: Bencion and Hershel
Sisters: Risi and Malchi
and 106 Aunts, Uncles and Cousins
(z"l - May their names be remembered for goodness)

Among the six million brethren who perished
and generations who would have been born.

Contents

Foreword

A human being does not *have* a story; a human being *is* a story.

If we each look at our own history, we see stories are not built from memories, but quite the reverse. Memories are built from the stories we tell about our lives. Some of the stories we tell about ourselves are tragic, while others may be joyous. All will consist of a journey, a struggle, a challenge, and hopefully growth in the end. We are creatures who need more than food and water. To thrive we need meaning, and to have meaning we need to know and tell our stories to ourselves and to those around us.

A man I once met told me, "I have spent my entire life learning, making mistakes, and growing. I have finally attained wisdom." He then added, "Sadly, I have no one to tell it to." Leah Roth has a story to tell. It is a story of love, of yearning, of loss, and of unimaginable pain. However, if one reads between the lines, Leah's real story is one of perseverance, courage, and faith. It is a story of overcoming the odds, losing everything, and then building again.

However, there is another story behind the story, which I believe sheds light on this beautiful and powerful memoir.

I first met Leah on the eighth night of Chanukah five years ago. Professionally I am a rabbi and director of Mishkan Miami: The Jewish Connection to Spiritual Care; it is a program funded by the Greater Miami Jewish Federation. Our program sponsored a project where families went to visit Holocaust Survivors in the Jewish community, to light candles with them, share Torah and a gift, and simply spend some time together. This program was called "Light up the Night."

My assignment was to go with my children and visit Leah. As we entered her home on that evening, pictures of the past adorned the wall. She took my children on a tour, sharing a bit about her life. Some of the pictures in this book we saw that evening. As Leah tells it in this memoir, it was clear to me then that Leah was "one tough woman"!

We had a few refreshments, lit candles, and then she escorted us to her work table. We sat down by her computer, which she had recently learned how to use. Leah showed us a major project she was working on. Her late husband, Menachem, had left tomes of handwritten Hebrew notes on the Torah, commentaries of great insight and erudition. She took the initiative to translate his material into her broken English, toiling hours every day on the computer; she feared her transcription was a never-ending project, and that she would never complete it. Reflecting later upon this, I realized that in this formidable project, Leah was trying to hold to her past in some way. The past weighed heavily upon her, and I sensed a woman who was trying to capture the entirety of her history, but simply did not know how. On leaving her home that evening, I felt sorrow for her losses and suffering.

Fortunately, the story does not end here.

Mishkan Miami for six years has run a series called the Refuat HaNefesh Fellows program, training volunteers from all backgrounds to become spiritual care providers. Volunteers serve in hospitals, long-term care, hospices or other settings. Some volunteers opt to visit Holocaust Survivors, and through this project some have created lasting relationships.

Menucha Meinstein called me the day before this program began, begging me to accept her, even though the course was at capacity. After her nudging, I reluctantly accepted her into the program. I consider this one of the best decisions I almost did not make.

We connected Menucha with our Jewish Community Services volunteer program, Two's Company, a program, which matches clients with friendly visitors. Menucha was matched with Leah, and a budding relationship emerged. Over the first year, Menucha heard Leah's stories. As a writer, Menucha felt it important for Leah to share these stories with others. They started with weekly writing sessions together. The meetings became more frequent. Leah moved into Menucha's home and essentially, Leah became a surrogate family member. Menucha dedicated herself tirelessly to writing with Leah, and a beautiful and profound relationship has emerged. Leah will tell you about how "Menucha is an angel sent from heaven," but Menucha states that "My relationship with Leah has brought new depth to *my* life."

In addition to the ongoing writing and visits, Menucha took the initiative to create a Bikkur Cholim Society in her synagogue, reaching out to all in the community. In this work as well, Menucha will tell you that although many people have benefited, she has benefited most of all, as her sense of humanity has enlarged in ways she could have never imagined.

That is the secret of bikkur cholim, of visiting those who are in need of our support. Objectively we are supporting them, but on a deeper level, we become the supported.

Two years ago I came to a special meal hosted at Leah's home. Menucha attended with her husband, along with other friends as well. Leah was a wonderful host, and the food was plentiful - chicken soup, roast chicken, potato kugel, and even brisket. It was quite a spread for a Sunday afternoon. Seeing Leah that day, I saw a transformed human being. Confident and happy, she wanted to celebrate the completion of a section of her book, a memoir of the Holocaust no less! She began to read to us selections of her book, selections, which you will read in final form.

We live in a generation that soon will have no Survivors from those darkest of days. So many people leave this world with their stories untold. As Leah approaches her own later years, she has developed the confidence to tell her story to the world. She has been given the voice she never had through her work with Menucha. To give voice to another is one of the greatest kindnesses one can give, and why this book is so special. In a unique way, Leah has been reborn. Behind our tears as we read her story, we celebrate her strength and her life.

May both Leah and Menucha be blessed with many years of health and vitality. Their relationship should be an inspiration to all of us, empowering us to share our own stories with those we love, and to patiently listen to those of others.

Rabbi Frederick L. Klein
Board Certified Chaplain, Master of Philosophy
Director, Mishkan Miami: The Jewish Connection to Spiritual Support,
A Program of the Greater Miami Jewish Federation;
Executive Vice President, Rabbinical Association of Greater Miami

Introduction

Remembering the Holocaust: A Woman's Voice

The unusual and nurturing partnership of Leah Cik Roth and Menucha Meinstein allows for the telling of a forceful and rich life story. The one, a survivor of the murder of Europe's Jews years ago, and the other, a teacher and writer born in a better time and a better place, forge a bond of friendship that releases a complicated and nuanced story. Leah Cik Roth's story is not an easy one to tell – in fact, it has taken her almost a lifetime to get it on paper. Some of her memories are the sweet tales of early childhood, others the tough memories of a motherless child, or an adolescent fending for herself. Still others are the stuff of nightmares – indeed, they come out in Leah's dreams. The telling of this unusual story reaches deeply into the fierce past and also projects the possibility of ethics and compassion into the future. A record of the past made possible by Menucha Meinstein's special gift of active listening in the present, *My Eyes Looking Back at Me* is, at heart, as much about memory as it is about the power of empathy, listening and caring.

It is the evolving intimacy of the relationship between the two women that gives this unusual book such an intimate feel. In telling the story of a life, rather than just a story of war, *My Eyes Looking Back at Me* resists turning "survivors" into artifacts of history, and instead restores a record of a fulsome life. Of course, every life story is unique and precious, leaving traces of the experiences, memories and thoughts of a singular human being. But there is something special in stories of those who lived through the Holocaust – who, against all odds, managed to escape the program of deliberate dehumanization and murder that was aimed at them, and went on to share their stories.

While it is true that all Jews under Nazi control were targets of genocide, Jewish men and women experienced the war years both as Jews and as men and women. For many years after liberation of the concentration camps and the German military defeat, the story of the Shoah was presented by historians in the aggregate. That is, we read what is referred to as "master narratives" – accounts of the Holocaust meant to represent the experiences of the Jewish people as a whole. Such accounts of the collective experience were deeply important, allowing for a broad reconstruction of the events of the past. At the same time, they had certain limitations. The researchers whose crucial work mapped out the Shoah as a historical subject were reluctant to attend to the voices of survivors. And the "master narrative" they constructed reflected, by and large, the experience of men.

Based on research, and relying largely on documents, these researchers mapped out the broad picture of the events that came to be called the Holocaust, or the Shoah, or the Churb'n – that is, the destruction of the Jews of Europe. For a long time, researchers were reluctant to accept the firsthand accounts of Holocaust survivors, preferring instead to build historical knowledge from "official" sources – in large measure, documents produced by perpetrators and abettors of the Nazi genocide. Survivor accounts, many historians believed, were too subjective. They were considered unreliable as evidence in reconstructing an accurate picture of the past. When historians did cite the memories and testimonies of survivors, they did so primarily to provide an illustration – vivid and emotionally gripping – of a set of facts that had already been determined from other, more "reliable" sources.

This attitude left many survivors feeling unheard and undervalued. It is a wonder that, with such reluctant listeners, survivors continued to speak and write about their experiences. Yet they did. Most survivors view bearing witness as a moral obligation – a debt owed those who were murdered and cannot tell their own stories, and an act of faith on behalf of those who will come after.

By now, researchers in all fields who study the Holocaust have come to see the irreplaceable contribution that survivor testimony makes to what those of us who come later can know of these unspeakable – and yet, spoken – events. And – thanks to the detailed remembrances of people like Leah Cik Roth– the fabric of the lives of Jewish women has not been lost. In taking us from pre-war Czechoslovakia to post-war Israel to contemporary Miami, Leah's memory pieces together a lost world. In her story, we see the rhythms of the domestic daily lives of women like her mother, her Aunt Chaya and her

Aunt Ruchel: the scent of the garden, the hum of the market, the preparations for *Shabbat*. Through Leah Cik Roth's eyes, we see food gathered, preserved, prepared; we see the weaving of wigs for religiously observant women; we see the precariousness of childbirth, the many challenges of women's lives, as well as the many acts of kindness that women performed. The attention to detail and the honest account of emotions offer a window into a lost world.

In Leah's account of the war years, we see the rapid assault of genocide on Jews and Jewish communities. Through her eyes, we see, too, the special vulnerability of women – for example, the young pregnant woman who gives birth amid the filth of a cattle car bound for Auschwitz, the selection of young mothers and their children for immediate murder upon arrival there, the humiliation of nudity and body shaving. But her recounting of survival, and of rebuilding a life and raising a family after the war, also reveals women's strength and resourcefulness.

"Often we think horrifying things happen only to others," we read in *My Eyes Looking Back at Me*. Leah's reflections remind us that horrifying things happen to people much like ourselves, to people who – like us – imagine they happen only to others. In inviting us into Leah's life, *My Eyes Looking Back at Me* makes an ethical call to readers, to imagine ourselves in these "others," to listen to their stories with compassion and also obligation to do what's right. Leah says it best when she reflects, "Whenever I am wronged, I speak up. When I see others wronged, I defend them."

Sara R. Horowitz
Professor, York University (Toronto, Ontario, Canada)

Sara R. Horowitz is the author of *Voicing the Void: Muteness and Memory in Holocaust Fiction*, the editor of *Lessons and Legacies of the Holocaust*, Vol.X, and the author of numerous articles on Holocaust literature and women and the Shoah. She served as Director of the Israel and Golda Koschitzky Centre for Jewish Studies at York University, and as President of the Association for Jewish Studies.

My Eyes Looking Back at Me

Insight Into a Survivor's Soul

PART I

Beginnings

Prologue: Tuesdays with Leah

Looking like Queen Elizabeth wearing a cameo brooch and a tight smile, Leah Roth is anxiously waiting for me on the hot pavement of her parking lot in North Miami Beach, Florida.

I roll down the car window as she walks briskly toward my car, pointing a worn hand with big rings and scarlet nails, and commands in her husky voice, "Park in my space, number fourteen, over there. I moved my car to a neighbor's empty spot...you didn't pay, did you?"

Proud and frugal, she doesn't want me to pay those three dollars for parking.

I feel a blast of heat as I scooch out of my air-conditioned car. The weather is its usual midday scorch, even though it is December.

Leah's no-nonsense handshake is as firm as her stocky frame, a hand that has both labored and nurtured. I lean down to hug her as our eyes connect. She cracks a wary smile. I like her, this noble, stern woman.

Raising her eyebrows above her glasses she says, "God sent you to me, and I need a lot of help to express myself in English."

I have come to visit Leah as a volunteer from the Greater Miami Jewish Federation's Jewish Community Services that comforts the lonely, the elderly, the sick, and dying. My job is to help Leah, an Orthodox Jewish Holocaust Survivor, to write her life story. I plan to use my method of assisted storytelling and guided journaling to help Leah overcome hesitation she may have in her revealing her life's experiences.

As we chat on the way to her apartment, her heavy accent makes me wonder how difficult helping her write in English might be. The vitality of her gait surprises me as I follow Leah to the elevator. In her sensible oxfords, she's walking faster than I am. This no nonsense woman is wearing a tailored white blouse tucked into a straight black skirt, accented with a fashionably wide belt. I'm thinking: Leah is a plucky, well-put-together Holocaust Survivor; not the bent over older woman I expected, but upright and vigorous for 85 years old, and certainly not sick and dying.

I follow this sturdy, full-figured, under five-foot-tall woman with soft edges, a fair, sun-spotted complexion with short curly blond hair through her front screen door. As we enter, I see another woman strategically sitting at the breakfast table. Leah introduces her as a longtime friend. As a widow living alone, Leah is careful with visitors. She doesn't know me; I know I'm suspect. The three of us chat over coffee about nothing in particular. She says, "It's good - the coffee." I lean in, listening closely to decipher Leah's awkward syntax. Her friend eyes me.

Leah is positioned on the edge of her chair with her arms leaning on the table as if ready to stand. Her light conversation leads me to believe she isn't one to reveal herself easily.

Leah asks, "From where does your family come? You have how many children?"

Closing her eyes, "An angel sent you to me," she murmurs.

Apparently, I pass her test when she asks me about scheduling our future meetings.

"It will have to be in the afternoon after my aerobic water class. I swim twice a week. It's my major exercise, and I can't miss it."

Leah does appear physically vital and strong.

"Tuesday afternoon works for me."

I agree to meet for three hours weekly – a big time commitment for me.

Leah's friend nods approval and excuses herself, "I need to be going now so you two can get to work."

After her friend leaves, Leah ushers me through her dining room. A candelabra used for *Shabbat*, the Jewish day of rest on the seventh day of the week, and her ceremonial silver wine cup decorate her buffet. Hand-painted porcelain plates displayed in the china cabinet are treasures from happier times.

"I used these things every Shabbat when my husband, Menachem, was living. I don't have company for dinner anymore, and my children live up north." She purses her lips and furrows her brow.

"I'm alone."

I sense she is more than alone. Even though she goes to activities and lives independently, she's a widow, lonesome among her treasures from times long past. Her traditional furniture is from the 1980s, with little frames of family snapshots carefully arranged on the coffee table. Leah gestures toward a wall with a lovely framed watercolor of iris flowers and next to it – scenery of mountains and bridges.

"These scenes I painted in the last twenty years. My favorite flower is the iris. Menachem was proud of me. He never failed to point out my art to our guests."

On the way to the computer room, I notice shelves piled with religious books and many three-ring binders.

Touching the notebooks lovingly, she says, "These are Menachem's notes, handwritten from his Hebrew-school teaching. I brooded over his passing for nearly three years. Then I transcribed and catalogued everything he wrote during his whole career. I still learn Torah from him every week through his writings."

I'm impressed with her vocabulary. "Transcribed and catalogued?"

"Tell me more about your husband Menachem. Did he have hobbies?"

"He loved music and played the violin for me and our guests. He was a Torah scholar."

Leah sits at the computer desk in the sunroom and hands me a bound journal she has written for her children. Thumbing

1990 Menachem playing the violin for Leah

through, I see lists of genealogy entries but very little of her personal story, yet there were statements of insight and perception.

"My wisdom did not originate from scholarly books or training with great masters. It sprang from confronting myself in the most extreme circumstances."

Waiting for my response, she comments, "They should know where I come from and who my family was. I want my family to know how precious it is to have family, to be close to your family." I hear her sadness, suspecting even more importantly, her longing to be remembered.

"I like what you've done. You have a good beginning for an important book. We can expand your story even further," I say.

I suspect she's holding back deep emotions from her tragic past. Once she begins to trust me, I'll carefully encourage her to reveal more details. I'm hoping to bolster her confidence and optimism through our interchange with my method of *Soul-Writing*, digging deeply into her reservoir of memory, helping her uncover her resources of endurance. I know it's a big responsibility, never having worked with a Survivor or even written a memoir. I question if I can really do this. A thought passed through my mind, "If your dreams do not scare you, they are not big enough" (President of Liberia, Ellen Johnson Sirleaf). I can do this.

Looking at over twenty printed pages, I compliment her. "What amazing computer skills you have."

As she leans forward, her eyes sparkle, "I began using the computer only two years ago, when I was eighty-three. It's never too late to learn." She's obviously proud of herself.

"You've already done a lot of wonderful work here. Where shall we begin?"

Straightening up without answering my question, she says, "Menucha, I want to finish my book while I am still here. I want to hold it before I die. Life is only one time. Let's work now."

She relates a few random events from her early life.

Important to Leah is that she was brought up in a religious home, in her precious small village of Brustury, Czechoslovakia.

More importantly, "I grew up without a mother," she says.

Then, hesitantly, Leah only touches on the Holocaust horrors of her teen years.

I'm sitting next to a woman who seems willing to trust me as a new friend. Her memories begin to surface. In spite of bitter sorrow, she cautiously reveals humble gifts of robust toughness from the grit of a tragic youth. I'm hearing her heartbreaking testimony, the inner journey of one who has survived. Leah suffers through every story she tells, reliving the painful emotions. Often she lapses into the language in which an event occurred before bringing it into English. Her deep sadness affects me. I must be constantly aware of the risk and consequences of opening old wounds. Am I sensitive and deft enough to avoid these pitfalls? Can she relive so much agony and sorrow?

We work four hours instead of three, leaving both of us drained and tearful. It's too much for a first meeting, but she can't stop telling me about her life, and I can't stop listening.

"Sometimes I get very tired," she confesses, "but I refuse to give up."

I also am weary, trying to hold in my emotions. Noticing my tears welling up, she touches my shoulder and says softly, "Is this too much for you, Menucha?"

The stoic sufferer is consoling me. We know it's time to stop. We've come a long way since our first handshake only a few hours earlier.

We end with another hug, both of us grateful for our new friendship. Driving home, I think about my little worries and how puny they seem as compared to Leah's life of sometimes unspeakable pain. Yet, I feel her optimism, knowing she finally is ready to talk, hoping she senses I am someone willing to listen without judging her.

I've joined Leah on her mission to help her remember, **Zachor**; to tell, **Emor**; that the Holocaust will never happen again, **Le olam lo yikra od.**

We begin meeting several times a week in her apartment, not just on Tuesdays. I see this is going to be a long-term project, as every day becomes a Tuesday. She's direct, insistent we work as often as my schedule allows. We begin with Leah's homemade cake (not on my diet), but I can't refuse her appreciation and hurt her feelings. I look forward to our ritual of friendship. Sometimes she prepares a big basket of pastries for me to take home to my husband Eddie, not understanding he has diabetes.

One day I invite her to my home for lunch to meet Eddie. I'm sure they'll enjoy each other. Leah resembles Eddie's late mother, also a short European with a roundish soft face who used to love to tell a good story. Both lived thrifty yet satisfying lives.

Leah says chuckling, "If you can make with your own hands, why buy? I love everything I have."

Later her philosophy changes when things become cheaper due the availability of manufactured goods.

"For this price, why bother? Time is money. I'd rather sit and read a book or knit. I read all the time."

At our kitchen table, looking uncomfortable on the edge of her chair, she remarks, "Such nice dishes for everyday? I love these pretty things. My mother taught me that."

As the three of us reminisce about parents and grandparents, our personal boundaries are merging. We are becoming closer friends. Something about her just takes us in, as if we'd known her for a long time. Eddie and I invite Leah to stay for Shabbat. She sleeps in our guest room and we attend the synagogue downstairs. She's appreciative when Rabbi Jonathan Horowitz recognizes her as a Holocaust Survivor, a "national treasure."

Soon, I convince her to stay for a few days at a time during the week, so that we can write intensively. We like her company. I get to know her through her daily routine. Leah's random stories begin to come out a little at a time, like a dripping faucet. I sense much of her tale remains to be told because she relates only dry facts, never how she feels about anything, even though I gently question, "How did you feel when that happened?"

Leah struggles to share her life anecdotally, with immediacy and intensity, emotionally demanding work for both of us. Putting events in chronological order is a challenge. Harder is evoking her deeper feelings about what happened and what they have meant. I am using my *Soul-Writing* method of guided journaling to help Leah safely reveal dark memories of her early life. How will I structure her story into a book? An outline seems impossible at this point with so little information, unusual names and places I've never heard of and couldn't pronounce.

My experience has taught me that if you create a halo of silence, people will trust you and tell you their stories. When someone feels safe, they will share their secrets. With trust comes love, a mutual opening of hearts as our bond strengthens.

Absorbing the horror she suffered, I begin having nightmares of my own. The unfolding of her life awakens new vulnerabilities within me. Could I endure what she had endured? I think not. Often I want to run from her story, but I cannot, and I will not abandon her. We are becoming powerfully connected through this holy work. We are both growing from our collaboration.

During the week, we often sit at my computer past midnight. We have uninterrupted writing time once the phones have stopped ringing. Since she shouldn't drive after dark at her age, our guest room is now her second home.

We are becoming inseparable best friends, spending untold hours together; writing, shopping, cooking, laughing, and chatting as women do. The guest bedroom gradually fills with her things and becomes "Leah's room."

We've adopted one another. Leah has become my "other mother," and I – her "other daughter." We mentor each other in many ways.

When we aren't writing, our home is the hub of late-night reminiscing as we share a beer and a bowl of popcorn. Relaxing this way encourages her to broaden her spellbinding life with more random vignettes. Each story reminds her of another and then another. Leah's memory for detail is astounding. I learn I must always have a pen and paper in hand when I'm with her. I never know when her wisdoms might just pop out. She rarely wastes words on small talk and nonsense, not even on the phone. Everything must have meaning. Eddie and I both love having Leah. Even though our parents are gone, and we're both great-grandparents several times, she nevertheless fills a generational void.

Leah now lives with us for most of the week, and we always spend Shabbat together. We adore Leah, and our old friends have become her new friends. We have had only one fight, and it was in the kitchen, about cooking. She likes fattening food, like chicken soup with noodles, cookies, and cake. She thought she should add olive oil to cooked Shabbat cholent, a stew of fatty meat and beans. I didn't. "It's my kitchen, my space," I laughed. We giggle a lot more now that she's so comfortable with us.

Next to my curio cabinet containing a collection of antique teacups from my mother and grandmother, Leah sits knitting a scarf at our kitchen table by the window. As she knits the details of her life, Leah reminds me of my grandma, also a strong-willed immigrant, with hands that never rest, hands that have created a life of valor, fought life's wars, nurtured children and created abundance — hands that have done much. One yarn leads to another, as each loop hooks to the next. Interlacing the details of her life is significant, and she bravely stumbles through one more insightful story. Leah begins to untangle the knots in her stomach, knitting her to my heart.

After cooking our meal together, we welcome Shabbat on Friday nights by lighting the candles, and Eddie leads us in singing special Shabbat prayers. We linger over a sumptuous Friday night meal in the dining room with salad, fish, soup, and chicken, complete with her details of vivid memories. Everything reminds her of something from her past, beginning with the tablecloths her mother, of blessed memory, used to make.

"This is like in pre-war Czechoslovakia, when we ate the best meal of the week on Shabbat" she tells us, "After fifty-five years of celebrating Shabbat with my husband, I have found the worst time for me, as a widow, is sitting by myself at the table. With you, I am no longer alone."

Sitting on the edge of her chair, ready to help serve, she never fails to thank us for the food and our friendship. I love watching her enjoy the food.

I often wonder why she perches herself on the edge of her chair and leans onto the table.

At night she waits for me to say goodnight and turn off the lights. She never closes the bedroom door because she painfully remembers the claustrophobic feeling of being helpless, locked into the ghetto, the cattle car and the gas chamber.

I like to think she feels protected with us, as she did before her young world fell apart. Bits and pieces of her story keep coming, and we struggle to knit them into chronological order while maintaining Leah's distinctive European, English-as-a-second-language voice. Finally I understand why she always sits close to the edge of her **chair**.

Psychologically scarred from the Holocaust, she is instinctively ready to flee on the spur of the moment. She doesn't realize she does it.

"Always remain vigilant and be aware," she often intones. "Everyone is not your friend. Trust no one except yourself."

CHAPTER 1

My Earliest Memories

Brustury, Czechoslovakia, 1930
(Presently Bystrytsya. Ukraine)

I was only five years old, but I knew something was wrong.

My father, *Tatuka,* unfolded a white handkerchief from his back pocket and put it in my hand. With a kiss, he sat me on the wooden chair next to my mother's bedside. Afternoon shadows from a kerosene lamp darted across her face. Though only in her early thirties, my mother looked old and weak.

In his softest voice, he explained, "*Leichuka*, your *maminka* is not well. Shoo the flies away from her face."

A single tear ran from the corner of *Maminka*'s eye. Feebly motioning for me to lean close, she rose on her elbow to kiss me and slipped back to her feather pillow.

"*Maminka*, I love you," I whimpered.

Early the next morning, sounds of whispering voices and sobbing from my four older siblings awakened me. Through sleepy eyes, I saw our Shabbat candles flickering from the floor, rather than on the table. It wasn't Friday night, our Shabbat. It was a weekday morning. *Maminka* was lying on the floor with her green shawl completely covering her, even her face. She didn't move.

Shivering, I moved close to my *tatuka*. "What's wrong with my *maminka*?"

He picked me up and whispered, "Your *maminka* has passed away."

"Passed away" meant nothing to me.

Grown-ups murmured, "The fish...she got food poisoning from the fish. She was so young."

Malchi and I later became sick and threw up for days.

I asked my seven-year-old sister Malchi, "Will we pass away, too?" Of course, she didn't know.

Soon our house was filled with people wailing. The commotion made me dizzy and even sicker. Ladies were coming and going, hauling large tubs of cold water from the well, distracting me from watching the older women prepare *Maminka* for burial.

Chaya Adler, my mother's eighteen-year-old sister held my hand tightly.

We stared intently as pious men took *Maminka* out of the house on a board. She was wrapped in her shawl. Walking very slowly, they carried her around our big yard, followed by a procession of sad townspeople. They passed the household storage shed and the carefully piled stove wood and my swing hanging from a tree. *Tatuka* walked behind, consoling my older brothers and sisters. Bitter sobbing muffled the dusty sounds of shuffling feet.

Today I understand that they lingered at every corner so *Maminka* could say good-bye to everything. They walked around the vegetable patch, her beloved flower garden, and through the front gate. She had been friendly with everyone. Even the priest's wife, with a newspaper tucked tightly under her arm, watched curiously as they carried *Maminka*, still sleeping under her green shawl, through the gate toward the synagogue.

Chaya eased her grip and took me back inside the house. Speechless, we watched from the doorway as the procession disappeared down the road in the crisp spring air. I didn't understand that *Maminka* was now gone forever.

The crying grown-ups were gone, and now the house felt strange and serious. Were we waiting for something else to happen?

I questioned Chaya, "When will *Maminka* come back?"

Chaya answered with a plate of potato pancakes to divert my attention. "Here, eat this. Have some more sour cream." Food was my comfort. This was not the only time in my life Chaya would be there to soothe me.

Overnight, our home became empty and unbearably sad. Confused and feeling alone, I didn't know how to express my gray loneliness. *Maminka* had adored me. Where were my hugs and kisses?

A five-year-old was not included in the ritual of *shiva*, the custom of Jewish bereavement. Standing aside, I watched *kriá*, a display of intense grief, as my father and my two brothers tore their lapels with loud, heaving sobs. They remained deep in prayer, shrouded in mourning for the entire week.

I had never seen my father cry before. His pain was so intense, it gripped me, squeezing my insides. Sitting in the corner with my sisters, we cried. I could hardly breathe.

Many friends and neighbors came to the house with food to nurture our motherless family. Father now milked the cow, did the gardening, and was in the house more to care for the children. He did most of the things *Maminka* had done.

Our white cow, Biala, died the next day. Grown-ups thought the cow had also been poisoned. Biala drank the water that we used to wash the fish dishes from our Shabbat meal. Nothing was ever thrown out or wasted, not even dirty dishwater. For our milk, Father soon bought a new cow we called Sula.

On the outside wall of the cowshed where Sula lived, there suddenly appeared a big long piece of white stone, curved on one side. My sisters told me it was our mother's head stone. It lay sideways through the whole summer until the snow came. I was afraid of this heavy stone, a constant reminder of my mother, my deep longing to hear her voice, yearning for her tender touch. Maybe there was a ghost hidden inside. Maybe it could grab me. When the slippery snow covered the mountain, my brothers took the marker away to place it on her grave. I was never taken to see her grave. The stone was gone, but not forgotten. Memories of *Maminka* and this stone shadowed me during my lifetime.

My father seemed to cry all the time, and it made me sad and insecure. With tears wetting his face, he told us about the beautiful handmade things *Maminka* had created: embroidered underwear, monogrammed towels, tablecloths, wall hangings, and tapestries decorating our walls.

It must have taken my mother over a year to make the white linen tablecloth I still have, now ivoried from years of aging. She had embroidered it in the early 1900s, before her wedding. There is a continuous pattern of stitched flowers with small, cutwork lace-embroidered circles. I am proud of her fine, meticulous work. Back then it was a custom for fourteen-year-old girls to begin making handmade things for marriage. This tablecloth was used just for decoration, put on the table only after the dishes had been cleared from the Shabbat meal. We never ate on it.

Every Shabbat, it was our family's custom to take a walk after lunch before we took our naps. For years, *Tatuka* wept on these walks as he told us stories about our *Maminka* so that we would remember her. I sensed that my parents had been very much in love by the way he spoke of her.

I had no idea that in years to come I would see death every day without the dignity given to my mother.

CHAPTER 2

Pre-War Czechoslovakia: My Precious Village

March 1925

I wonder if my mother was happy that I was the third girl, instead of another boy, born in our small two-room house in Brustury, Czechoslovakia. I arrived just before the Jewish holiday of Passover in the early spring of 1925. My parents named me Lenka, a Czech name meaning light. Cute and chubby, with blond curly hair and hazel-green eyes, I looked like my father. My family tenderly called me by my Yiddish name, *Leichuka.* My name would be altered many times during my life. In school, my Czech name was Lenka as on my birth certificate. Some adjustments in Hungarian (Lily) and German (Elka), were made to fit my circumstances and different locations during World War II and even thereafter. In Israel, I changed my name to Lea. Now I spell my name *Leah*, like in the Torah.

I was the fifth child in an active family of two boys and two girls: Bencion, 9, Hershel, 6, Risa, 4, and Malchi, 2. My favorite was my oldest brother Bencion, my protector. He resembled our mother with her dark brown hair.

We lived in a small house built by *Tatuka* just before I was born. Our home was in a tranquil country village situated in the Carpathian Mountains near the Polish border then in the southeastern part of Czechoslovakia. There were about three hundred families in our village. About one hundred families were Jewish and the rest were Christian.

Tree-covered mountains and forests hovered on both sides of our pastoral lands. Dirt roads led to homes, most with small porches. The elite traveled in buggies. Horses pulled wagons with benches for ordinary people. A single bus carried travelers to surrounding villages. My mother's sister Ruchel and my uncle Hershel Lebovic had a lumber mill. Uncle Lebovic and the local priest owned the only two cars in the village. Our Jewish neighbors next door had something even more special – a truck. It had to be cranked for the motor to start just like the bus and both cars. Children had fun standing around to watch the cranking. We would wait for the car to make the first noise when the motor started up.

The main toy in our yard was a wooden swing that hung by twisting ropes from a leafy tree. Twirling round and round was so much fun. Risi and Malchi often played with me on a teeter-totter our father made for us. I was clever and athletic for my age, and games with balls were the most fun for me. On idle days when the older kids were in school, I enjoyed playing alone, building a house and making bread with mud and stones. My grief softened as I remembered how to be the carefree little girl I had been before my mother died, but it never left me. Anguish from my mother's death has stayed with me my whole life.

Maminka's sister, Aunt Chaya, lived next door. She had married an older, widowed cousin who had grown children. She told me she wanted to have her own baby but he didn't want more children, so they didn't have any. Too young to understand what he had to do with it, I wondered why she wouldn't just have a baby on her own if she wanted one so badly. I didn't think about asking anyone. Aunt Chaya cared for me as if I was her own child, and I felt loved.

After I walked to her house in the snow, she would take off my shoes and place me on a shelf above the oven to warm my little feet. She sang lullabies to soothe me as she wiped away my tears. Sometimes, when the windows were open, she would hear me crying and come running to comfort me. Aunt Chaya knew I loved to eat, so she would prepare special food just for me: warm blintzes, thin pancakes filled with homemade cheese, kreplach, and dough pockets filled with cheese.

"Can I have more sour cream and potato pancakes?"

I knew Aunt Chaya would give me whatever I wanted. She was always happy to put food in my tummy, as *Maminka* had. She also sewed beautiful dresses and bloomers for me. Wearing these pretty clothes on Shabbat and other special occasions made me feel special. Aunt Chaya grew as dear to me as I was to her. She was like my second mother, and I – like her daughter. When her husband was away on business trips, she would take me into her bed because she was afraid to be alone. I still remember Aunt Chaya in my private prayers.

We were friends with everyone in our village, although both Jewish and non-Jewish children mixed only at school, not at weddings or funerals. The priest's wife had been friendly with *Maminka*. It was unusual for a Jew to have a Christian friend, especially one married to a Russian Orthodox priest. This couple was generous and shared their well water with us. The bucket always hung over the well, inviting us to help ourselves.

Our other neighbors were Russian and German peasants. I was never aware of anti-Semitism or any friction because of cultural or religious customs until I was older and lived away from home. In fact, our neighbors helped us on Shabbat by lighting the stove fire for warmth and milking our cow, because Jews aren't supposed to do work on Shabbat. As young children, we were instinctively aware of our differences. A Jewish home could not be mistaken for the one of a gentile. Jews had *mezuzot* on their doorposts, special handwritten parchments containing a prayer from the Old Testament honoring One God. The Russian Orthodox community had crosses on their rooftops. The church sat next to their cemetery, and they had their own priest.

We had two synagogues with one rabbi for both, our own cemetery, and a *mikveh*, the ritual bath. My father went to the *mikveh* every Friday before Shabbat. In the morning, my family went to the older, larger synagogue. I used to walk with my father and carry his glasses because he wouldn't carry anything on Shabbat. His glasses were made differently than today. They had no side temples, only a nose clip. Upon arriving to the synagogue, I knew to go up the tall stairs to the windowed women's section. Men and women sat separately for prayers. If a woman wanted to listen, she had to open an inside window so she could look down at the men's section. From our upstairs view, we saw the sparkling crystal chandeliers lit with candles for the Friday night service. They had burned out by morning.

Men would not have breakfast before prayers. There was a break in the service when congregants left the synagogue, walked to members' homes to have schnapps and cake, and then would return to finish their prayers. *Tatuka* would only eat in certain homes, where he trusted the kosher observance.

Christians had their customs and we had ours. We were respectful of the diversity among our neighbors. On their holidays and at funerals, we observed long lines marching somberly down the road. With devout expressions on their faces, they carried crosses and special flags, walking in a procession to their church. The priest had long hair and wore a black robe with a matching tall pointed hat. In Brustury, everyone married within their own community and most families had several children. Many mothers from both communities died in childbirth, leaving children just as lonesome as I. We were classmates in school; whether they were Jewish or not, we had to be friends with them.

Our rural mountain village was divided into two parts by the wide and cold Brusturyanka River. Because it was turbulent, I waded and splashed in the safety of shallow inlets with my brothers and sisters during the warm summer months, even though we girls didn't know how to swim. We wore our old underwear instead of bathing suits.

Bencion warned me, "Don't go out too far. The water can quickly become deep." I was obedient.

We improvised floats by knotting together the legs and sleeves of men's long johns, then blowing them up like balloons and tying them off at the neck. We would lie on top of them like rafts.

"It's my turn now," I would insist.

All afternoon we would have fun playing and skipping flat stones over the water from the riverbank before we would come home cold and hungry for a bowl of warm bean soup with corn bread and butter.

Many tourists came through our village during the summer on the way to the lush mountains. Shepherds played musical instruments while happy milkmaids yodeled along their way. The visitors needed places to sleep and food to eat. Villagers rented out extra rooms in their homes, looking forward to this additional income. Affluent tourists were teachers and intellectuals from all four sections of Czechoslovakia, from west to east: Bohemia, Moravia,

Slovakia, and Carpathia. In the mountains, there was a big hotel where the tourists would stay.

It was exciting for me to start school. Once we went on a fascinating field trip from the outskirts of Brustury to the Polonini Mountain pastures to see how peasants milked their cows and goats. Animal stalls smelling of freshly cut hay were kept extremely clean. We also watched them make hard cheese from sheep's milk called *Bryndza*. They shaped it into large round discs. Recalling the sharp deep flavor of this cheese still makes my mouth water.

In warm weather, Christian families from our village would go to their second two-room homes in the surrounding mountains to work their summer crops. They grazed livestock in the meadows owned by the townspeople, including my father. The farmers would prepare hay by cutting and drying the grass in the sun, then bundling it into bales for the winter months. It was brought down the mountain on sleds after the first snow. My father would receive bales of hay for his cow in exchange for rent for his land. At the same time, farmers would bring their livestock and chickens back to their homes in Brustury.

In the mountains, they used to grow vegetables for their families. Everyone grew their own food. Jewish households had at least two gardens. As a small rural farm community, we ate only what we could grow. In the backyard we had vegetables: onions, cabbage, green beans, peppers, kohlrabi, kale, radishes, corn, tomatoes, cucumbers, and our main staple – red and white potatoes. Father would hire workers to tend our vegetable garden. In the front of the house, in a smaller garden, we grew fragrant flowers: red roses, white carnations, and lavender. I looked forward to Friday afternoons when I would clip the most beautiful blooms for our Shabbat table. I would take my time to place them in a vase, one by one, until I thought they were perfect to greet that holy day.

I would prepare food to feed the geese before the Shabbat candles were lit. I would pick greens, cut them into small pieces and mix them with corn. Our fifteen geese were fed in the morning before going to float on the river for the rest of the day. Each family would mark their geese with a special cut between the webbing to show to whom they belonged if they strayed. Our geese had two cuts in the web of the right foot. They always knew to come back home where they were well fed. During the winter, the geese were kept in a special coop and were fed corn to fatten them up. The cooking fat rendered from geese was enough to last for a whole year. The birds were kept on ice until they were roasted or smoked. The dark goose meat tasted sweet, similar to that of ducks.

We were self-sufficient except for bulk items such as flour, oil, sugar, salt, yeast, chocolate, cocoa, coffee and tea, which we would purchase from the deliveryman who used to take his wagon to warehouses in the nearby cities of Tiachovo (presently Tiachiv, Ukraine) and Chust (presently Khust, Ukraine). He would come back with the goods and drop them off at the shopkeepers' where we would pick up our orders.

The Jews of Brustury kept strict kosher dietary laws and had their own grocery stores, butchers, tailor shops, shoemakers and barbers.

The grocery store was busiest on Thursday afternoons, with women shopping for food to cook for Shabbat. The store was owned and run by a husband and wife. Sometimes elder children would help their parents stock the shelves. Dry food was stored in big burlap sacks, dispensed by the workers to the customers. The store had a monopoly on yeast used for Shabbat bread, and a percentage of profits would be donated to the synagogue. To sell cigarettes and liquor, a special license was required. Both cigarettes and liquor as well as sugar were sold at fixed prices and taxed by the state.

The butcher would buy livestock from the owners and the Jewish ritual slaughter took place before the carcass was given to the butcher to prepare the meat for sale. This was a very expensive treat we could afford only on Shabbat. The butcher had a huge cleaver that he would use to cut up the meat on a big tree stump at the back of the shop. Today it would be called a butcher block. With the purchase of meat, he would give away the bones for *cholent*, our special hot Shabbat beef stew cooked overnight. The bone marrow gave it a special flavor, one we anticipated all week.

When I was eight years old, Sula, our cow, gave birth to a calf. The baby was allowed to nurse for eight days and then was sold to the butcher. I cried when they took the baby away from its mother. I felt sorry. We couldn't afford to feed two cows, but Sula gave much more milk for months after the birth. Some people raised goats instead of cows because a goat ate less and needed less space. I knew two families who had goats and drank goat's milk instead of cow's milk.

I used to love to visit the shoemaker whose home was always warm with laughter. We would watch the father, Zalman, sitting in the kitchen on a small low chair in a corner, hammering nails into worn shoes with his rough, polish-blackened hands. A friendly man, he always asked me where I was going. He wore a dirty apron over his short, stocky frame and a black *yarmulke,* a skull-cap worn by orthodox Jewish men. The children would sit around him sing-ing school songs, and he would always tell jokes. Unlike in my home, there was a lot of laughter there. On the small shoemaker's table lay tiny wooden nails, a hammer, and small pliers, with shoelaces hanging from a hook. He had outstanding memory. He knew to whom each pair of shoes belonged without having to write down their names. Back then, because shoes were so expen-sive, we could not afford to throw them out; instead, we had to have them fixed. We could afford to buy only one pair of shoes a year. The shoemaker's daughter was my close friend from school. Her mother would feed us slices of bread with honey. It was yummy. It felt like a real home.

Yankel, the Jewish tailor, made suits for men. Customers brought him fabric from a fabric store. Suits were made to exact measure – one for every day and the other for special occasions. All men's suit jackets were styled the same, not with rounded front finishing like today, but rather with square "cor-ners" in front. Yankel worked together with his sons, who were learning as ap-prentices. Once I went to the tailor with *Tatuka* to have a new suit made for Passover and "Uncle" gave me red and white candies. Children called him un-cle because he was an older, friendly gentleman. I was welcome everywhere I went with my father. I went back with him for fittings several times. These were special outings for just me and my *Tatuka.*

The men and boys would go to the hunchback barber's kitchen for short haircuts before Shabbat and holidays. When I was little, I would ride with Bencion to the barber as his passenger on the front handlebars of his bicycle. I felt very important accompanying my brother when he would come home from yeshiva, a boy's school for higher Jewish learning. The barber seemed to look right through me. He was scary. I guess because he was different. He had a short leg and a hunched back. I'd never seen a person with a deformity before.

A young Jewish boy Hirsch would pick up our village mail from a post of-fice in another village and would deliver it to our homes on his bicycle, even on Shabbat. My father would reprimand him for riding the bike on Shabbat be-cause he was strictly observant. Hirsch surely wouldn't be a match for either of my sisters. When the streets were muddy from the rain, he would have to walk. We received mail every day. Letters and packages were sent through the post office. We had no phone or electronics in those days, so all communication had to be handwritten or be passed through by word of mouth.

Dr. Drexler lived about seven miles away, in the next town. We had health insurance, so I could go to the doctor when I needed medical help. I would walk seven miles to his home office, which was in his house, and back. When someone was very sick, the doctor would find out about it by word of mouth and travel there in his two-wheeled horse "chariot." Doctors would receive the same respect as teachers.

Our teachers, both men and women, lived in our Brustury village.

Some families had many children and made use of the one midwife in town.

The German midwife Erika was a busy woman and had no family. She was impaired with one short leg and a significant limp. Thoughtless children mimicked her uneven walk. Erika was renting a nice room in a well-kept house. I saw it once when she invited a few girls for milk and cookies. She loved children and would always sing songs with us. We knew she was a lonely, depressed old maid. One time she went to the river to try to end her life. At the last minute, she was rescued by a kindly person.

Our house in the newer part of Brustury had a large kitchen with a roomy pantry and a big bedroom that I shared with my parents until I was five. After that, I too slept in the kitchen on a crowded bench with Malchi and Risi.

Our kitchen had many functions. It had a brick oven for baking and a separate stovetop for cooking. Two pails of well water for drinking and cooking stood on a small bench in the corner, near the door. Long benches with hinged seats were used for sitting at the kitchen table. One chair at the end of the table was my father's. Only he sat in that chair. No one would even come near it when he was away at work. At night, we would convert the two long benches into beds by opening them at the hinges. They were hollow inside and could hold two small mattresses filled with hay, a blanket, and thin pillows. Each bench would make a bed for two or more children. There was no heat at night, but goose-feather blankets kept us toasty warm. On winter mornings, the windows would be covered with frost, forming patterns of beautiful white trees and flowers. Risi and Malchi shared one bench and Hershel and Bencion slept on the other. Even a table in the corner could be opened to become a bed.

The centerpiece of the kitchen wall was *Maminka*'s framed needlepoint with red and blue words stitched on a white linen background. These Hungarian words spoke to our hearts: "Foolish is the man who worries. Foolish is the man who cries. Life is short, and the grave is long and dark." This would remind us that no matter how much a person worries, life passes and, eventually, ends. Worry changes nothing. Action accomplishes everything.

A small embroidered satchel hung under a large mirror in the dining area, a bag that held a comb, a brush, and a small mirror, shared by the whole family. I remembered how *Maminka* used to love to brush my hair in the kitchen at night. She would make me feel special when she kissed me and said, "Your hair is so nice and shiny. You have beautiful curls." I felt special and knew that she loved me.

Our father was the only person in our house to have a toothbrush. The children didn't even have a toothbrush to share. In those days, most people lost their teeth to decay at a young age. I once found my mother's dentures in her bedroom drawer after she had died.

Our next-door neighbor pulled teeth for money. Through the open windows, I could sometimes hear people scream during the process.

Our house overlooked the Brusturyanka River from a high bank. We could see Grandfather Adler's house on the other side. Most houses like ours were built of timber with roofs made of wooden shingles. Our house was small, had no running water or an indoor toilet. We had no electricity, telephone or radio. Our lifestyle was primitive by today's standards. There were no trash cans as we had very little garbage. There was no canned food or wrapped paper cartons. The only trash was worn-out shoes or clothes that had been thrown down the riverbank. Potato peels, carrot tops, and leftover cooked food was given to hens and geese.

Our bathroom was an outhouse in the backyard. Every Friday afternoon, before Shabbat, children would cut leftover community newspapers into squares for toilet paper. We would put the squares into a cloth bag, which hung on a rusty hook. We used to take turns cleaning the toilet bench and the floor. Everything in the whole house was made tidy and clean in honor of Shabbat. We washed the wooden floors, changed the kitchen towels, polished the furniture and covered the table with the white linen cloth *Maminka* had made before she got married.

Kerosene lamps lit our home. We had two stoves. The cooking stove in the kitchen was made of bricks. The older kids had to scrub the shiny iron cooking top until they could see their face reflections on the surface. For the bitter cold winter, there was an iron heating stove in my parents' bedroom. Everything required hard work. Our home was spotless. When I was older, my job was to scrape ashes from beneath the stove grill once a month. It was dirty work. We would mix the ashes into the soil of our vegetable garden.

A big lamp hanging over a rectangular kitchen table glimmered with a dim circle of light. Its thin hand-blown glass covered the flame. Soot from the fire had to be cleaned from the glass every day. It cracked easily. When I was older, I would often be sent to the shop down the dirt road to buy a replacement cover.

The kitchen was the larger of the two rooms. It functioned as a living room as well as the kitchen. The other room, which was a bedroom during the week, would become a dining room for Shabbat meals. We had both an attic and a cellar. In the attic, we would store old clothes, Passover dishes, used bottles, along with onions and garlic that were braided together with ropes that we hung from the ceiling. In the cellar, we would store potatoes, cabbage, beans, and beets for the whole winter. Carrots were buried in the sand on the floor to keep them fresh. In another separate food pantry, next to the kitchen, we kept our cornmeal, flour, sugar, and dishes. In the shed, outside the house, we kept our bathtub, laundry supplies and big utensils used for kneading bread. Next to our house there was a barn with our dairy cow, geese, and chickens.

Our laundry was kept in a tall barrel that stood over a flame that warmed the water. After soaking awhile, the laundry was boiled all night long before being washed, then rinsed in the clean river.

Everything had a place and everything was in its place.

My grandparents, the Adlers, raised their family in the house across the river. Aunt Chaya grew up there with my mother and nine other siblings. As the eldest son, mother's oldest brother Uncle Bencion inherited the house.

Bencion and Chaya were popular given names. Uncle Bencion lived with his wife, Aunt Hinda, and his unmarried sister, Aunt Hansee. He passed away from an illness when I was only seven, so my memory of him is limited to a framed photograph that was hanging in their bedroom.

My father, Shlomo Cik, from Sepinka, Romania, and my mother, Elka Adler, were married in Grandfather Adler's house in the early nineteen hundreds. The marriage was arranged by their parents. I understood they liked each other from the very first sight.

My father would always talk about my mother with fondness. At one time, he described her Shabbat appearance to us: she wore a black silk scarf with long fringe and beautiful clothes. In his eyes, she was delicate and feminine. He was proud of her skills in homemaking and her ability to speak five languages – Yiddish, German, Czech, Hungarian, and Russian. In our home we spoke Yiddish and our parents spoke Hungarian if they didn't want the children to understand their conversation. Father, taller than Mother, had a reddish beard and mustache and always wore a three-piece suit with a long jacket and hat when leaving the house. Softspoken and polite, he was a humble gentleman, regarded as an intelligent man, often writing legal papers for the Russian peasants. Father also spoke several languages: Yiddish, German, Czech, Hungarian and Russian, as well as Romanian. He worked as an accountant for Uncle Lebovic's timber mill in Brustury and for the synagogue.

When the Adlers arrived to Brustury, it was still under the reign of the Austro-Hungarian Empire. They bought large parcels of land. They were smart and very wealthy. They built themselves a spacious house, much bigger than ours, as well as a synagogue and a ritual bath for the first Jewish families who settled in Brustury.

Aunts, uncles and cousins lived in nearby villages and visited one another often. Our whole family was close. When we had a visiting rabbi, our family was privileged to gather with other townspeople at Grandfather's house to celebrate Shabbat and Jewish holidays. For a wedding, all Jews in town would be invited with all their children.

I often pleaded, "When can we go play at Grandfather's house?"

"Soon," I was told, "on Shabbat afternoon, for sure."

"What will we play?" I asked.

"We're going to play the button game," Malchi said.

I loved the colorful buttons and I especially enjoyed winning them. Everyone had a button collection they would bring from home. Sitting on the ground in a circle, we would dig a small hole in the dirt and try to flick our buttons into the hole with a snap of our finger. Only one snap was allowed per turn. If someone's button went into the hole, everyone had to pay with his own button. The goal was to win the most buttons. I cried if I lost. If I won, I felt grown up.

1880 Postcard of Grandfather's House in Brustury, Czechoslovakia

My grandfather's big house, across the river from us, was the heart of our family activities. It was a single-story building on a big property with gardens, trees, and a deep water well. The outer buildings included an ice shed and a barn for cows, hens, and ducks. It even had a separate shed for domestic helpers and a basement storage which could be accessed from the side of the main room through a door that would open in the floor.

A tall ladder provided access to the underground cellar that was the size of the whole house. From the outside, there was a short flight of stairs that would be used to bring in the merchandise.

This basement kept the food cool, preserving potatoes, carrots, cabbage and other produce throughout the winter. It was chilly and smelled damp.

Creepy families of bugs lived among the big heavy wooden barrels where beer was being aged. Refrigerators had not yet come to Brustury. Our life was simple and we were resourceful.

Every day on the way to school, I walked with my friends over the bridge past Grandfather's house. We also went this way to the big synagogue.

The biggest room of the house was used as a community center by townspeople of all religions, a gathering place for various events. It had another important function of a hall for Jewish weddings where all eyes would be on the beautiful bride dressed in pure white. The bride's hair was adorned with pearl ornaments to be later broken into smaller pieces and given to all the ladies and young girls as good-luck gifts. I thought, someday, I would also make a beautiful bride. There was lively dancing to violin music. I was allowed to stay up late and eat delicious food. After chicken and geese, we would gorge on a honey loaf, apple strudel, and sweet fluffy cakes.

The smaller room of the house was used for many things, even a tavern. A wall painting in big letters was a reminder to customers to drink: "If you drink, you will die. If you don't drink, you will die." The government mandated that the tavern remain open on Saturday, our Shabbat. After their payday, gentile men would come on the weekends to get drunk and have a good time. My uncle Bencion hired a non-Jewish man to work on Shabbat to serve beer and vodka.

Grandfather's house was a busy place during the entire week. On Sundays, it would become a room for the local elite, where they would come to play bridge, sing, and play their musical instruments. My cousins who played violin would perform both folk songs and classical pieces.

Children would sit outside on the ground watching silent films projected onto a brick wall. The first time we saw a Charlie Chaplin movie, our jaws dropped open in amazement. It was a miracle to see silent moving pictures on the wall. Weather permitting, we would watch the grown-ups play billiards and bowl at an outdoor bowling alley in the side yard, where they would also drink. Young boys would help set up the pins and retrieve the balls. They were paid in tips for their work.

Shabbat was a sacred time at Grandfather's. There was a happy atmosphere in the meeting room where families would come to share the warmth and wisdom of the Shabbat table. Occasionally, a spiritual leader, Rabbi Yisroel Hager, the Vizhnitzer Rebbe, would come from Romania to celebrate and encourage the Jews of Brustury to be strong in their faith. We used to go to the Rebbe's class at Uncle Bencion's where adult men would sit at the table to discuss and study Torah. This was a gathering of Orthodox Jews with their spiritual leader.

For hours, they would sit and listen to the Rebbe's discourses on Torah, the Five Books of Moses and the Talmud, our Jewish laws and traditions. Then they would sing and dance around the table. In the other room, Aunt Hilda enjoyed seeing the children play and laugh. She treated us to luscious goodies: a warm challah, braided Shabbat bread, dipped in sweet wild honey and crunchy red apples kept us quiet. Sounds of those innocent happy times when I was six years old still echo in my memory.

Traditional Shabbat foods like chicken, beef and goose were a special treat. During the week we ate simple foods like soup, potatoes, corn, and beans from our garden. Holiday food was a potluck dinner prepared by my aunt Hilda together with other women. They would bring steaming hot *cholent,* sweet kugels, warm casseroles of noodles or potatoes, and delicious cakes. I still love fresh cake. It was a custom for the Rebbe to taste the food before it was served to others.

On Shabbat afternoon, children would play next to the drinking Christian men in the spacious hall. Workers would come by train to my grandfather's pub to drink and socialize. Usually they would end up in a fight. Malchi, Risi, and I would huddle in fear in the corner.

This room was the scene of many barroom brawls. Once a man chased another until he fell on the floor with blood on his face. Someone yelled in Russian, "Hit him again. He's still alive." I was only six years old, and those loud, scuffling men frightened me. We would stay in the corner until the injured man was dragged outside. Even if I had to go to the bathroom, I would to wait until the fight was over. I was afraid to run past these huge angry men, worried that they could hit me by accident. Once we felt it was safe to leave, we would run away, back to our quiet little house across the river.

Brustury had distinct seasons. In the fall, before the bitter winter months, shepherds and farmers would move back to town to once again live among the Jewish people. Every spring, when the snow melted, around the time of my birthday, the swiveling river would overflow its rocky banks. Many houses and bridges in its path were swept away, but our home was protected from the flood waters because we lived on the incline. I clearly remember seeing boots, broken branches, roofs, and uprooted trees moving swiftly in the current.

Once, when the Brusturyanka overflowed, I had an especially happy time with Bencion. The river was dirt brown and treacherous.

"Leichuka," Bencion said, "let's go on the bridge to watch the river flood."

The two of us, bundled up against the chilling wind, stood in the middle of the bridge with others from the town. We all had the same idea.

Bencion stuck a nail into the end of a long pole to snag floating branches and tree trunks for firewood and then carefully dragged his catch sideways to the bank. This was a dangerous and exciting adventure. He knew these wood scraps and logs would help my father heat our home and provide much-needed kindling for the stove. This time, my elder brother also caught a whitefish that we prepared for the Shabbat dinner. He hit the slippery, writhing fish on the head. At home he split open the belly to remove the guts. It was ugly.

"Not for me," I said. "Maminka died from fish. I don't like to eat fish because it has a lot of small bones that get stuck in my throat and make me choke."

"You don't have to have it, but the rest of the family will enjoy the fish for Shabbat."

Today I will eat only fresh fish with the bones removed.

Brustury had severe winters. When the river froze, workers would cut out pieces of ice with a long saw and use sleds to deliver the chunks to Grandfather's ice shed. It was built using logs filled with tree sap that insulated the hut like a refrigerator without a motor. This ice was brought to the cellar to keep the barrels of beer cold during the hot summer months. Big blocks of ice were kept in the ice house and lasted as long as five months. Warm beer didn't sell so well.

When the ice on the river was thick enough, we would skate on it for fun. My sisters would hold on to me as I would wiggle along on shaky skates too big for my small feet. Our family had only one pair of skates and one sled. Walking across the frozen river was more fun than crossing the bridge. It was exciting to watch hefty horses pull sleds with children across the frozen water to the other side.

Men sawed holes through the ice to fetch drinking water and wash clothes. Even the children had to carry large pails of water to their houses. We were expected to do our assigned chores. I dragged along with my sisters, following their every move.

Someone told me, "It's easier to carry two pails at once, one in each hand, because it balances you out." It really wasn't! During wintertime the ground was slippery and treacherous. The goal was to get home safely without spilling the heavy pails. The river was closer to the house than the well.

We had special clothes for winter. Children wore a one-piece underwear suit made of warm knitted material, fashioned like overalls. It had buttons across the back waist to attach the drop seat so we could use the bathroom without undressing completely in the cold. On top of my bulky underwear were full-length stockings, a dress and a heavy coat, with a wool hat and mittens. I wore hand-me-downs from my sisters that *Maminka* had made.

"All these layers make me look fat," I would whine.

Adults would say I was adorable and used to call me "the little one." Vain and aware of my appearance at an early age and painfully self-conscious about being short and chunky, I tried not to eat too much. Risi, who was skinny, had told me that food made me fat. Father saw to it that Risi got extra chocolate. My other sister, Malchi, was chubby like me.

My Uncle Lebovic's mill, in the old part of town, was the main industry of our village.

When it snowed in the mountains, tall pine trees would be cut down and into logs and then slid down a chute carved into the icy hill. Horses then dragged the wood to the Brusturyanka River. Slippery frozen snow helped get this heavy job done. There were warning notices near all the roads, cautioning locals to stop and watch for logs rolling by with great speed. Everyone knew that these signs were made by *Tatuka* and placed on the road by his workers.

Electrical saws, a brand-new technology in Brustury, allowed workers to cut logs into planks for export. Large pine trees yielded different-size boards. They were cut, measured, and stacked high with separations, permitting the boards to dry.

Loggers lashed seven or eight tree trunks together to form a raft. Burly lumberjacks stood on the makeshift platform and paddled the wood down the waterway toward the port, where it was sold. Father measured the length of wood to determine the price. Most of the men in our town used to work at the mill. Since he was their boss, Father would calculate the workers' wages based on the number of logs.

About 1933, when electricity finally became available in Brustury, Aunt Ruchel Lebovic took my class on a field trip to the water wheel and we watched it generate power. She explained how the water force rotated the wheel and the wheel turned the generator, making electricity for the community. I was eight years old when this marvel brought electric light to many houses, but it had not yet reached our home. We still used kerosene lamps.

Warm memories of Brustury are still in my heart like the light of those lamps.

Even without my mother I felt protected then. Life was predictably comfortable.

I reminisce about the many stories Aunt Chaya told me of the house across the river that we affectionately called Grandfather's house. Mother's parents, Joseph and Risi Adler, passed away before I was born. From Galicia, Poland, they were among the first Jewish families to settle in the region. They immigrated in the mid-1860s. Our mother, Elka Adler, was born there in the late 1890s. I can't be sure of exact birth, marriage and death dates because all records were destroyed during World War II. Thus, my parents' exact ages are unknown. We only knew what we were told to tell the school about our own birthdays. We knew when my brothers had a bar mitzvah at age thirteen and that my sister Risi was born on the fourth night of Chanukah.

Brustury can't be found on present-day maps. It's now part of Ukraine. The Russians burned down my precious village during World War II, when they fought with the Hungarians. It's a lost world, yet their fires could not burn the memories from my formative years: summers of laughing and playing with my friends as we climbed the tall mountains, gathered wild strawberries and picked blueberries on the hillsides.

CHAPTER 3

Cinderella in Brustury

Aunt Chaya, my mother's younger sister from next door, stepped into *Maminka*'s shoes to care for us. Within a few months my mother's older sister, Aunt Rivka, visited from Ungvar, Czechoslovakia. Seeing Rivka stunned me. She looked exactly like I remembered *Maminka*'s face, with dark brown hair and tender eyes. Seeing Aunt Rivka was also a bitter reminder that *Maminka* was gone. Six months had dimmed my memory of *Maminka,* but she definitely was not forgotten. I missed her warmth when she held me on her lap. Rivka's presence reminded me that my mother was dead and was not coming back. I was aware that everyone felt sorry for me.

As a child, I must have read the Cinderella story a hundred times. I identified with her because I felt I was an abandoned orphan like Cinderella. I was insecure without a mother and needed love. I knew my father loved me, but he was distant and strict and was only home on Shabbat. I would sit on his lap while he ate and he would carry me to bed on his shoulders.

There were no pictures of *Maminka* for me to hold. In those days, Jewish law was interpreted by the Orthodox to prohibit personal photographs. Some took them anyway. I still grieve that we have no photo of my precious *Maminka*. There are no photographs of either of my parents, my siblings or of Aunt Rivka.

My father carried a passport with his photo when he visited his parents in Sepinka, Romania, located near Sighet and bordering with Czechoslovakia.

The immigration authorities required a document with a picture. That photo was taken away from me in Auschwitz, along with my other belongings. I resembled my father. He was handsome, with hazel-green eyes and distinguished in his gray three-piece suit and the black hat worn by Orthodox Jewish men. Religious men never went out of their homes unless they wore their suits.

In Brustury, families would help each other. We followed the orders of our grandfather, Mendel Cik, from Sepinka. He sent his daughter, Tzirel, to care for us until my father would remarry. Even though she was only eighteen years old, we called her Aunt Tzili. She pampered me for the rest of her life and we came to adore one another. As my mother's substitute, she helped our family for a year after *Maminka*'s death, just before I began first grade. When her responsibility with us ended, she left us to return to Sepinka to get married.

It was only one year later, after Maminka had passed away, that my widowed father took a trip to Hungary and returned home with a new dark gray suit and a big mink hat. We knew married men wore these special hats on Shabbat and holidays. To our surprise, he presented a wife-woman to us children, Frimed Fixler, firmly announcing, "You shall call my wife *Mamuko*," which meant mother. Without question, we did so, at least for a while. All of us, except for my brother Bencion. At fifteen, he was defiant about having a new mother. Refusing to obey this new rule, he blurted out, "She is not my mother."

Taller than my mother, *Mamuko* was a good-looking woman of about 30. Looking like she was dressed for Shabbat, she wore a dark wig covered with a pretty kerchief, a tailored dress, high-heeled shoes, and gold earrings. Soon *Mamuko* became chubby around the middle and changed from a city woman to a pregnant village woman, wearing only a plain scarf instead of a wig, a housedress and low-heeled shoes. I didn't like a strange new woman in our kitchen. She was not my mother and I still fondly remembered *Maminka*.

Taking on a family of five children was a very hard first job for a young married woman. On Thursday afternoons, she would walk to a small grocery store to buy yeast and dark unbleached wheat flour to make bread for the whole week as well as bleached white flour for *challah*, braided Shabbat bread. Thursday nights she would begin her preparations for baking. A small amount of flour and yeast with a little water mixed in it caused it to ferment overnight until early Friday morning. Her day would begin at 3:00 a.m. while it was still dark and the family slept. After quietly making the fire in the oven, she would make two separate bowls of dough from the yeast mixture with flour and then knead it by hand. Kneading heavy dough was hard work. The bowls were covered with a dish towel and a feather pillow on top to keep them warm while rising for a couple of hours. While it was rising, she would begin to prepare soup, chicken, and kugel, a potato casserole, for a Shabbat meal. It was the only time during the week we had a small portion of meat.

When the bread rose, she would knead it again before shaping the brown dough into round loaves. The *challah* dough for Shabbat bread required special braiding. Long ropes of dough were braided into single loaves. Housewives took pride in the beauty of their braids, with each one more beautiful than the week before. Once the wood would burn down to coals, the oven was just the right temperature to bake the bread. We would awake to the wonderful aroma of freshly baked bread. The extra dough was used to make special round flat breakfast bread that looked like a pizza shell. It was our breakfast before school; warm bread with melted homemade butter made from milk from our cow, Sula. We would make butter when Sula gave extra milk. Taking turns, even young children helped make butter from cream that was separated from the milk, using a plunger-type butter churn.

My stepmother was soon overwhelmed with a new baby, housework, and a brood of children not her own. She became cranky and angry but I loved the new baby and helped take care of her. Father insisted on naming her Elka, after my mother. I don't think Frimed liked this idea.

There was continuing friction and resentment between Bencion and our *Mamuko*. Discreetly, Father had placed our mother's beautiful clothes and jewelry in a trunk covered with her handmade tapestry, locked for safekeeping. Bencion was eager to open it, but *Mamuko* was against it. Lucky for him, it was time to go away to a Jewish school in Pressburg, Slovakia. His absence reduced tension in the house. Two years later, my other brother, Hershel, when he became 14 years old, also went away to study.

I did not understand the sudden change of getting a different mother. How could Father just bring home a "mother" who wasn't loving and kind to his children? Father tried to distract us with new outfits. It didn't work and they did not make me feel better.

All I remember were new clothes and shoes that we wore on Shabbat. Malchi and I had matching outfits. Our blouses were red and the pleated skirts were royal blue. Big white buttons joined the blouse to the skirt and the new shoes were made of shiny black patent leather. Risi's dress was dark red with a big sailor collar with white stripes.

I still cried loudly, "I want my *Maminka*."

Our way of life changed with this cold woman in the house. Even though she slept in *Maminka*'s bed, she wasn't a real mother. Everything was different to me. *Mamuko* had to plant and care for the vegetable garden, tend a cow and chickens, and bring water from the river while caring for the house and the children. She was pregnant most of the time, although I thought she was just fat from eating too much. One day, I heard her screaming from behind the bedroom door. I didn't know she was having another baby. The midwife was in there with her.

Many times when we called her *Mamuko*, she would become angry and reply in a harsh voice, "I have a name. My name is Frimed." I decided not to call her anything. My father muttered, "How can I take out your stubbornness?" But he never spanked me. I think others thought I was a willful child. When I was mad, I would stomp my feet and yell, "No!"

Over the next eight years, there were five new babies. I loved the first one, little Elka, the most. As she grew older I began to take her to school with me. She was especially cute and my teacher loved her. My Elka would sit quietly in a chair next to me and listen to the teacher.

On Shabbat, both Friday night and Saturday morning, we would recite our prayers of thanksgiving and awe. Father was a captivating speaker and would entertain us with stories from the Torah.

Those Shabbat interludes were especially important to the children, as Father was away working at the mill most of the week and pleasant days with our stepmother were rare. On Shabbat we would sing songs and dance for *Tatuka*. He read his German newspaper, *Der Spiegel*, sitting at the dining-room table.

Tatuka never discussed the political events sweeping the European continent that he read in "Der Spiegel." We were isolated in rural Czechoslovakia and ignorant about the brutal storms to come.

From my early memories of Jewish observance, I developed deep appreciation for the warmth of our customs. Our tradition instilled within me an internal discipline that served me throughout my life. There was a time for everything. Every season had ritual holidays. Shabbat was strictly observed according to the Torah. I vividly remember those Shabbat days, Father laughing with me and my two older sisters. We were so happy when he was home. Shabbat was fun and carefree, until each of my sisters left to learn a trade. They had finished eighth grade and there was no high school in our town. Each sister went to live with a different aunt in Czechoslovakia to work as a dressmaking apprentice. Risi went to my mother's sister, Aunt Rivka in Ungvar. Two years later, my sister Malchi went to Aunt Mindya Mermelstein in Koshelie. Everything changed. When I was 12 years old, I was alone with my stepmother, four new half-brothers, and my little half-sister, Elka. With my brothers and sisters gone, no one from my family was there to protect me.

Angry at life, my stepmother bitterly placed her burden on me. When I would come home from school, she never asked me about my day. To avoid staying at home, I told her, "I have to do homework with my friends." Czech was the official language in school with German as a second language. It was fun to practice with my schoolmates.

"No, you shall work in the garden. The vegetables are overgrown."

Crying with resentment, I would yank out the weeds as I watered the plants with a trail of tears running down my face.

Eating supper alone at a small table in the pantry, I felt abandoned. Happy mealtimes with my family were gone, except on Shabbat, when *Tatuka* would come home. He was a weekend father. The house was peaceful at that time with everyone on their best behavior, even my stepmother. My father was distant and didn't show me much love. Although I knew he loved us, there was no hugging in our house. Aunt Chaya hugged and kissed me a lot when I was small. Throughout my life, I still yearn to be loved.

During the rest of the week, Frimed would belittle me with ugly names. "Stupid girl," she would say, pointing to my heavy legs, "You are not a normal child." I have come to believe that God gave me heavy legs to support my exhausting walk through life so that I would stand tall and proud. I was no longer the cute little girl protected by older brothers and sisters. I was only twelve, and had become like Cinderella, doing the hard work and being verbally abused and ridiculed. I felt worthless and angry. I only cried to myself and, eventually, became a sad child.

Tatuka would always remind Frimed of our mother's ways. Livid with jealousy of *Maminka,* my stepmother would curse me, "Your mother should be thrown out from the bowels of the earth."

With hostile eyes, she would scream at me, "You will never grow tall. When you cry, no one will hear you. No one will see you. No one will care. You will always be alone."

I learned to hold back my tears, rarely crying. I had become the Cinderella in my book.

We could never be mother and daughter, though I cared for her children and helped with housework. For her own reasons, she resented me. She was a bitter woman who didn't even show warmth to her own children. She did not like my independent nature. I was becoming stronger as I got older. At that time, children were taught to be seen and not heard. I, on the other hand, would speak up.

The more she called me names, "a midget, the little twerp," the more I felt unloved. At the time I did not understand exactly what she meant. Now I do. Her tone of voice and those hurtful words stuck with me throughout my life. She was sorry she married my father, but had she remained single, she would have been looked down upon as an old maid. Back then, couples did not marry for love, but only for security, hoping to grow to love each other. Father's priority was to have someone care for his first family and also to have more children as he followed religious expectations.

While she never spanked me, she whipped my soul, leaving me bruised inside. It's too bad that I only remember bitter times, with little laughter or comfort, but happy times were a few.

I was forced to grow up quickly since my older sisters went away for four years to learn dressmaking. There was no one else to help. Caring for several young children at a time prepared me to be organized from an early age before my teens. Each year brought more responsibility as another baby was born. Our two-room house seemed to get smaller and smaller. My older sisters would help out when they were home. I also became more defiant and disobedient, just like Bencion. I had to defend myself against *Mamuko*'s rages.

Once, in the eighth grade, Frimed's brother came from Prague to visit. He brought rubber boots for all the children, except for me. Instead, he gave me his son's used high-school textbooks. But I was so happy to have those new books, which I took to school to show my teacher. He admired them, and told me, "The school cannot afford to buy them for everyone." With the help of these books, I was privileged to learn science, history, arithmetic, and physics, in addition to my regular elementary schoolwork. Books made me smart, so I studied whenever I had free time, thinking this would prepare me to pass the exams to finish high school. Sadly, that time never came.

Once grumbling to Father, I whispered, "I hate being taken advantage of and feeling lonely."

He stepped close to me and whispered a Yiddish proverb. "We're supposed to put on a good face. Pretend. Pinch your cheeks to make them appear rosy." That meant, keep your feelings private.

One time, when *Tatuka* was working near the river, I brought him lunch. Alone with him, I whimpered, "It's hard to live at home. I feel used. I need a change."

In this moment of tender privacy, he moved close to me, affectionately brushed my face, kissed me and softly said, "Leichuka, we have to pretend to the neighbors that all is well. They do not need to know our personal situation." Everything private about the family was hidden. If people knew, it could hurt your reputation.

My father was loyal to his wife. I felt invisible, with no one to talk to. I envied other children who had a "real" mother. *Maminka* had loved me so much, and every day I was painfully reminded of her absence.

CHAPTER 4

School Was an Escape

Through bitter cold winters with many snowstorms, we would walk to school across the bridge for twenty to thirty minutes each way. I would look forward to going to school, a reprieve from my heavy work schedule and verbal abuse. Learning to read was my greatest pleasure.

Losing my mother at the age of five left me with a lonely void throughout my life. I began school at the age of six entering the first grade in September of 1931. My two sisters, only eight and ten, took me to school on the first day, in place of my mother. There, the door was opened to reading, writing, and learning, distracting me from my deep loss. Malchi and Risi did their best to comfort me while still dealing with their own sadness.

There were two schools in town. The one far away from my home was for Jewish, Christian, and German children. On my way to and from school, I looked over my notes to memorize poems. We had to memorize everything by heart. The other school, close to our house, was for the local Russian children. It was three times larger than ours. Since the Russian families had settled in Brustury before the Jews, they were more numerous than us. We spoke Russian to these families. Even the village mayor was Russian.

The official language at school and in the village was Czech.

The Czechoslovakian government funded both schools equally, and attendance was mandatory. We all learned the same basic subjects. The children in the two schools barely spoke to each other as we felt how different we were. They were taught in Russian, and we were taught in Czech. Customs at home were different, and mothers cooked different foods. Our chicken soup, cholent, and challah were the most special.

The Russian school used to host functions such as school plays and town and country elections that we attended jointly. I remember the excitement in the village during the re-election of the president of Czechoslovakia, Thomas Masaryk, in 1934, when I was nine. It was believed he was good for the Jews. Jewish people honored him. Even the street name by Grandfather's house was named after him.

Early on weekday mornings, Jewish boys used to go to Hebrew school for supplementary religious studies. They would carry lanterns to light their way. Attending public school during the day, they would go back to Jewish school at night. The boys' education was a priority in every Jewish family. At fourteen, many young men would be sent away from their home to *yeshiva* in Bratislava, Slovakia, a full-time religious, sleep away school for advanced religious studies.

In the afternoons, Jewish girls from wealthy families would go to a girls' Hebrew school to learn to read Yiddish and Hebrew. Since my family couldn't afford to send my sisters and me, our father used to teach us to read and write Hebrew whenever he was able to come home from work at night. We used to repeat our Hebrew lessons over and over again, until we would get them right. By soft lamplight, we would learn to read our Jewish prayer book and to recite special blessings of thanksgiving. Father was strict, criticizing me for writing Hebrew script too small. Very precise in all things, he also had an el-egant handwriting. He taught me well – till this day, I try to write with bigger letters. *Tatuka* used to get irritated when I would mispronounce God's name in Hebrew. Though I would become anxious when he was impatient, I knew he loved me because he sat only with me when he taught me to read and write in Hebrew and Yiddish. Once he told me how disappointed he was when Bencion had sent him a letter with misspellings. *Tatuka's* own handwriting was distinct and beautiful to read.

When I was growing up, I knew God was everywhere – in the street, in the garden, in the river – everywhere. I knew God was watching everything I did. We as children were taught not to question what our families did or why we did it. Our faith in God was basic to our lives. There were no questions and no one questioned anything.

✡

At night, as we would walk home from school, it was not only dreadfully cold, but also dark because there were no streetlights. I wore a coat that the teacher had given me. Despite that, we were not afraid. We walked in lines and were watched over by the girls behind us who lived farther away. In those days, there was no fear of boys or men who might be hiding in the woods, waiting to kidnap young girls.

There were two rooms in my school for learning and a big dirt play yard in the back. During recess we would play volleyball, boys and girls together. I was very good at it and loved playing the game. The kids would always put me in the top corner where I would push the ball over the net. I was a better player than the boys and popular among the kids.

We also played jump rope where two girls would turn the jump rope and the third one would jump over it back and forth. I was the best jumper. I could jump and count up to eighty until my feet would get caught in the rope.

My spoiled friend, Rosie, was the only child of a refined mother from Vienna. She had everything she wanted, including a fancy decorated sled with a seat for only one child. Sometimes she would let me ride her sled down a big hill. I was envious that she had everything, especially a loving mother, father, and grandfather. One day in school I was angry about something and I beat her up. I knew I was stronger than she was. She fell to the ground on her face and was injured, with a bloody nose. I was afraid from then on that her father would come after me but he never did.

During Christmas time, the teachers would give us a list to mark off the clothing that we would receive from Prague that rich Christians would donate for the cause of the less fortunate. Once I checked that I needed a warm coat and dresses. Other times, I would check something else.

When we weren't writing and had to listen to the teacher, we would be told to sit straight with our hands placed behind our backs. There was a lot of discipline in the school from the teachers. Punishment was the embarrassment of standing in the corner or staying after school. I would often have to stand in the corner for talking with my neighbor. The naughtiest children would receive a slap on the palm of their hand with a thin stick. I never did. Our room had students through the fourth grade with two of us sharing a bench and the attached desk with an inkwell on each side and a trough to hold a pen or a pencil. We would learn to use pens only in the second grade. In the first grade, each of us had an erasable black tablet that we wrote on with white chalk. We tried hard not to drop the tablet because if it were to break, we could have been spanked for carelessness, and our parents would have had to pay for a new one.

Every morning I, along with other students, had to show the teacher my clean hands and fingernails. It was also important to show a handkerchief.

I sat with my best friend, Esther, the shoemaker's daughter. We were close since the first grade. I was always placed in the first row because I was the shortest in the class.

The school bathroom outside had three compartments: one for the boys, one for the girls and a separate one for the teachers. We would raise our hand

with two fingers, indicating we had to go to the outhouse. Sometimes, I would raise my hand to go to the bathroom just to have a break.

Lunchtime was also recess. We used to bring a lunch snack in our school bag, a piece of bread or corn bread with butter and blueberry jam, and maybe an apple. My punishment at home was to go to school without a snack. Many times my friend Rachel would share her bread with me. Frimed was hard on me.

The fifth grade was like high school, with a different teacher for each subject. We learned arithmetic and algebra, chemistry, music, physics, botany, geography, history, reading, language arts, and writing. My best subject was language arts. I liked taking sen-

Lenka at 10, 1935 - her only pre-war childhood photo

tences apart to learn Czech grammar. I sat with Ruchel Katz throughout the entire eighth grade.

I loved music, but I didn't have a nice voice. When they tried us out for duets, I was never chosen. I couldn't bring up my voice. Every teacher was required to play a violin. We would sing national and folk songs. I was better at reciting poems by heart.

School provided me with the opportunity to discover myself and try new things. In the sixth grade, we had after-school classes in arts and crafts where we learned to knit, crochet, sew by hand, and paint with watercolors. The teacher showed us how to measure distance with our pointer-finger, to measure landscape distance on the paper. We learned to make simple items such as aprons and pajamas. Drawing class was my favorite, and I still try to sketch and paint. *Working with my hands let me think through things that were on my mind. My hands were never idle.*

Despite my concealed grief, I continued to develop skills of endurance and grew into a more confident young lady.

At twelve years old, every girl needed pocket money for things like sweets, school supplies, and shoes. My father could not give me pocket money and an idea came to me for a business. I would take candies, chocolate, peanuts, and even some flavored cubes used for making sweet drinks from a grocery store and sell them to my classmates. I would calculate the price per piece to guarantee a profit after paying back my debt to the grocer. I made a special cloth bag to carry the sweets and the notebook where I would write down the names of the students who bought my candies and couldn't pay right away. This made me a successful vendor during recess. No one at home asked where my cash came from and I didn't tell them. My top customer, Ruchel Katz, was also my best friend and desk mate from the fifth to the eighth grade. Years later, I even introduced her to her husband in Tel Aviv. Today we're still close friends.

On Purim, a holiday celebrating Jewish survival, more money would come to me. It is a Jewish custom to hire children to deliver gifts of food to friends and the poor. We were taught to be caring and thoughtful of others, even though we had little for ourselves. I delivered baskets, each with a china plate full of sweet goodies, covered with a clean white embroidered napkin, and received tips. I used this money to buy new black laced school shoes and fabric for Aunt Chaya to make me clothes.

When Hershel went away to a religious school, Bencion joined the Czech army while my sisters were still away from home working as apprentices. After graduation, Hershel also went away for military training.

I always wrote letters to Bencion and Malchi, and they answered with news of their lives. Bencion and Hershel finished their two-year military training and returned home to Brustury. By that time there was no room for them to sleep in our small two-room house. They stayed next door with Aunt Chaya. She had a big empty house with six rooms, as her stepchildren had grown up and moved away.

When *Maminka* was alive, she had financial help from her parents. The extra money paid for a lady who would come every day to work in the house. I did not understand why help from our grandparents ended upon her death. Now we were poor. We had a person who came to our house once a month for the big laundry of sheets, towels, and tablecloths. In the winter, they were hung in Aunt Chaya's attic to dry. During warmer months, the sheets and the towels were stretched outside over a line to be bleached white by the sun. I loved the smell of the sheets and the towels drying in the summer mountain air.

Bathing was a Friday afternoon event. We would have a bath and get clean clothes once a week before Shabbat. We would save our new clothes to be worn for the very first time on Shabbat or other Jewish holidays, never during the middle of the week. For weekly bathing, a large tub would be placed in the center of the kitchen for the smaller children. Cold well water was heated in a pot on the stove and poured into the tub. The children, up to six years old, washed in the same bathwater, one after the other. After moving the tub into the pantry, Mamuko would change the water for each older child who bathed separately. Women would go to the community ritual bath near the synagogue, and in warmer weather, men would bathe in the river. The river was the most fun!

In the summer, the Christians would take our cow to graze in the mountain pastures. It had to be milked every morning and night. I would take the long walk alone to watch them fill up the bucket. In observance of Jewish dietary laws, milk from other animals was not allowed to be mixed in to stretch the volume of the cow's milk. I carried the heavy pail of milk back home, trying not to spill it. My stepmother and I would alternate mornings, but at night I would trudge up and down the hill by myself.

On the path to and from the pasture, I could look over to the mountain to where my mother was buried. The trail was covered with gravel. Sometimes during the summer, I would leave my shoes at home. Tiny, sharp rocks would cut into the bottom of my little feet. One time it hurt so badly that I sobbed loudly and bitterly for my mother knowing no one could hear me. Did she hear my loud screams?

✡

While World War I ended in 1918, the Treaty of Versailles in 1919 created the new nation of Czechoslovakia from the Austro-Hungarian Empire. Our life in Czechoslovakia was predictable until 1938, when the fascist Hungarians, allies of Nazi Germany, took over parts of it threatening to harm the people. Until that time, children in school were educated in Czech. Once under Hungarian control, we were no longer able to buy books in Czech. They even tried to erase it as our spoken language, because Hungarians always thought that Czechoslovakia had belonged to the Austrian-Hungarian Empire that ended in 1919.

In 1939, after Germany invaded Poland, all of Carpathia and some of Romania became part of Hungary. Hungarian became the official language. War had changed the landscape and the culture.

It was only as I entered adolescence that I became aware of the tumultuous political and military events drastically changing Central and Eastern Europe.

Everything changed to Hungarian: lessons in school, signs on the storefronts, street names, and the language spoken on the street. The Hungarian police replaced the Czech authority. The new regime watched over people in the village, the forests, and the fields. It was easy to recognize the Hungarian police in their black hats with a cluster of huge colorful feathers on the right side. Influenced by the Nazis and their followers, they were arrogant and forceful. We were now called "the dirty Jews."

The rise of Hitler (may his name be erased) and the event of *Kristallnacht*, November 9-10th in 1938, known as the Night of Broken Glass in Germany and Austria, which foreshadowed the Holocaust of European Jewry, were unknown to us because my father never spoke about the wave of violent anti-Jewish pogroms throughout Germany and Austria. Homes, hospitals, stores, and synagogues — the heart and soul of the Jewish community — were demolished and burned down.

Life in Brustury was no longer peaceful. Normal life had been suffocated by harsh treatment from the Hungarians. Father became restrictive and nervous about our walking outside at night. We saluted a new flag and children had to learn the new Hungarian language in school. When I finished the eighth grade in Brustury I was not impacted as much as the younger children who were still in school. The new regime began with the new school year in September.

CHAPTER 5

Sneaking Away Forever

In the summer of 1939, it was my turn to leave home as I turned fourteen. Feeling lost and unimportant, I knew I needed a change, desperate to escape the pain of my stepmother's constant insults. I had no hope of further education as public school had ended for me at the age of fourteen. They could not afford to send me to high school in the nearby town of Tiachovo. Boys' education took priority. My idea was to sneak away for good before my parents would uncover my plan.

I knew *Tatuka* would be sad to find out I was gone when he came home on the weekend. He was caught in the middle between his wife and love for his children. I shared his attention with nine others. My four older siblings were away and now Father was there only on Shabbat. Even then, he rarely spoke up on my behalf. It was my idea to try a different life.

After having been away for two years learning to sew, Malchi and Risi came back home to Brustury and slept in Aunt Chaya's house next door, waiting to be married. Father had bought them a sewing machine to share so they could earn their own money. Knowing I wanted to leave home, Risi and Malchi convinced me to go to live with Aunt Mindya Mermelstein in Koshelie, just outside Chust. My father and Aunt Mindya frequently wrote letters to one another. *Tatuka* told me Mindya was an important person in Koshelie because her husband Yaakov was a rabbi of two synagogues and the local authority on Jewish law. He was also the town *schochet*, a ritual slaughterer.

Malchi and Risi helped me secretly organize my getaway. With there being no privacy in our two-room house, my stepmother overheard us whispering. In a manipulative, warm tone, Frimed tried to persuade me not to leave.
But I was a determined and defiant girl, and her attempt failed. In revenge, she
tried to discourage me by hiding my favorite green Shabbat dress, hoping to
change my mind. I had only three more dresses. The next morning, realizing
I was leaving regardless, she left the dress outside on the front porch. Maybe
she felt sorry for me. Perhaps, she would not mind me leaving the house, but
she needed my help, and it was hard for her to see me go.

My sisters helped me pack the few clothes that I had in a produce carton
with my three dresses, a nightgown, two bloomers, socks, and my Shabbat
shoes. As a going away present, Risi gave me my first pair of silk stockings and
her blue straw hat.

"Here, Leichu, take this for good luck."

I felt so grown-up. Traveling was a new experience, but I had mixed feelings. I was sad, scared to leave everything behind — my family, my school, my
friends, and my home. I did not sleep well that night.

Afraid of what lay ahead, I cried as my sisters took me to the bus station
early in the morning. There was no good-bye to my beloved *Tatuka*. He would
never approve of my plan.

My sisters asked me, "Leichu, do you want to change your mind?"

"No, I will go to Aunt Mindya's in Koshalie."

Maybe this would be my only chance to get away.

Malchi bought my bus ticket. My sisters told to me to get off in Chust, at
the Jewish grocery store to meet "the skinny family friend with the long black
beard." In my eyes, almost all the men were tall with long, black beards. In the
late afternoon, I arrived at the yard at the back of the grocery store. I bravely
got off the bus. Malchi told me the man would have a single-horse wagon. I
waited over an hour. "Did I get off at the right place?" I kept asking myself.

Finally spotting him on his wagon, I walked over and in a grown up voice
said, "I am Malchi's little sister."

"Climb up," he said.

Nervous, I sat in the back of the wagon, squinting to see where we were
going at dusk. I was anxious and tired. We bumped along the road for several
miles. How did he know where to go in the dark? It took about an hour to
reach my aunt's house in Koshelie. The man didn't say a word to me or to his

horse the whole time.

I knocked on the door not knowing what to expect.

"Look who is here!" Aunt Mindya shrieked in Yiddish.

She was not expecting me. I was relieved when she welcomed me warmly. Lacking self-confidence I didn't say much. She prepared a nice dinner for me and her only daughter "Miss" Suri, my 24-year-old beautiful and elegant cousin. She was the spoiled older sister in their family with three younger brothers.

I thought my *Maminka* would have cared for me in the same way – with modern clothes and laced-up boots with pointy toes. Like her daughter, Aunt Mindya was also elegant.

After a few weeks, I began to make new Yiddish-speaking friends. I even learned to ride a two-wheeled bicycle. Aunt Mindya did not approve of girls my age riding bikes. It was not ladylike for a girl to ride a boy's bike with a bar. Being a tomboy, I was not physically timid. Back home only Jewish boys were allowed to ride, and not every family had a bicycle. I explained to her how much fun it was for me. Finally, she let me enjoy this activity on a girl's bike. Later in life, riding a bike would become a blessing, a useful skill that would once save my life.

Aunt Mindya was a resourceful woman. She made me a winter coat from the one her son had outgrown. By turning the fabric inside out and attaching a warm fur collar saved from another son's jacket, she created a warm coat. It felt brand new. She even bought me a dress and new shoes.

"Thank you," I said with a smile, even though the shoes looked like black work boots for a man. They weren't shiny and feminine like Miss Suri's or even those I saw in the window displays. They were ugly, high shoes, handmade by a shoemaker in Chust. I used them anyway because my others were worn out. For the first time in many years, I felt like I belonged somewhere. Aunt Mindya cared for me like her own daughter, even though I knew I would never be her favorite. Their home became mine, and I felt that I had made the right decision.

My brother Bencion wrote that he was going to marry a girl named Blumi in Ganich, Hungary. We were invited to the wedding, the first wedding of my immediate family. I was ecstatic at the thought that *Tatuka* and the rest of the family would be there. It had been too long since we were together.

Aunt Mindya's dressmaker styled a red winter Shabbat dress for me though it was a summer wedding. It wasn't as special as Suri's. She hired the same skinny guy with the wagon to take four of us on an eight-hour ride from Koshalie to Ganich. We brought Aunt Mindya's cakes along with gifts for the newlyweds. When I saw *Tatuka* at the wedding, he hugged and kissed me. It had been a year since I had seen him and my siblings.

Celebrating Bencion's wedding, *Tatuka* and I danced with great happiness. I laughed when dancing with my sisters and even my stepmother, Frimed, who was on her best friendly behavior. We ate an extravagant wedding meal of challah, goose liver with chopped onions, baked meat, chicken soup, and many honey cakes. When the celebration was over, we had a long eight-hour ride back home in the dark, arriving at sunrise.

In January 1940, I was nearly fifteen. There was a job opening at a factory in Chust where my aunt sent me to learn to weave all types of baskets made for export. The owner, a wealthy Jewish man named Dunkel, brought basket-weaving instructors from the Hungarian country village. They taught our group of forty young men and women. I had not been in school in Brustury long enough to learn Hungarian. I learned to basket weave by imitating the teacher, and my quick hands allowed me to follow along.

During training, the company gave the students room and board in private homes near the factory warehouse. After four months, when the training was over, Dunkel sold me straw to take back home to Koshelie so that I could start weaving on my own. I would send the finished baskets to the factory, and they would purchase them. I was not good at basket weaving, because I didn't like it. I just wanted to get the darn baskets completed so I could get paid what little they were offering.

While I lived with Aunt Mindya, she taught me how to do *chesed,* acts of kindness for others. Since her husband was a kosher slaughterer, he received extra pieces of meat from the butcher. On Friday mornings, Mindya would wrap the meat she could spare in big grape leaves from the backyard as wrapping paper was in short supply. She would send me to deliver these small meat packages to widows and other needy families. They used to thank me, grateful for the only meat they had for Shabbat, and maybe for the whole week

Once, when cleaning Mindya's elegant bedroom, I found an old rusty can under her bed, in which she had hidden her precious gold jewelry with diamonds. On Shabbat, she used to go to the synagogue dressed elegantly, wearing fancy jewelry from the tin can under her bed. It was a custom for Jewish people to buy gold and diamonds as a safe investment that could be exchanged for cash, property, food, and even one's life. People were prepared in case they needed to leave their home quickly.

Mindya was stunning when she would dress up, wearing her jewelry and a beautiful silk black scarf. As a religious woman, she completely covered her hair. She wore a wig with a scarf over it to maintain modesty. I admired her character. I was also impressed as I watched my humble aunt kindly teach illiterate women to read Hebrew in the synagogue.

Within a few months, Aunt Mindya found another opportunity for me. I was to learn the trade of wig-making from Mrs. Chaya Shönfeld. She would train me to make wigs, a craft more delicate than basket weaving. I would have to move to Mrs. Shönfeld's house in Chust, a town nearby. Aunt Mindya and Mrs. Shönfeld agreed that every other Shabbat during my apprenticeship

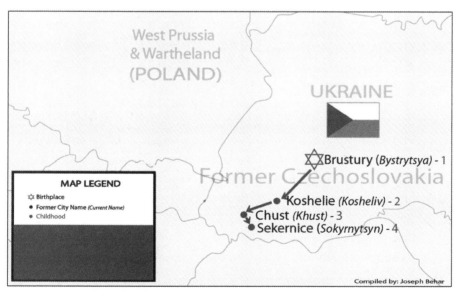

For Complete Map - See Appendix, page 232

I would walk back to the comfort of Aunt Mindya's home. It would take me over two hours.

Having a skill was considered preparation for the rest of one's life. Knowing a trade, you had certainty for the future. With this marketable skill, I could support myself, be independent, and not require handouts from others. More formal schooling was not a possibility. On top of it, I had left all my books at home in Brustury.

CHAPTER 6

A Wig to Cover the Hair

September 1941

I was young and inexperienced, only sixteen and a half years old. Aunt Mindya had my best interests at heart. Leaving her home again to live with total strangers made me nervous. She sent me from Koshelie to Chust, with the familiar "taxi service." Where was he taking me? My new family would be the Shönfelds, where Mrs. Shönfeld would teach me the trade of wig making. It was early afternoon on a chilly fall day when I knocked on the door of the wig-maker's apartment. Her good-looking husband Morris greeted me. He had a black beard and was taller than my father. Being a religious man, he wore the usual dark suit. As I entered, I saw Mrs. Shönfeld waiting for me at the work-table in the kitchen. She wore high-topped laced black shoes, a striped house-dress and a kerchief on her head.

"How are you, Leichu?" she questioned with authority.

Feeling shy, I said, "Aunt Mindya Heftman sent me." They shared a glance. I felt uncomfortable.

"Yes," she said, "we've been expecting you." Moving closer, with her strong voice of authority, she explained, "You'll be replacing a girl who fin-ished her training and left for a job in Budapest."

Her forward manner surprised me, and not knowing what to say, I could only mumble, "Thank you."

The wig-maker's husband said, "The girls working here call my wife Maestra, out of respect for her artistic skill and superior social status."

"Oh."

Mrs. Shönfeld sat me down at her worktable in the kitchen with a bowl of soup and a piece of dark bread while quietly explaining our arrangement in Yiddish, as serious as if she were reading a contract.

"You will work for three years: two years for room and board and the third year I will pay you wages at a monthly rate for making wigs. Once you complete daily household chores, you will sit at the workspace in the kitchen with other girls and make wigs."

I nodded, sensing she was already impatient with me. Maestra made it clear I wasn't to waste her time.

"Do you understand?"

Intimidated, I lowered my head and answered, "Yes, Maestra."

Gesturing with her hand, she said, "I will teach you how to do it."

She was my boss and there was no choice. There was nothing I could negotiate; it was not proper to speak up.

I told myself, "Whatever it is, I have to do it."

Our "contract" was not in writing. Would this someday be a problem? At sixteen, I didn't know the meaning of a contract. In the meantime, there would be food to eat and a bed to sleep in while learning a trade. I was relieved to be able to earn my own keep rather than live on charity of others. I would do what was expected of me.

It was apparent from the beginning that our relationship would be impersonal, yet we would both benefit. Maestra taught me a skill. I served their family purpose. It was easy for them to take advantage of an insecure, poverty-stricken girl forced to grow up fast. They did not ask me about myself or try to draw me out. They were not curious about my family or where I used to live. Since I was only their live-in apprentice and house worker, they were certainly not interested in my opinions. I knew my place and it was not being part of their family. Housework took as much time as did learning the intricate skill of wig-making. Their rented apartment was a modest three-room unit offering no privacy. To be alone, I slipped outside to the back yard.

Slowly, my courage to stand up for myself grew, as did my feeling of independence.

There were six people in the apartment. The Shönfelds' first child, daughter Shaindy, was a year younger than I. Even though we shared the same bed, we did not become friends. Shaindy had her own friends from school. We slept in the same room with her brothers, Shmuli, 13, and Yaakov, 10. Within a year, Mrs. Shönfeld arranged for me to sleep in my own bed, a makeshift straw mattress, hidden in a pullout bed under the wig-making table in the kitchen. During the day, this bed space would be transformed back into a workbench.

The room where the children slept was used as the dining room on Shabbat. It was heated by a tall, decorated wood-burning stove. A large bookcase held Mr. Shönfeld's holy books. At the bottom right end of the bookcase, there was a small cupboard with two shelves, where I was allowed to store my few belongings.

A big credenza displayed fancy dishes that were used only for Shabbat. During the afternoon on the day of rest, I enjoyed reading next to the warm tall stove in the corner, while the family napped. Sometimes after Shabbat, they would include me in a card game. My sisters had taught me to play rummy.

Thursday, the day before Shabbat, was a day I dreaded. It was my day to go to the butcher with a live chicken that Mr. Shönfeld had purchased at the market. He would hand me the plump, clucking hen with her long, sharp claws.

"Take this to the schochet's house so that we can have it for Shabbat. As you pluck the feathers," he said kindly, "be sure to get them all. Mrs. Shönfeld wants to cook a clean chicken." I squeezed the wiggling bird tightly under my arm.

At the shop, the kosher slaughterer would take the chicken, pluck a few feathers from its neck and, in an instant, slice the neck open with his special kosher knife. Then he would quickly throw the bird to the ground. It was icky to watch sticky, red blood drain from the open neck. I would collect the clean chicken feathers and, perhaps, feathers from ten or twelve other hens, to sell them to the women who couldn't afford goose and duck feathers for their pillows. The money would buy me a skirt or a blouse.

Preparing for Shabbat early Friday morning would find me hauling heavy buckets of freezing water from the well to warm on the stove. I would sweep the wooden kitchen floor before scrubbing and drying it. Loose floating hair from the wigs was everywhere, even in the soup.

I distinctly recall one Friday morning when Shaindy was studying for her high-school exams before everyone was up. I envied her because she was privileged to study and did not have to wash floors. Her parents adored her the same way my father loved me. It was a bittersweet experience. She had schoolmates and would go to their homes for tea parties. My companions were my co-workers and we had no place to go. I knew my place.

Another Friday morning, after a heavy snow, when the family was still asleep, I went to the well wearing rubber galoshes that I secretly borrowed from one of the Shönfeld boys. The boots got wet inside so I put them on the hot stove to dry. Naturally, they melted, filling the house with the smell of stinking burned rubber. When Maestra awoke to the putrid smell, she was furious.

I had to explain, "I used the galoshes because I did not have any of my own."

Mrs. Shönfeld didn't scream or call me names. She put on a face of shark's teeth, laughing with angry eyes. She was a bitter, overworked woman and had no patience for me or my mistakes. Mrs. Shönfeld's reaction made my stupid blunder even worse.

Maestra's husband was a religious man and, like my father, wore a fancy fur hat on Shabbat. Studying each day at the synagogue, he would come home for lunch. Occasionally, he would take his wife by the hand to their bedroom. Through the thin walls, from our worktable we once overheard her loud complaining, "Don't shame me at my age."

We knew something private was being discussed.

Later we heard her say, "I don't want to be laughed at."

We didn't quite understand what was going on, but we knew it was something to do with having babies. At forty, I figured she didn't want more children. A baby at that time in her life would have been a burden.

One time she asked me, "Did my husband ever come close to you?"

"He never did," I replied. Why did she ask?

On the side, Mr. Shönfeld had a jewelry trade, buying and selling gold on the street. He also ordered materials for Mrs. Shönfeld's wig-making business. Shabbat was the only time he would spend with his family.

After cleaning the house in the morning, I had to wash small loads of laundry by hand once a week. Bedding, towels, and tablecloths were washed once a month by a laundry woman. Once they were dry, I would iron them. For a small girl ironing stacks of laundry was hard work. Ironing included bulky sheets and shirts washed during the week.

The iron was heavy and bulky, weighing over four pounds. It was hollow inside, where I would place hot coals from the wood-burning stove. Once, when the coals were cooling off, I decided to go across the street to refill the iron with coals from the burner at the ritual bath. It always had hotter coals than the ones from the Shönfeld's smaller English stove. I refilled the iron and started back home.

Coal iron from the time period

As I was reaching for the door, someone on the other side slammed it open against me. Losing my balance and falling to the floor, I dropped the hot iron on my calf and burned my right leg. The smell of my flesh burning filled my nostrils. In searing pain, I dragged myself back across the street to the house and collapsed from the shock of intense pain. Mrs. Shönfeld came out, looked at me, irritated with disgust. She did nothing to help me — no sympathy, no medicine. I could not work for several days. The raw wound took weeks to heal. This burn left a scar on my right leg and a deeper one in my heart.

On occasion, windows had to be cleaned. Once, I accidentally broke the glass in the kitchen window. Mr. Shönfeld's face became angry, his eyes narrowed, and his mouth puckered.

With a strong voice, he threatened, "You will pay for the repair."

Mrs. Shönfeld looked at him with an expression understood between them and stuck up for me. In this instance, I felt protected.

Staring out the window, she explained with a sigh, "Sometimes accidents happen."

What a relief. No payback was required.

One of the three rooms in the apartment was the parents' bedroom with nice maple furniture. While making their twin beds, I couldn't help but notice Maestra's personal belongings. On Mrs. Shönfeld's side was a nightstand with magazines. *Look* magazine, in Hungarian, was on top of the stack. I had to sneak to read these magazines, an opening to a world beyond my understanding. I had learned rudimentary Hungarian, overhearing conversations from women who would come to Mrs. Shönfeld's wig shop and from the city people in town. I knew enough vocabulary to understand the main points. The magazine advertised a bottle of Coca-Cola for the equivalent of five cents. What was Coca-Cola? At that time I knew little about Hungarian culture or the world at large. There were articles about Hitler, anti-Semitism, and the war. I was more interested in beauty advertisements for lipstick and nail polish for ladies. Still not fluent in Hungarian, I didn't fully understand the impending doom for the Jews.

On the other side of the room, Mrs. Shönfeld had a vanity table with three drawers and a trifold mirror in which she could see herself, as she would powder her nose, apply rouge, lipstick, eyebrow pencil, and the finishing touch – a fragrance of lilac. She was tall with a good figure, and noticeably conscious of her appearance and her shape.

She would tell us, "I love bread, but I have to watch my figure."

She wore a dark wig and dressed elegantly when she went out in the evening with her Hungarian girl friends.

On Shabbat and especially holidays, she looked well made-up and attractive, wearing nice clothes, a brown mink coat, and matching soft leather gloves. During the week, she worked in a housedress with a kerchief on her head.

On Sunday mornings, washing Shabbat dishes was a long and dirty process. After bringing full buckets of water from the well, I would warm the water on the stove, divide it into two large round pails for meat dishes, and then place them on the worktable. One pail was for washing and the other for rinsing. I used that warm water, baking soda, and a rag to wash the dishes. We did not have special dish soap. If food or grease had hardened on a dish, I would scour it with white sand from the river. After rinsing, I would dry the dishes and put them away in the large three-door buffet cabinet standing next to the pantry. The family followed strict kosher rules, keeping meat and dairy dishes separate. The fancy meat dishes were used only on Shabbat or holidays. We ate dairy meals during the week, served on "milk" dishes. These dishes were washed and rinsed in the "dairy" set of pails.

The two other girls and I sat at the wig-making table for six to twelve hours a day, six days a week, depending on the number of wigs we were making, washing and fixing.

Sitting at my work place on a hard wooden chair, I could hear how Maestra dealt with customers. Young religious brides would come with their mothers to order their first wigs. It was customary for Jewish women to have their hair shorn after the wedding before they covered their head with a wig, a kerchief, or a hat. Covering the head was for religious identity and modesty. The wig-maker was an important person in the community.

I heard how gentle and persuasive she was as she spoke with the brides in Hungarian or Yiddish, depending on their language at home.

"I will make you a beautiful wig, matching your hair perfectly. Would you like the same style you're wearing?"

"Yes. I need one for Shabbat and the other, a cheaper one, for every day."

Nodding her head in agreement, she would say to the mother, "You have a beautiful daughter. So, I can fit you into my schedule, when is the wedding?"

A sale was certain when the bride permitted her to cut swatches from her hair so she could match the wig color exactly. Their cash down payments were not hidden from us, but rather placed in the center of the table. We wouldn't dare touch Maestra's money. She was teaching me and the other wig-makers a silent lesson – don't take what isn't yours. Was this a test?

While sitting at the worktables, the three of us followed Maestra's strict rules – no one is allowed to talk while working, except about the task.

We would remain quiet, but sometimes we'd giggle only to be reprimanded.

"You'd better pay attention to your work," she would say. "Time is short."

After the client's head measurements were taken and the swatch of hair was cut, the dimensions were used to make the undercap, the foundation of the wig. Only Maestra did this precise work. To begin constructing the wig cap, Maestra would choose the right size of wooden head from many she had on hand. Strong lace netting covered the block to form a cap. The sewing had to be delicate for comfort on a bare shorn head.

Once the cap was made, it remained on the wooden block as we meticulously knotted Italian hair to the net with a fine needle. This is the work I learned to do. Three to five hairs at a time were intertwined into the net of the cap. Eventually the whole cap was covered with hair. The artistry was in knowing where to knot in more or less hair. The front and bottom required more hair than the top and sides. An entire wig took me the better part of three to four days to finish. Only Maestra herself styled the wig before delivery. I felt pride when she would request me personally to craft a new wig for her. It was a big compliment.

It was clear to me that Mrs. Shönfeld was a hardworking woman. She struggled to support her family of five and me. She had two other certified wig-makers that were on salary, but only I lived with the family as an apprentice. The expertise of creating stylish wigs for Orthodox women served me my entire life. As an adult, I became a highly paid wig and toupee maker after the war, always working for established businesses. I grew to appreciate my skill and everything I learned from Mrs. Shönfeld.

Before holidays, Mrs. Shönfeld would share some of the goodies like chocolate and fruit she would receive as tips from her clients. Then Mr. Shönfeld would lock them up. Sweets such as honey, chocolate, nuts, and candy were always kept under lock and key in their bedroom. Normally, Mr. Shönfeld would decide when to share these treats. It was a puzzle to me. Why, on the day of Day of Atonement, a fast day, was his private cabinet unlocked? I felt it was a setup. Was this how he tested his children or was he testing only me?

On Fridays, upon completing the wig work, I would be sent walking to her customers' homes to personally deliver their washed and styled wigs before Shabbat. With my tips, I bought clothes and shoes. I felt independent and grown-up with these small indulgences, and even bought my own lilac toilette soap and undergarments.

While not a member of the family, I still observed their private life, very different from my home in Brustury. One evening, Mrs. Shönfeld snuck out with a girlfriend to a movie, a pleasure forbidden to Orthodox women. Maestra's elderly mother overheard a neighbor gossiping about her daughter's un-Orthodox behavior. Once, when her mother was visiting, she told her in a stern voice, "It is not appropriate for you as a religious woman to see movies. I'm embarrassed that my daughter has become the talk of the town."

I overheard her mother complain that she felt ashamed. "It doesn't matter whether you did it or not. It's enough that the women are blabbing and giving you a bad name."

She cared for her elegant mother, who lived alone down the street, with great respect. Mrs. Shönfeld's father had left for America alone. They never heard from him again and never mentioned him in their conversations. Running away for a better life was considered cowardly.

Friday nights, after Shabbat dinner, we would all walk to visit Maestra's mother. Shaindy stayed overnight with her "Bubby" every Shabbat so her beloved grandmother wouldn't have to eat alone. Among ten grandchildren from her five children, Shaindy was the darling. I was friendly with the grandmother's other children, and I know they resented this favoritism.

My own grandmother lived far away in Sepinka, Romania. I only saw her twice.

I learned from Mrs. Shönfeld, a surrogate for my own mother, how to respect others. She demonstrated charity by offering a friend who opened a restaurant, the use of her oven to bake cheese Danishes. She took pride in helping others.

On a lovely summer day sitting at the worktable, one of the girls saw a man's figure through the open window.

"Who is that man in the yard?"

Having recognized my father, I felt dizzy.

I shrieked, "My *Tatuka*!" and bounded from my chair, running outside into his open arms.

Mrs. Shönfeld did not invite him in. It was a lack of respect and a reminder that she still didn't care very much for me or my family, whom she didn't even know. I still had not earned my way as part of their family. I was only an employee and a boarder.

I visited with *Tatuka* in the yard for only a short break from my work. Overcome with emotion, we hugged and kissed. We both cried in our embrace. He looked me over with approval noticing that I had grown taller. A warm expression and teary eyes told me how much he missed me. I sobbed in this magnificent moment.

I did not know this was the last time I would ever see *Tatuka*.

My life would change forever when a letter came from my brother, six months later at the end of 1941. In it, Bencion wrote that our whole family had been forced across the Polish border by the Hungarian Niloshes and killed with bullets. They murdered my father, my stepmother, my brother Hershel, sister Risi, four half-brothers, and my dear little Elka. I couldn't stop crying. Later I learned most of my schoolmates from Brustury were also killed there. I wanted to run after my lost family, but it was impossible since Jews could no longer ride trains. I could do nothing.

I did not know then that thousands of Jews were being killed. After this, it became politically quiet for a couple of years. Temporarily, the Hungarian police stopped harassing Jews.

I overheard the Shönfelds speaking with one another about the progression of the war. They talked about the German military being deep in Russian territory, and told stories of how the Russians sprinkled water on the Germans during the bitter winter, causing them to freeze to death. The Jewish people hoped that the Germans were losing the war and that they would be safe. These were only fantasies that never materialized for most.

Until now, I was privileged to live a protected provincial life.

CHAPTER 7

In the Big City

September 1941–1944

My life went on. I lived with the Shönfeld family in Chust for almost three years, from September 1941 until July 1943. I learned many new things about life in a big city brimming with opportunities for adventure and luxuries for a few. Work was abundant for people like me, despite the economic disparities. This was quite different from my precious little village of Brustury, where almost everyone was equal. To me, the big city was irresistible with people acquiring riches, very different from my little village, where people were close and knew each other from generation to generation. Chust residents lost contact with one another over time as the city grew and prospered.

The main synagogue was a stunning two-story building on a long block with the rabbi's house, the ritual bath, the home of the religious judge, and the kosher slaughterer's quarters.

Lining the adjacent streets, there were small stores with big display windows showing clothes, shoes, and toys. Factories manufactured expensive furniture, men's prayer shawls, candles, and even soap. A large hardware store was filled with building materials such as hinges, nails, window glass, scales, and tools. A radio and a liquor store were next to a fabric shop. The fancy Crown Hotel down the street catered to tourists and dignitaries. One street contained a big block-long marketplace selling vegetables and fruit, chickens and eggs as well as livestock and horses. That was where Mr. Shönfeld shopped for the family. Running the wig business, Mrs. Shönfeld was too busy to go to the market most of the time. Customers gossiped about a husband shopping for his wife. Back in those days, women did all the domestic work.

When I was fifteen, my teeth and gums started hurting. So I went to a Jewish dentist. He told me I had several abscesses. It hurt a lot when he filled my cavities without any anesthetic. Being a friend of the Shönfelds, he didn't charge me any money. I knew I was charity. He suggested that I brush my teeth daily. I went to the apothecary and bought my first toothbrush and toothpaste with my tip money. They also had makeup, so I treated myself to a reddish-pink lipstick. I felt grown-up wearing this makeup when I went out with my friends.

Chust had two train stations and several coffee shops. The small station was in the middle of town, the larger one – about an hour's walk away. Special horse-drawn taxi wagons, carrying four or six passengers, took riders to and from the train station. Bells jingled from the horses' bridles, as they clopped along the street. Trains whistled at each stop, as they passed from one part of Hungary to the next, this time from Brustury to Budapest. One-way with several stops took twenty-four hours.

Once that train brought my beloved sister Malchi who was seventeen. A letter from her told me exactly when she would be passing through Chust from Brustury on the way to visit Aunt Ruchel Lebovic in Budapest. The train stopped at the small station in the middle of town near the Shönfelds. I hopped on and kissed her. We were excited to see each other and chattered non-stop until the porter came around and asked to stamp our tickets. I didn't have one. Lost in conversation, I forgot to get off at the station, so I had to ride to the next city. We were so scared. Would the train man take me to jail? He couldn't throw me off in the middle of the ride. I got off at the next stop, bought a ticket, and caught the returning train back to Chust.

Down the middle of Chust was a promenade where women of means would parade on Shabbat afternoons wearing their fur coats and beautiful wigs made by Mrs. Shönfeld. I used to imagine them brag about their husbands and children and even talk about their servants. These fancy city ladies dressed to impress, unlike poor women from my village. Being stylish and in vogue was important in Chust. Seeing this parade each Shabbat made me conscious of my appearance as well. Even a poor young lady can develop a taste for pretty clothes and furs. I used my small earnings from tips to buy a few new things. My first outfit was a dark blue skirt with a sky-blue blouse and a wide red belt. Wearing my new outfit on Shabbat made me feel proud while walking together with my new friends on the promenade. Boys our age would stand on the side and whistle as we passed by.

Hanging from electric light poles, loudspeakers would crackle with Hungarian folk tunes, alternating with military marches. From these sounds I picked up the lyrics of local popular music. I can still speak street Hungarian.

I wanted to make new friends and connect with peers my age, but I could not. No one in Chust knew of "the new girl." Finally, in the city, I found two sisters my age – Chana and Mindy. We became close. They were orphans living with a neighbor. The sisters introduced me to other young people.

From far away we could see a castle standing high on a hill outside the city. For fun on Shabbat, boys and girls together would chat and giggle, as we'd climb to the top to sing songs and eat our snacks. Once Aunt Mindya reprimanded me: it was forbidden to carry on Shabbat. I didn't care. She had no control over me. And Mrs. Shönfeld really didn't care either. She had little interest in my private life.

I was 17 and I wanted to have fun with my friends. For entertainment during the week, we used to hang out at the movie house and the ice cream parlor next door, where we would bring pastries and other homemade desserts. I had no parents to restrict me. A boy whom I liked worked at the ice-cream parlor. He would refill my cone on the sly. After work at the Shönfelds, I would take off to be with my friends. Two years had now passed with the Shönfelds, and I had matured.

In 1942, when clients would come to the wig shop, they were just starting to talk openly about political events occurring as far back as 1938. With serious expressions, they would gossip, almost in denial, about the Nazis' brutal treatment of the Jews in Germany and in Poland. They would also talk about *Kristallnacht,* the Night of Broken Glass, which had occurred on November 10 in 1938. It was unthinkable to believe that synagogues had been set afire and demolished by the Nazi Gestapo, who were swept up in nationalistic fervor. Holy Torah scrolls and rabbinical books were stacked in piles, doused with gasoline, and burned in bonfires, torching the very soul of our identity. Windows in Jewish shops and homes were violently smashed, robbed, and shattered with sledgehammers by the Brown Shirts. Hitler's private bodyguards, along with enlisted German civilians. The rampage killed up to 200 Jews and 30,000 were sent to jail for a few months. Next, the Nazis imposed exorbitant fines on the Jewish people to repair the damage.

Could this really be happening in civilized Germany? Until now, our people would not accept what we would later know as truth. They were unable to understand how something so violent could happen; how there could be planned incidents of cruelty and brutality. If you hadn't seen it with your own eyes, it was impossible to understand. In the stores, shoppers spoke as if the stories were just rumors. Then I learned how wrong they were.

One day, at the end of 1941, I received another horrific letter from Bencion confirming these rumors.

Heartbroken, Bencion wrote to me he was finally able to go to Brustury to recover at least some mementos that had been left behind in our home. Aunt Hilda saved whatever she could carry with her to her house. Furniture was left behind, free for the taking. Bencion was able to bring back to Ganich our roaming cow to produce milk for their children and save Mother's bedding, hand-embroidered linens, and her gold jewelry, including the ring with three blood-red rubies. This was all my family had left of our personal history.

Longing for family, I took some time off work to visit Bencion. Aunt Mindya paid for my train fare to Ganich, as Jews could temporarily ride the trains again. First, I visited my brother for a few bitter cold weeks during December 1942 and then continued on to Brustury in January 1943 to see for myself what was left of our house.

Not emotionally strong enough to go by myself to see our little house one last time, I asked two of my school friends to accompany me. As we approached what was left of my home, I shivered as my eyes fell upon the open front door and broken windows. It was dark and empty inside – a lost world. I broke down sobbing and could not enter the house or the yard. I was in shock. I didn't have to go in to know that everything was destroyed. This terror was now real for me.

Even though Bencion had written to me, even though he had talked to me when I visited him in December 1942, even though I heard people in Chust talk about destruction, even though some men and women in Chust had disappeared, the reality did not hit me until I saw my own home in ruins. My hope was shattered. To this day, remembering this scene makes me cry and my heart ache. My childhood home and my world of innocence wounded, never to heal.

My friends and I went back toward Aunt Hilda's house, where I recovered for only a day before I returned to Bencion.

I couldn't stay in Brustury any longer. It hit me too hard. There was nothing left there for me. I felt empty, alone — a terrible void passed through me.

Aunt Hilda was born in Czechoslovakia and had papers to prove she was a citizen, as did some of my school friends. Many Jews hurried to Budapest to obtain their certificates, blindly believing that official documents would save their lives. The Hungarian police took away Jews for any reason, papers or not.

Often we think horrifying things happen only to others. It's hard to understand the evil you have never witnessed, but only heard about. Some events are too horrific to imagine. It was easier to believe what you saw with your own eyes. And *see* we would.

We knew that in 1938 Germany had taken control of parts of Czechoslovakia. In 1939, Hitler annexed Hungary, taking over the area where I was staying in Chust; it became Hungary. Germany gave an ultimatum to the Czechoslovakian government to surrender the rest of the country. In 1940, as part of the continuing occupation of Czechoslovakia, we began to feel the menacing presence of the Germans. They came and ordered people onto trucks. Eventually the Hungarian military moved all the Jewish people into ghettos, a small barricaded section of a city where Jews were confined. There was little food, no stores, and abusive military control. People would starve and die on the street. From the ghetto, they would be shipped off to the Nazi "model" concentration camp, Theresienstadt, in Czechoslovakia, near Prague. Others would be sent to Auschwitz and Birkenau in Poland. The Hungarian army took many Jews from Carpathia between 1941 and 1942, but I was still with the Shönfelds. Only half of our people in Chust were left.

Our family members who escaped this roundup were Malchi in Budapest, Bencion's family in Ganich, and me. The Nazis couldn't take all the Jews at once. Had I been home with my father, I too would have been among the slaughtered. It was my first escape from death.

The region did seem to quiet down from the end of 1942 until mid-1944, when the Hungarians, under great Nazi pressure, stepped up their role in Hitler's Final Solution to rid Europe of every Jew. They transported an estimated 400,000 Hungarian Jews to their death.

I knew that one transport train carrying Jews was taken to the Polish border, but because of Raoul Wallenberg's intervention, it was returned to Chust. I took food, sent by townspeople and cooked in the Rabbi's kitchen, to the train just as it arrived. I later learned that the Swedish diplomat, Wallenberg, made this happen against all odds, to save some of the Hungarian Jewry.

Crying inside, with no one to confide in or ask for advice, I knew there was no one to rely upon except myself. From the age of five, I had no mother to hug me. Love from others was short-lived. An extended family of aunts, uncles, and cousins could never replace my parents and siblings. My life was like playing a game with my favorite flower, the daisy, pulling the petals, one by one: *love me, love me not.* It always ended in *loves me not.* I had no one.

Before every holiday, especially Passover, my job with Mrs. Shönfeld would become intense. There was extra work with the wigs, as ladies wanted to look their best for the holidays.

"We must spend most of our time on the wigs. They are more important than housework," Maestra commanded.

Once when I was dressing to go on her errands, she sarcastically asked, "How long will your toileting take?"

She didn't expect an answer, and I knew she was impatient, but I tried to look attractive.

Once I overheard a customer whisper to Mrs. Shönfeld, "Doesn't she look lovely?"

That gave my self-confidence a real boost. I could be an attractive young lady.

Before Passover, our holiday celebrating God's deliverance of the Jews from slavery in Egypt, we would work the whole night to finish the wig orders. It was hard to stay awake.

My eyes were strained from looking at those tiny knots of three hairs for hours on end while knitting them into the wig cap. She never taught us how to cut or style the wigs. This was the artistic expertise of the Maestra. I used to turn the light hanging from a hook on the wall toward my hands so that I could see through my tears as I thought about my family.

Our reward for staying up all night to finish wigs was to have a warm bath in the Jewish women's bathhouse. Mrs. Shönfeld would pay for this luxury. I would have preferred to go to a movie. During the night, she would feed us with hard candies and chocolates to keep us awake.

For nearly three years, ending in July of 1943, I would often walk for two hours from the Shönfeld's back to Aunt Mindya's house in Koshalie for Shabbat. Young and spirited, as I was walking, I got lost in my thoughts. I shut off my memory to quell my fears. Deluded into thinking I was safe forever, I laughed frivolously with Cousin Suri when I arrived.

With tears running down her face, Aunt Mindya scolded me in a loud angry voice. "Your parents have been taken and murdered by the Hungarian military. What you are laughing about?"

With irritation, I talked back. "Can't I laugh once in a while?"

I was hurt to always be reminded of bad things. My sorrow was locked deep inside. By acting normal, I tried not to show it. Just like *Tatuka* taught me. I had to go on, but I cried every night under my feather quilt, alone in my bed.

If only Aunt Mindya knew — a young girl doesn't want to remember only awful things. Sometimes I needed to pretend it didn't happen and laugh it off, though the shadow of dread followed me.

One Shabbat, Suri surprised me with a gift. It was a fine new black silk skirt she had made just for me, with small red, blue, and white flowers embroidered on the hem. She also gave me my own bar of soap as a present. Suri knew life had treated me harshly and that I was grateful for any present.

By now, everyone knew what was happening to Jews all over Hungary.

"What is going to happen to me? I am alone."

CHAPTER 8

On My Own

Our Chust community began to talk in fear about the roundups of Jews. Sitting by the table making wigs, I overhead women whispering in disbelief about the rumors I already knew were true from Bencion's letters, that the Jews — entire families — were loaded onto military trucks and taken north to the Polish border, where the Germans were in control. Chust was finally experiencing the feelings I had been having for a couple of years. Only Aunt Mindya knew my fear because my father was her brother. Sharing late into the night, we tried to comfort one another. Most people if they weren't directly affected, were still in denial.

A few boys and girls managed to escape from being taken, but not my Risi and Hershel. People said the German SS - *SchutzStaffel*, the Nazi Party's protection and security service, – made the women, men, and children undress before chasing them into a river where they shot them with rifles. This massacre also claimed my family.

The river must have become a flowing red graveyard. Other victims were forced to dig deep ditches that then became their own graves. Terrified, they were lined up and shot. They would fall into the mass grave.

A handful of young wounded people waited until dark before they managed to crawl out from among the dead and escape into the forest. Others had already been taken to a bordering city, Kamenets Podolski, in Ukraine, Soviet Union, where they were gassed.

Some young Jews who escaped these killing ditches found their way back to nearby cities. They told their stories to anyone who would listen, but no one wanted to believe what they had not seen. The locals called the escapees *meshugeners,* crazy people. Rumor, now fact, continued. They came back from hell, yet no one paid attention. When I saw a stranger walking in the street, I looked at his face, trying to recognize my father, my siblings or someone from my town.

I knew the scenes of mass murder were true since my family had been captured still in their wet clothes, not yet dry from the laundry. I later heard this from people in Brustury who had been left behind. It must have been after Shabbat when clothes for the week were washed. Acquaintances would not want to accept the news from Bencion's letters.

Will they come for me?

I was crying most of the time, distracted from my wig making. Mrs. Shönfeld saw my suffering and tried to divert me by sending me walking on errands. Walking outdoors helped me release some of the anger from my scrambled mind, so that I could again focus on my work with the wigs.

On Friday nights, when I was with the Shönfelds, I would go outside on the porch during the meal and cry. I knew if they saw me crying, it would upset the happy Shabbat meal, the only time everyone sat together as a family. I tried not to stay away too long. Where were *my* parents? I wasn't hungry. The Shönfelds and most city people still denied the rumors of Jews being slaughtered, even when Polish people came to the house begging for food. It happened there, but not here.

Once, a young boy came to ask for food.

"What did you eat at home?" Maestra asked him.

"I had delicatessen."

"You must have come from a family of means."

She offered him what she had – a bowl of bean soup.

Thank God, I was reassured that Malchi was safe in Budapest through her letters, but no one else seemed to care. When *Maminka* died, I became less of a person. With my father and family now gone, I had become an orphan.

Mr. Shönfeld saw that I was wearing a gold ring with rubies that I brought back from my visit with Bencion. He asked me to sell it to him. I was offended, since it was the only memento from dear *Maminka*. I always wore it so it would never accidentally disappear.

We heard that young, healthy, agile boys formed groups in the east to run away to Russia. Others applied for citizenship papers, believing that that identification would protect them. Legal documents didn't help.

I turned eighteen in March 1943, nearly four years after leaving home. I went to Ganich for the second time to visit my brother Bencion for Passover in April. I stayed longer than expected because I wanted to remain close to my favorite brother, now my only brother. He was still my protector. We hugged and cried as he showed me the treasures saved from *Maminka* that he had been able to bring back from Brustury. Even Sula, our cow, seemed sad in her stall. Bencion walked with me to the rowboat on the river that took me to the train station in the next city. Chust was now my only home.

"Leichuka, be very careful. We don't know what's going to happen. God will protect us." As tears puddled in his eyes, he tenderly held me close, "I love you, dear little sister."

I did not know then that I would never again see my brother, Bencion, his sweet wife, Blumi, and their two precious babies. They would all later perish in Auschwitz.

I returned to the Shönfeld family on one of the last trains that Jews were allowed to ride. It was a few weeks later than Maestra had expected me, and she was furious.

Shaking her head and looking at me sideways, she sarcastically said with a rising voice, "You *finally* came back?"

She made another crack in my soul.

The situation for Jews in Hungary had changed drastically. The government was now under total German control and Jews felt hunted. Food was becoming scarce. The Shönfelds had no garden at their city home like we had in Brustury, and had to rely on store bought food.

I was only able to remain with the Shönfeld family for six more weeks. Jews became immobilized, not allowed to travel by train. Local citizens had taken over Jewish stores and factories. Shopkeepers were banned from selling merchandise to Jews.

Maestra sent me to the grocery store to buy bread for their family.

The proprietor, who knew me and knew that I was Jewish, politely said, "My dear miss, we have bread, but we are not allowed to sell to Jews." There was plenty of bread spread out on the counter.

I felt my face puff red with embarrassment. Shamed at my helplessness, I turned away and slouched out of the door. This was the first time I personally felt the stinging disrespect of anti-Semitism.

Buying food was nearly impossible and the Shönfelds could no longer afford to feed me.

Maestra told me, "You have to leave and find another place to live." She couldn't look me in the eye. I felt ashamed as well as angry at life and at her. She didn't want me anymore.

I was terribly angry that she sent me away during the third year, when it was my turn to be paid a monthly salary. My co-worker, Toby, was paid because her father came to collect her wages. I had no protector. My father was dead. I was mourning. I didn't have the nerve to speak up or the knowledge to advocate for myself. Was she punishing me for staying away so long? Or was she using my absence as an excuse. This would not be the last time that someone would take advantage of me. Nothing could ever be the same. Nothing!

Maestra gave me supplies with which to begin work on my own – a wooden head and the needles. She made me use my own tip money to buy the hair and cap material from her. I left without my wages for the third year I had worked.

Tools of wig-making - Knüpfnadeln Ventilating Needles and hair, on Maminka's tablecloth

On the street, I saw Jewish men who had been beaten up by Hungarian youths. Finally, everyone believed the reality they saw, that anti-Semitism had come to Chust. Local civilians openly mocked us. Even the grocery man who had taken over the Jewish store openly hated me.

Luckily, I had one option. My father's cousin, Faige Ruchel Cik, heard about my plight and came to Chust to rescue me. She took me by horse and wagon to her big house in Sekernice, which is presently Sokyrnytsya, Ukraine. She shared her home and her food with me. She was worried about her husband who had been taken away by the Hungarian police to work for the government cleaning streets. We had to be vigilant along the way back, watching for intimidating local police. We could spot them by the large plume of colorful shiny feathers cascading from their black hats.

Once safe in her house, I was not allowed to go out at night because she was afraid that the cruel Hungarian Niloshes, the intimidating local police, would take advantage of me. Faige was afraid of them for herself as well. They peered into our homes through the windows at night before we had pulled down the shades. Who were they looking for?

Faige was able to offer me refuge for about six weeks. To protect me, she took me to live to my cousin Mali Cik's house just before Sekernice became a ghetto in April of 1944. Faige went to live with her brother, Mendel Chaim Cik[1], on the next street in Sekernice. She was safer with her brother who was a college graduate. He was an important person in the community.

The Hungarians had also taken Mali's husband to the slave labor camp to clean streets. Mali was left behind alone to care for their four children. She was afraid for herself and her children and was relieved that I was there to help.

Mali sheltered me from the police, also forbidding me to go out of the house by myself, even during the daytime. We knew that my beautiful girlfriend Peppi, walking alone, had been caught by the Hungarian Niloshes. They took her to police headquarters, where she was humiliated – her beautiful long wavy blond hair shaved from her head. I was afraid they would catch me and do the same.

Ultimately, we all became prey to their blind animal rage.

---

1   See Appendix page 237

PART II

Ghettos & Camps

CHAPTER 9

"For the Good of the Nation"

March 1944

When my cousin, Mali's husband Hershel, was forced into a Hungarian labor camp, she was left terrified, alone, and helpless with four youngsters, all under the age of ten. As a nineteen-year-old orphan, I came to love this family. It was my own.

I had been with Mali for about six months when, on the day after Passover, in April of 1944, German troops united with Hungarian police to create the Sekernice ghetto, formerly Czechoslovakia, now Hungary. Loudspeakers blared, "*Achtung! Attention!*" The drumbeat from the trucks commanded us. "No Jew can leave town. Remain inside your houses." We were only allowed to go outside to use the outhouse in the backyard. We had become prisoners in our own homes.

All over Europe, this scene was repeated many times as Jews were driven into ghettos. There was no escape. Now families were being rousted from their homes in nearby villages and hustled into Sekernice. We were trapped.

Early one spring morning, heavy, angry noise from the street led us to peek out Mali's windows from behind the curtains. We saw military men with guns pointed at a crowd of grim-faced, bedraggled families. I gasped and held my breath to push down my rage. The street was filled with hundreds of frightened people wearing heavy layers of clothing. Jews of all ages had been walking throughout the night with stooped shoulders and vacant expressions, carrying their children and heavy bundles. Most families traveled on foot with few possessions. A few walked next to their horse drawn wagons that hauled their large bundles and bulky mattresses stuffed with hay, camouflaging their valuables.

We had no idea that thirty to forty people would be forced into each single-family house. They burst through the unlocked front door of Mali's home, telling us of the night's terror. We knew none of these uprooted strangers who crammed into our home, eventually sleeping on the floors in Mali's large six-room house. Tensions escalated as petrified men returned from the synagogue from morning prayers into this mounting chaos.

In one day, Sekernice became a ghetto, surrounded by guards with guns and big dogs.

Fear and hunger outlined these refugees' faces. Parents held tightly to their wailing children as Mali and I squeezed our family with her four youngsters into one bedroom. We each slept with two of her children. Worried what would happen the next day, we really didn't sleep the whole night.

The next morning, the military soldiers ordered adults, and even babies, to wear a yellow six-pointed star on our clothing to identify us as Jews. I had to find yellow fabric to make stars by their exact measurement specifications. When I found Mali's best yellow damask tablecloth in the linen credenza, I was relieved it would be enough material for us and several of the other families. I had learned how to sew by hand in the sixth grade and first made a pattern to cut the six-pointed stars. We were told we were going to be relocated. Mali prepared nonperishable food in the kitchen with what she had in the house. I worked the whole night, shedding tears onto the fabric as I stitched these stars of scorn to our outer garments.

The Hungarian police in their green uniforms and colorful hats once had been our protectors. Now, allied with the Germans, they became bullies and thugs, brutalizing anyone who dared to speak out or try to escape from the town. We were held in our Sekernice ghetto for a few weeks. Nasty and rude, these police were attacking their own countrymen who happened to be Jews.

People were corralled to stand for hours in or around the synagogue. If someone moved out of place, they would hit them with the butt of their rifles. We dared not rebel. The next group of incoming Jews slept outside the building or wherever they could find a place to lie down on the bare ground with their bundles. Families desperately clung together.

Stunned into submission, we followed orders without question. Mass murder of Jews was in its full swing. Husbands and fathers who spoke out in defense for their wives and children were taken to military headquarters and tortured. Some returned with bleeding wounds and broken bones. Others never came back. Women were left waiting for their husbands and children cried for their fathers' comfort.

The gentiles in town moved about freely with obvious curiosity, watching the plight of their Jewish neighbors. From rumors, they heard that we were going to be displaced soon. Some of our neighbors waited for us to be taken. Then they would invade and loot our homes and businesses. As bystanders, most did nothing to help. Even if some wanted to assist us, they knew they would be risking their lives.

The Hungarian militia stuffed as many Jews as they could into the largest synagogue. There was a temporary makeshift bakery in the ghetto. I volunteered to work in the bakery, helping to prepare the dough for bread. I had to be escorted by a guard to and from this work.

A washing station for clothes was set up across from the synagogue, not for washing clothes, but for dipping them. It was mandated that we use it to sterilize our clothes in what was a putrid- smelling liquid. To appear to obey orders, I gave them only two of my dresses. They came back stinky and crumpled. I had to wear them anyway.

Knowing what had happened in Poland and Germany and anticipating the same for Hungary, many Jews had already started to hide their valuables. Money and jewelry could be concealed in a bar of homemade soap, or even in a bottle of goose fat. Coins and precious stones were sewn into the linings of clothing and valises. Maybe jewels could be used to buy favors of food or even a few more days or weeks of life. Unlike parcels of land, these valuable gems were transportable and easily hidden in all possible places, even in body cavities.

Sekernice, Hungary, became one ghetto of many in Europe. The miserable ghetto life lasted but a few weeks. Jews were forced to live in a small landmass in a sectioned off part of the city, isolated from the non-Jewish population. It was dirty and unhygienic. Meager food was rationed at under 200 calories a day. Former homes were pillaged and taken over by the Nazis. Jewish "abandoned" homes were auctioned off on behalf of the Reich. Jews were collected until they were deported and eventually killed, except those who were strong enough to work for the German war machine.

It was after Passover when German troops burst into our homes, yet politely announced in German, "For the good of the nation, your families are being relocated for work to help the war effort." Cynical and condescending, they politely challenged, *"Nicht wahr? Isn't it right?"* They were trying to deceive us. We knew they had no intention of bettering our lives, but we were afraid to disobey with rifles being waved in our faces.

During the commotion, Mali whispered to me, "Please, go up to the attic and hide my Shabbat clothing. Then go to the backyard and bury the fabric I bought to sew the children's new underwear and shirts."

This I could not do. Had she forgotten that no one was allowed to go outside except to the outhouse? Somehow, I slipped her things to the Christian neighbor without being seen. Soldiers were everywhere, shoving people.

Knowing we were going to be moved, Mali continued to prepare travel food, noodles, and flatbread with many eggs. Eggs were still plentiful from the hens in the yard. She baked as much bread as we had flour.

Later, I saw Mali talking to her friendly Christian neighbor, who risked his life to visit us and check on our well-being. Mali and his family had been friendly neighbors.

"Please, take our silver and my jewelry, the sewing machine, and fabric for safekeeping until we return," she pleaded.

I asked Mali to give the neighbor *Maminka*'s ring and tablecloth. Mali trusted our kind neighbor with her precious possessions. Did she have an alternative? Would he keep our valuables safe, holding them until we returned? Will he give them back to us? People were naïve, thinking they would come home again. There was no way to know. There was no other choice.

Just before we were forced out of our home, I put on three dresses, and my new brown coat, in case I lost my suitcase. It was in vain. When the Hungarian military reserve came for all the people in our house, we were required to line up in the street, before being taken with the others. Townspeople laughed and spit on us while standing in front of their houses, yelling, "Look at your homes for the last time. You will never see them again." We were the butt of their bad jokes, not knowing what to believe.

Mob mentality prevailed as people acted without caring or feeling about the consequences to their victims. When they took us out of our houses, we prayed for a miracle that never came. I could hear my heartbeat pulsing in my ears.

Why did God abandon us?

The soldiers announced, "You are being sent away to work for Germany."

No one knew where we were actually going or how long we would be away. Our minds could not comprehend what was happening. The day after the announcement ordering us to prepare to leave, a troop of Hungarian soldiers with guns on their shoulders, clubbed and whipped us as they marched us to the other side of town. As we gathered in the schoolyard, we heard the SS barking orders over loudspeakers: "Bring your candelabras and gold into the school building."

Even though people were stupefied, they opened their bundles and threw valuables onto a big pile of candelabras, Chanukah menorahs and silver Kiddush cups, the goblet we used to bless the Shabbat wine. I had nothing to give.

I forgot one of the children's rucksacks in the house and attempted to go back to get it, but it was impossible to make my way through the tight crowd. We could not risk losing one another.

The Hungarian military had set up guns on the rooftop of the schoolhouse. It was the first time I had ever seen a machinegun, and it was pointed right at me. Germans selected Jews to collaborate with them against other Jews as informers. They were given white armbands and the job of keeping order. They in turn were ordered to select other Jews to join them. They forced us into long lines and we were as scared of them as we were of the soldiers. Fearing for their lives, they did as they were told by the Nazis.

A Hungarian soldier ordered a woman to take off her fur coat and give it to him, leaving her wearing only her dress in the cold. Everyone had to remove the gold wedding rings from their fingers. The Hungarian militia made sure our family heirlooms would remain in Hungary. Losing our valuables, we had no bargaining power for another meal. Perhaps, if we were lucky, we could beg for another day of life.

I was just a naïve country girl with no money or valuables, only a small suitcase. After knowing the fate of my family, I constantly feared that the Germans would take away the most valuable thing I had – my life.

This was a nightmare in the daytime. I was experiencing the fear my family must have suffered when they were snatched from their homes in wet clothes three years ago in 1941. Faige Cik, her brother Mendel and their family were also part of the roundup. They found us in the line. I reached out to Mali's precious children and we clung tightly to one another. There was no place to run or hide. Mendel Cik had already been taken into a slave-labor camp later returning to Sekernice and ending up on our same train.

It all happened so fast. We shivered as we stood in line holding our bags. At nightfall and at gunpoint, we were marched for hours to a cattle train.

The SS soldiers merely "followed orders." After the war, the Nuremberg war crime trials declared "following orders" as an unacceptable excuse. We writhed under the fear of their cruelty.

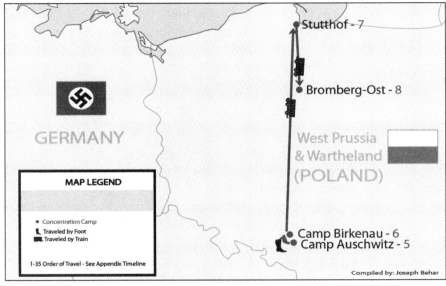

For Complete Map - See Appendix, page 232

CHAPTER 10

Train to Hell

Thirsty and hungry, everyone crowded toward a single water spigot in an open field. No one stayed in line. When I came to the water pump, someone shoved me from behind. Tripping and falling face-first against the metal pipe, my front tooth was chipped and I tasted blood. Against the darkening horizon, we saw the vague silhouette of railroad freight cars in the far distance. Soldiers shoved with butts of their guns. Dogs growling at our heels kept us walking.

Dragging my heavy, swollen feet through the cold night, I finally reached the waiting cars. They were cattle cars. Terror stricken, I cringed as soldiers yelled that we must climb up into the car. We were whipped as they pushed people up into the open mouth that seemed to absorb more people than there was room, until not one more person could fit. With no loading ramp, everyone required help to get up into the high opening. It was especially painful for the elderly. Once inside, our bodies pressed against one another, just like livestock. Were we going to be slaughtered? Families desperately tried to stay together, though some were separated. I was able to remain with cousin Mali, her children, and the other Ciks.

The iron door slammed shut. I heard the metallic banging of chains locking us in. With everyone crammed tightly together in a putrid box with a low ceiling, I could hardly breathe. Wheels screeched. The train lurched forward to an unknown destination, and children screamed in the strange darkness.

Old women moaned. Frightened men, once protectors of their families, had lost control, their masculinity shattered. I had no choice but to succumb to this inhumanity. We couldn't explain to the *kinder* what we didn't know ourselves, and if we had known, we wouldn't have told them. How can you explain to the naive little ones that we are captured like sheep and taken by our enemy?

At nineteen years old, my world had completely fallen apart. I held my breath to push down my anger. During the entire trip, "what will happen to me next?" was on my mind. "

Rumbling on the train for days, we passed through Humenné, Slovakia. Over eighty people crammed together were forced to stand, pressed next to one another during those harrowing days. There was no room to move or sit. No air to breathe. No water to drink. A barrel in a corner of the car served as a toilet. Everyone — men, women and children — had to use the toilet barrel in front of all the others, if they could make it there. Otherwise, we soiled ourselves. We were packed in like cattle. The stench of urine and feces flowing under my feet was overwhelming. An old man leaning next to me was dead. He eventually fell to his knees. A woman had slumped against the wall. I think she died, too. With weakened cries and dazed eyes, we were specimens of humanity at its worst: vomit on the walls, sweat mixed with tears, a hopeless brew of life clinging to itself. My family, Mali and the children, pressed to the far side of the tomb in an effort to avoid the stink and embarrassment. Privately, I fought to be released one way or the other. We had completely lost our rights of human dignity.

Small horizontal neck-high openings with metal bars provided little circulating air. There was no escape through those narrow slits. Mali and I held tightly to her inconsolable children. We could not comfort them. She passed a letter to me that she had written earlier to her beloved husband. In it, she told our horrible story. I pushed her addressed and stamped envelope through the small opening into the cold night air. We prayed a stranger would find her note and mail it. Maybe it fell into the hands of a Nazi.

A young mother gave birth to her first child during the trip. She was at the far end of the car near the toilet barrel, which was surrounded by men. Her laboring screams pierced the airless cubicle. Although I had heard my stepmother's screams in labor, I knew nothing about where babies came from. I once read a book in Hungarian about menstruation. It happened to me when I was fifteen at the wig maker's house. Confused and ashamed, not knowing about my body, I found rags to use. I was afraid someone would see a stain on my dress.

The child's birth was humiliating for the laboring mother with men all around. I never heard a cry from the baby. Before the mother saw her tiny infant, it was compassionately not allowed to take a first breath. I think someone put it in the toilet barrel. Sadly, this young new mother died before we arrived at *the hell*, as did several others in the rolling hearse. These would not be the last deaths I would witness first hand.

It was hard for me to keep track of time. Had it been two days or three? Day and night were the same, except during daylight when I could see mountains through the narrow bars at the top of the car. I recognized the tall Tatra Mountains in Slovakia, where I knew that well-off families vacationed during the summer and skied in the winter. We were traveling north, approaching the Polish border.

The train ground to a stop. The outside chain clanked, and the heavy door scraped open. A lightning of shock passed through me when I saw the German SS standing before us with their rifles pointed at our faces.

The leader yelled, "If one of you tries to escape, we will kill everyone in your transport."

Five or six prisoners were ordered to bring water from a nearby pump to our car and then empty the foul toilet barrel. I wondered if they saw the baby. When I realized that Germans had replaced our Hungarian guards, an even greater terror gripped me. I finally realized, with stunning clarity, that our lives were in peril. No one attempted to escape.

We were locked in once more. The train clanged forward again for days. No food and little water.

As the train slowed down, I glimpsed a tall arch through the narrow opening at the top of the rail car. Hanging in the arch was a big sign — *Arbeit Macht Frei*: *Work Makes You Free* — reminding us of their "work for the war effort" message, deluding us into believing there could be a way out.

Before the train lumbered to a halt, I saw the word AUSCHWITZ looming in the distance. The heavy metal doors scraped open to blinding morning light.

Soldiers barked orders for us to get off of the train. "*Schnell! Schnell! Fast! Fast!*" Inmates, wearing black-and-white-striped pajamas with white arm-bands, boarded the train to collect our suitcases and rucksacks, even before we were off. Prisoners lifted the stiff corpses and threw them off the train. I can't forget the sound of these souls, once filled with tears, as they hit the ground with a collective thump, one after another.

I held my breath, clutching my pocketbook to my chest.

Trying to warn young mothers, the emaciated inmates whispered in Yiddish, "Give your little ones to the grandmothers." Mothers, fearing separation, still embraced their children. We did not know that their babies and elderly grandmothers were destined for immediate death.

No one realized that the inmates were Jews, like us. They knew what was waiting for us behind the gate, where we were selected to live or die. With intense anger, they questioned us: "Why did you come here? Didn't you know better? You should have committed suicide."

These words hit me in the worst way. I did not have a clue as to what awaited us.

I wanted to scream, "God, why did you let us come here?"

How could we have known?

Thousands of dazed men, women, and children from many Czech ghettos, now part of Hungary, oozed from the string of cattle cars into a noisy, chaotic crowd, trying to avoid the bodies littering the ground. Forced into submission, dogs snarled; beastly dogs on leashes, held by shouting SS men aiming rifles toward us.

"Throw your valises and food to the side of the field," they screamed.

That's when I lost my pocketbook with all my family photos. Items not left on the pile with the suitcases such as photographs, important papers, and jewelry, were also confiscated. Without personal documents, we were nameless.

I was no one.

Everyone — everyone sobbed in terror as we saw thousands of captured Jews pushing from all directions, stepping over dead bodies strewn like trash – a trauma imprinted in my mind's eye and on my heart. I can never forget. We obeyed orders, afraid of joining those lifeless white faces at our feet. There was no escape from this shocking scene.

I believed the hot sky crumbling upon us was fire from hell.

As we were pushed toward the main gate of Auschwitz, the SS separated us, men in one line and women and children in the other.

Terrified mothers feared losing their precious little ones as the SS blasted orders, "Men – to the left! Women – to the right!"

Mali's children clung to us. Starving babies shrieked. Mothers frantically tried to keep their families together as drunk SS soldiers viciously pulled babies from mothers' arms to separate them. I guess being intoxicated made their jobs easier. I didn't see what they did with the babies. In the camps, I heard from other inmates who had been in Auschwitz since 1942, that the small babies were yanked from their mothers' arms by drunken soldiers and thrown over the fence into an open fire.

Hell had opened and we were shoved in.

The SS guards roughly wrenched wives from their husbands' arms. Young women, including grieving mothers, were led to a gate where the cruel medical officer, Dr. Mengele, and other officers stood on a raised ramp, giving them a better view of us. Mengele, a death emblem on his hat, a swastika on his collar, carried a pointer, which he flicked at his whim to direct our destinies.

My turn came quickly as I held my little cousin's hand. I felt as though Dr. Mengele stared straight through me. Good looking, but with cold eyes behind his mean, expressionless face, in an accusing tone, Mengele said to me, "You are young; this is not your child."

I just looked down, frozen in my fear, remembering what my father said about "putting on a good face." Even though I held tightly to my cousin's five-year-old daughter, she was snatched from me and sent back to her mother, in the line with children and older women.

The Germans had no use for children or men and women who could not endure hard labor to support their war effort. They chose only those who appeared healthy – from fifteen to forty – for work. Prisoners fabricated their ages to be younger than forty and older than fifteen. The able-bodied were separated from the rest of the inmates.

Later, I learned that children under twelve and women over forty were sent immediately to the gas chambers. Young mothers, mourning for their lost children, suffered unspeakable agony. I understood what had happened when I saw them running from gate to gate for glimpses of their stolen children. With broken hearts and beaten souls, these mothers constantly wept as they were forced to work without regard for their yearning despair. Their bitter heartbreak would torment me for a lifetime.

Dr. Mengele determined my fate. He became known to the prisoners as the "White Angel," for his chilled, cruel demeanor and his white gloves. Jabbing his gloved finger close to my face, he motioned for me to move to the right. I can still see his stabbing eyes looking deeply into mine. To this day they haunt me. I was panicked, fearing his motion. What did right or left mean?

The rumor was that those sent to the left line went to their death. Looking strong and capable, I was spared though frozen in place. My instinct for survival moved my legs.

The left line became a fire in the sky. Smoky clouds rained ashes. My earlier vision of hell's fire cracking from the sky proved to be real.

Ordered to form lines of five, the SS chased us forward, "*Schnell! Schnell!*"

I heard classical music and saw marching inmates in striped pajamas playing instruments. It was so out of place — an attempt to confuse us further? Instead of crying, there was music, as if we could hope to be reunited with our loved ones after we passed through the gate.

"The epitome of irony" – Prisoners Orchestra in Auschwitz.

To terrify us, the SS watched closely for any disobedience, ready and willing to shoot us. Punishment for anything and everything was death. With brisk gesturing and loud voices, they choreographed our movements, as if every step had been planned. They wrote on clipboards. They documented our precise whereabouts. And we danced to their nightmarish tune.

"Take off your clothes and leave them in a pile over there. Put every item you love in the pail."

Take off all my clothes? Right here? Now? In front of everyone? I had no choice.

We were on display. I was allowed to keep my shoes. It was unbearably cold. Even my brain was frozen. Shamed and cringing with embarrassment, I hunched forward to appear smaller to hide my nakedness, as if I could make myself invisible.

Our hair was shorn, sometimes yanked out with cold manual hair clippers that quickly cut hair to the skin. Both male and female prisoners shaved our hair, even our pubic hair, removing all remnants of our identity to complete our humiliation. Guards peered into our mouths for gold teeth that would be pulled.

We all looked alike, unable to recognize one another. Robbed of our dignity, we were no longer innocent. I stood shivering with a crowd of nude women and no place to hide. Sisters clung together. I had no one. Mengele's penetrating stare traced our trembling naked bodies as he determined whether we were capable of hard labor.

He again approached me with his white-gloved hand, pointed to my legs with his stick, and asked, "Are your feet always so swollen?"

Trying to keep my face quiet, I quivered. "Nooo — only from the hard trip."

With his forefinger, Mengele gestured for me to go with the rest of the group. Once again I had been saved from certain death in the gas chambers. We were marched into a large room in a barrack.

Then he interrogated us further. "Are there twins among you?"

Many girls stepped forward. There was a rumor that twins would have certain privileges. This was incorrect. Twins underwent many medical "experiments" with no anesthesia, tortured by German doctors.

It was reported, by those who were lucky enough to survive, that large pharmaceutical companies conducted chemical tests on those child prisoners not yet gassed. The companies paid the government for this "research." We also heard about other grisly, bizarre medical experiments.

Auschwitz came to be known as a human processing factory. If you were doomed to die, it was immediate, on the day you arrived. If you lived, you were thrust into gruesome horror. We never knew what the next minute would bring.

How could this be happening to me? What have I done wrong? What is happening to the world? Where is merciful God?

I did not know until the next day, when I saw flashing sparks and black smoke coming from a tall chimney, that all the children and their mothers, including my cousin Mali and her little ones, had been shoved into the gas chambers and murdered on that very first day. My promise to take care of them was broken. Guilt consumed me.

My family was now smoke and ashes.

Of my family in the cattle car, only I survived.

CHAPTER 11

Twelve Hundred Naked Women

Late Spring 1944

We were given an ugly, short-sleeved, baggy gray dress to wear, without underwear or a covering for our shaved heads. Hairless heads all looked alike. I was allowed to keep only my shoes on as they looked under our tongues for diamonds. Ordered to stand and march in straight lines of five, everyone wanted to be next to someone they knew. Sisters tried to stay together. I had no one to be close with.

After being processed at Auschwitz, we were marched for about two miles to Camp Birkenau. These camps were referred to as one site, Auschwitz-Birkenau.

On the way to camp Birkenau, we were forced to walk through a dark puddle of disinfectant that soaked our shoes to ruin hidden keepsakes: pictures and documents some girls had concealed under their innersoles. I had nothing left to hide.

No stragglers remained as we walked our straight lines. Along the way to my left, I noticed an open space as large as a football field, strangely packed with people, mainly older men and young children. I waved to a third-year Jewish college student I had befriended before the ghetto in Sekernice. He used to visit me at Mali's house. He had an impaired short leg, but that didn't matter to me as he was nice looking, kind, intelligent, and interesting to talk to. He didn't recognize me without hair in that stupid gray dress. I understood something terrible was happening when I saw him with the very old and very young, standing in a dazed trance, stooped from fear and fatigue, waiting for something unknown. We passed by. We were gone. They would be gone forever. This scene shadows me even today whenever I see crowds of men, standing, praying in the synagogue. No one knows why I wipe my tears. I am different. I was there.

Two teenagers wearing striped dresses worked in the hot sun, sitting on a heap of stones, hammering rocks into smaller pieces. I wondered why they were doing that, but I dared not ask.

We arrived at Camp Birkenau hungry, thirsty, and tired to the bone. They marched us to a group of military-type barracks. My barrack was "A." As I stood in line for the counting, the reek of burning flesh filled the air. I was so hungry. My hunger and the smell of burning fatty flesh tormented me. Am I to die now?

Our building was one large room holding more than 500 girls on three tiered bunk beds. Each tier had only a wooden plank without any mattress. Ten girls slept on each level, five side by side, the soles of our feet touching the other row of five prisoners. Each plank had two blankets for five women prisoners in our row and no pillows. It was impossible to turn over, so we slept on our left side all night long. Stinging red bugs crawled out of the wall next to my bunk, biting me through the night. I was itchy for days.

A shrill whistle pierced the still dark morning. We hurriedly marched to the dirt field, lining up in rows of five, waiting to be counted by the SS women who stood guard with their leashed dogs trained to attack those who misbehaved. The counting had to be exact. If a girl fainted or died, we had to support her erect until the counting was approved. If it was off by even one person, it was repeated until it was correct. During the day, we were forced to stand or sit outside on the barren dirt ground until evening. The weather made no difference. We lost all concept of time with only the sun as our timepiece.

There was nothing green, not a bird, a butterfly, or a flower; just ants and an occasional worm beneath my feet.

If a girl disobeyed during the counting, talking, or not standing up straight, she was forced to kneel on a brick for hours at a time.

The first day, one of my friends bravely asked the Jewish warden the whereabouts of her parents.

"When can I see my mother?"

Without a word, the warden looked down while feebly pointing her finger toward the chimney.

I never knew that people could be burned.

This brutal truth traumatized me. Those sparks were the remains of people! I was petrified. My heart broke for the thousandth time and I was dumbfounded, petrified beyond the ability to respond, but only for a moment. Something deep within me rejected hopelessness and despair. I thought that one day I might be free. A desire to live raged through me. I must be free, and every second mattered.

This I knew for sure: "I will do everything I can to live beyond this horror."

During painful periods early in my life, I had learned to suck in my emotions and lock them down. Private tears were the secret of my soul.

The Germans took anyone that they judged to be weak away, out of the line. There was no room for tears or whining in the camp. The sickly were taken away and we never saw them again. Alone with my feelings, there was no escape except through my mind, no one to soothe my fears or wipe away my tears. I wouldn't give up.

I muttered, "Where is God? Where is God?" There were no answers. I heard an echo of my father's words, "It's better not to ask questions." I felt abandoned by God when I saw holy men, women, and children disappearing to the gas chambers. Yet I am alive. From that point on, I seldom had time to think about God because of the knocking pain of hunger. I was trying to fill my belly. Hunger overtook everything else.

Just like me, all the other girls now had lost their mothers. Not the only one alone, I was no longer embarrassed to be an orphan. Others no longer felt sorry for me. I was like everyone else. We had all become orphans. It made me feel better, but I was ashamed of my thoughts. Now other girls shared my life's long sorrow, and I knew theirs.

Mali and the children were no longer alive. Deep rage filled me, but I dared not show it.

Not until the second day at Birkenau did I taste food when one meal was finally served in the evening. A big wooden barrel on the floor provided soup for our whole barrack of prisoners. Many bleak wooden sheds were lined up in the field where prisoners were crammed together on three tiered wooden bunks. Jewish inmates, rounded up in 1942, two years earlier, were responsible for our whole group. The bosses were the *capos*, Jewish inmates selected by the Germans to be intermediaries, forced to supervise the Jewish prisoners. They doled out our meager meals, pouring a thin soup into one large metal bowl to be shared by all ten girls on our hard plank. They counted out only one ladle per person. Ten girls shared this one dish of watery soup that seemed to be made from some kind of leaves and a few beets or carrots. I searched for a sunken piece of potato only to find sand on the bottom. We were never given spoons or cups. The girls sipped, passing the bowl one to another. The more aggressive girls sipped twice. We didn't like those girls who took more. Our stomachs rumbled for food. We were in pain from starvation, the Nazis' quiet weapon.

Hunger made us fight for every drop. It's hard to understand the suffering from starvation unless you have experienced it. I kept telling myself, "Hold on or you won't last."

In the darkness, we took turns groping our way over now damp floors to a foul-smelling wheelbarrow stationed in the middle of our barrack. Clumsily, we maneuvered to relieve ourselves, squatting like animals. We were far beyond embarrassment.

To maintain our humanity under such harsh conditions, some of us formed special bonds. One was fortunate if she had a sister or a close friend from home. In the beginning, I had no one to comfort or to be comforted by. Endless evil days of hatred consumed us.

There was nothing except death.

Waking up in the morning meant I hadn't died during the night.

My aimless eyes wandered toward a small sobbing girl. Suddenly, I recognized a familiar face – Cipora, from Sekernice. She was small and skinny for her age. I had known her family before Sekernice became a ghetto. Without her mother, who had done everything for her, she was lost, hungry, and tearfully frightened. Cipora inched close me, clinging and crying in relief at finally finding someone she recognized. Five years older and more mature, I took her under my wing. Since we both had no one, we were a spark of light to each other. My empathy possibly saved her and it certainly helped me. Caring for another person took my mind off myself. Cipora became my special little sister.

So many others had a sister, a mother or an aunt to rely on. I helped Cipora in any way I could. We became family.

Looking around the barrack, I realized I was stronger than the other girls. Hardships from age six onward had become my school of survival. I still had some hope. I chose to fight and remain alive. "Oh God. Help us...do you hear me?"

Girls, who lost faith and gave up, went to touch the electrified fence to die.

One morning, while waiting for the count, a few girls were randomly selected to stand in a separate line. They were forced to have numbers tattooed onto their forearms. The rest of us remained in line to receive a different kind of number. I pushed Cipora in front of me. She received a dress with number 38,619. Mine was 38,620. Our rumpled dresses had our numbers glued on the left sleeve. Left meant death. Once called Leichu, I was now number 38,620. We were never called by our real names, only by the numbers on our dresses. Our names were replaced as part of their dehumanizing process.

Later we learned those of us who did not have a tattooed number on their arm had been condemned to be gassed, our bodies incinerated in a crematorium. Our remaining bones would be crushed into fertilizer, evidence of our very existence buried forever. As they didn't need us to make their death quota for extermination that day, we continued our daily work routine. They kept their quota. It was estimated that over six million Jews were murdered during the Nazi's Final Solution.

When we were given bread, I took both Cipora's and my portion and hid them inside my dress, under a belt I had made from a cord that I found on the ground. There was no other place to conceal food, as the dresses had no pockets. This way, our bread would not be stolen by another girl or eaten all at once. When Cipora felt hungry and sick, I gave her only a small swallow of bread. We learned to eat just a bite to quiet down the hunger and then wait a while.

Most girls, ill and ravenous from lack of nourishment, ate the whole chunk at one time. When they fainted, they were taken away. I used survival skill number one: give the impression of good health, show no sign of illness or weakness, and never whine for attention. The guards constantly removed the troublemakers, the feeble, and the sick, to the death chambers.

Cipora and I shared water from a bottle I found, filled from an open pipe near a toilet hole. I tied the bottle to my waist with a rope. We were warned not to drink this water because it was contaminated. Taking a chance, we drank it anyway and neither of us got sick.

They wanted us to suffer.

At nineteen, I had been living away from home for five years, learning to fend for myself. Life had been hard, but I became resourceful and knew how to tolerate suffering.

In Birkenau, our breakfast was dense, dirt-brown bread and a little black coffee with no milk. At the time, we were sure they were spiking our coffee with something to make it so bitter. It was rumored that the bread contained sawdust to stretch the quantity. To us, the bread was life. Later, it was rumored that the coffee was spiked with bromide or other chemicals to stop our menstrual cycles. The bread allotted to us while we stood in line was in the shape of a brick, each brick split between three girls. This was our only food for the whole day, until our evening watery soup.

The huge camp was divided into smaller sections by tall, electrified barbed-wire fences. During the long day behind the fence, I walked to the next building in the same yard where I called out my sister's name, just in case she might be there.

"Malchi! Malchi! Malchi!"

Thank God she wasn't there. Was she still safe in Budapest?

During the day, when the guards would decide it was time for us to use the latrine, we were escorted by female staff and an SS soldier carrying a rifle on his shoulder. There was no "bathroom," only holes in a bench outside placed over a large pit. The SS men watched us as twenty to thirty girls crouched at one time. There was no toilet paper, or water to wash our hands. After each group used the public hole, the guards marched us back to our barracks in the usual tight lines of five. People with sunken eyes and pale faces fell right and left from disease, hunger and fear. They were removed, gassed, burned, and ground up. All evidence of our former existence buried.

Each day, on my way back from the stinking pit, I looked for relatives and friends from other barracks passing by. Trying to find my relatives or anyone I knew, I asked every group I passed, "Which ghetto did you come from?" I heard that a transport had arrived at Camp Birkenau from Budapest. One day, passing the oncoming line, I got lucky. I called out the name of the ghetto

"Sighet" (presently Sighetu-Marmaiei, Romania), and my first cousin, Ettu Felberbaum, heard me. We had never met. She also had come from Sighet, Romania, on a transport to Birkenau. She was assigned to a different barrack. We had no further contact in Birkenau. Finally, I had proof that I was not only number 38,620, but also a person with a family.

On the opposite side of the barbed-wire fence, we saw groups of inmates called White Caps. They wore white kerchiefs as part of their prison uniforms. Their job was to sort the clothing from the dead at the crematorium. Sometimes the inmates stole clothes. Walking back from work, they would take a chance and throw sweaters and dresses to us over the fence. One time, I caught a gray sweater and pulled out some of the threads to detach the sleeves. I gave them to Ettu as I was walking in the line to the hole, and kept the vest for myself. This was the last time I saw her in Auschwitz.

Several incidents stand out in my mind. Some girls had been in the camp for several years and wore clothing from victims' suitcases. I couldn't believe it when I saw an inmate wearing one of my three Shabbat dresses from my bundle, a bitter reminder of my stolen life.

Another time I overheard one of the Polish girls crying loudly to our supervisor. She complained that an SS woman had written her number on a clipboard for an infraction. She knew this meant certain death. The SS had their way of keeping track of everyone. Soon she disappeared. I was fearful this could happen to me.

Once I saw a male prisoner walking among the women. He carried bread seized from the kitchen for his family in case he could find them. It was strange to see a man in the women's section. He was lucky to escape detection.

One day we found stinky herring barrels from the kitchen, sitting empty in the yard. The girls scavenged, finding nothing but a salty substance, which they ate. Some of them died from it. The stench kept me away from the barrels. We never ate herring in the camp. It was probably for the SS guards.

Birkenau was a harrowing, painful time where escape was unthinkable — impossible. The only way to be free was to touch the fence and be electrocuted. Girls who had lost hope chose this as an escape from this smoldering hell. Somehow, a glimmer of hope always sustained me until the next day.

Four to six weeks after we arrived, we were told we needed to shower in order to be disinfected. They lined us up in a field in Birkenau. Gestapo officers came and called the girls in alphabetical order by last names, instead of our numbers. This was most unusual. Girls were instructed to run to the other side of the field when they heard their name. Cipora's last name was Adler, coincidently, the same name as my mother. My little camp sister and many others from my ghetto were already on the other side and I was afraid of being separated from my friends. My last name was Cik. If they read it as Zik, my name would be on the bottom of their list. I knew to never be last. When I heard someone else's name called, I took a chance and ran to the other side where Cipora stood. There was no time to think about the potential consequences. Fortunately for me, I was not noticed by the German soldiers.

Which side was better? It was always a guess. If we were lucky, we survived.

During that selection, we did not know we were being sent to the gas chambers. The Germans, as obedient people, always needed to fulfill their daily quota for killing. Their allocation for this day was for 1,200 women to die. We just followed orders as usual, marching about an hour from Barrack *A* in Birkenau to the Auschwitz showers.

Twelve hundred shivering women were crammed into a large, windowless room and told to undress. We were shoved into the shower room. The doors slammed shut with a hollow echo. We wailed. We prayed. We waited . . . for the water to burst on us from the showerheads in the ceiling. Nothing happened. Turning a handle on the wall produced no water. I tried. Where was the water? I did not connect the fire coming from the chimney to this cavelike room, yet intuition led me to understand I was going to die. Cramped in a room with naked, wailing women, not knowing what to expect next, I felt hot and dizzy, rooted in a puddle of urine, standing nowhere, staring at others, but not seeing. Petrified, helpless, screaming voices echoed, pleading to God, *Shema Yisroel,* a prayer central to the Jewish faith declaring there is only one God. Others were sobbing through *Vidui,* the last prayer recited before death. I never gave in to feeling completely helpless. I didn't know the *Vidui,* so I screamed and cried loudly, *Shema.*

This place was a giant death factory for dry, shriveled souls, a very large room disguised as a shower room. Trembling with cold fright in the steamy room, we stood wearily for the whole day and night without circulating air. The room became stifling hot from the heat of the adjoining crematoria. I saw some bleachers in a corner. Cipora and I climbed on them. Sleep was our escape. We hoped for a miracle. Early in the morning, we were awakened with familiar screaming shouts: "*Schnell! Schnell!*" "*Get out quickly!*" Cipora helped me stand up, and we were moved back outside to a nearby holding yard. I was dazed from screaming, fear, and heat. Not in my right mind, I couldn't comprehend what had happened. Even though it was summer, I felt a chill on my sweaty naked skin.

What's happening? Does God have pity on us and have a change of mind?

A transport of children had arrived during the night, and the Nazis set a higher priority on killing those innocents.

It haunts me to this day. I can still hear the chorus of screeching children from where we stood in the field outside. Their shrill, primal screams faded into empty space as poisonous gas sucked the life's breath from the lungs of these young martyrs. Very...very slowly...their voices faded. Within half an hour . . . silence.

My ears still burn with the memory of their shrieking.

Hell had opened.

But why, God, the little children—those innocent souls?

Where was God? Maybe God was crying for us, but left us. People died like fumigated cockroaches.

Amazingly, my life was spared again. Surviving the gas chamber was a true miracle.

I hugged my sweet Cipora, and we fell to the ground. My world contracted to its smallest dimension, squeezing out all possibilities of light. We had been so close to death, feeling small and diminished, yet gratefully spared.

The SS ordered us to a grassy field. Fatigue and nausea filled me as I realized we had been in the gas chamber and were now saved. Now I knew why I had not been tattooed. It wasn't necessary for those scheduled for murder. From the very beginning, we had been selected for the death factory in Hitler's Final Solution. I understood where I had just been. I was standing in blood on the field, but I could not explain where it came from. Was it mine or someone else's?

We were pushed into a building large enough to hold 1,200 women and given striped dresses to replace the gray ones we left in the pile. This dress felt like a gift rather than a demand. I don't remember if our numbers were applied to the dresses.

The White Cap supervisors had hung their clothes on hooks while they bathed. I saw underwear sticking out from someone's pocket and I took the panties. They made me feel warm, but I was afraid they would find them on me. I was desperate, cold, and naked under my thin dress. Taking this chance could have meant being severely beaten by the White Caps. After the gas chamber, what did I have to lose except the little dignity I had left in me? I was still scared.

That same day, in June of 1944, the SS marched our group to a train that took us from Auschwitz-Birkenau to another camp, Stutthof (presently Sztuotowo) in Poland. We had been in Auschwitz for about six weeks. The guards gave us bread and salami for the trip. As hungry as we were, some girls chose not to eat the salami because it wasn't kosher. God knows I felt that eating this non-kosher food was the worst thing I ever did. Even in this excessive depravity, Jewish values remained with me.

We rode in an open coal car to Stutthof and saw civilians in the passing countryside, living their ordinary lives: children playing near their lit houses; cows grazing in green grassy fields, flowers covering the ground, and trees appearing strong and hardy. This normalcy was strange after having been locked up in the camp, hidden away from the color and texture of ordinary life. Was this an illusion after my near-death experiences in Birkenau?

Those German people who saw us did not seem to care. They saw that we wore striped clothing and were riding in the open train like cattle. As spectators, they closed their eyes and their hearts to reality. We felt like captive animals. I guess, to these bystanders, we were.

Midsummer 1944

Our group arrived the next day at our new holding camp, Stutthof, near the northern port of Gdansk, Poland. Soldiers surrounded us from every direction when we got off the train. We found ourselves standing in another open field. Were bullets coming next? They marched us to the barracks in rows of five, with rifles pointed toward us as if they were chasing swine to the slaughter. The surroundings were barren as far as we could see. No one dared an escape.

Conditions at the new camp seemed less harsh here than at Birkenau, even though we saw more gas chambers. Our midday meal was the same watery soup and a small brick of bread, but now we had a bowl and a spoon. I had water to drink and soap for a shower every night before bed. This was a luxury, even though there were no towels. We dressed while still wet, with no underwear. Sleeping conditions were better with our own separate bunk beds.

The morning would begin and end with a count of the prisoners. All day, every day, we would stand outside in a dusty, sandy field doing nothing during long, hot summer days of boredom. We weren't allowed to go back into the barracks. Were they holding us for another selection? The older girls among us thought of ways to keep us busy. One of the prisoners had been a gym teacher, and she led us to exercise in the heat.

One day a new group of SS officers made another selection, another quota to feed their grinding war machine. We were forced to stand naked outside in the yard in front of five pairs of roving eyes. These Nazis determined our fate. I held myself tight, hiding my shame as my knees went weak. I was able to stay standing.

I looked stronger than Cipora standing next to me. She was younger and pubescent thin, having not yet developed as a woman. We were separated and taken to different rooms. I never saw her again at Stutthof. Looking weak, she was not chosen for work. I couldn't help her.

I rehearsed my thoughts many times. Cipora's parents will be so proud of me when I tell them the story of how I helped her stay alive by comforting her, being her companion and not letting her die; they will be so happy. They will love me. I could not say good-bye to my beloved Cipora. I worried what had happened to her. I missed her close to me.

To deal with the hunger that never stopped, one mother encouraged the SS guard to take advantage of her daughter. An extra piece of bread might possibly save her young life. I saw that they had extra bread. A relationship with a Jew was very risky for a German soldier.

The next day, on July 15, 1944, the SS transferred a thousand of us by railroad to Bromberg-Ost in Bydgoszcz, Poland, a sub camp of Stutthof. We called it the Bromberg camp, Brano, for short. We arrived at night, extremely hungry, yet none of us was fed until the day after – more thin soup.

This small barrack had five rooms, each of which held twenty-two inmates who were assigned specific jobs. My group worked in a bomb factory.

We were in Brano during the Jewish high holy days of repentance, Rosh Hashanah, and Yom Kippur. What were we repenting? Someone had smuggled in a few pages from a prayer book. Those of us who knew how to read Hebrew read the prayers aloud before we went to work. Sitting with my father at the table as I learned Hebrew by kerosene lamp shadowed my memory.

I slept on a wooden bunk bed with my own thin mattress, a pillow, and, for the first time, my own wool blanket.

The camp's SS headquarters and the main kitchen were also part of this camp. These facilities were surrounded by a fence, with a German soldier always guarding the perimeter from their watchtower. The guards did not seem as cruel as in previous camps. There were also underground bunkers to protect us from the Allies bombs, which never came. Once, sneaking deep into the shelter, I found several potatoes lying on the floor that must have been stolen from the kitchen. I quickly ate them raw, like apples, before anyone caught me. They were delicious.

The SS commandant of the camp was nicknamed "the pipe guy" by the girls. He always smoked a pipe and had been appointed as camp administrator after being injured at the front lines. I knew he had family nearby, not because I ever saw them, but because someone had asked "Daddy" for a doll with long, dark hair. I volunteered because I knew how to make wigs from my apprenticeship with Mrs. Shönfeld. I thought maybe they would give me extra bread. I was given a doll and a pile of human hair, without the right needle. I wondered whose hair it was. The *capo* in the SS office provided a smallish crochet hook. Sitting in the soldier's office all day for three consecutive Sundays, I didn't work in the factory and completed the doll wig. For this work they did reward me with extra bread. Finally, I was someone special. Thank you, Mrs. Shönfeld, for teaching me a trade.

CHAPTER 12

A Heavy Price to Pay

Fall 1944

Some of the girls in Birkenau were from my same ghetto in Sekernice, Hungary, near Chust. Already friends from the past, we became close and tried to help each other when we could. It felt good to have friends. My ability to speak German that I had learned in the upper grades in Brustury resulted in my being chosen as the leader in our barrack room. There were four other rooms of prisoners. Most women in my room spoke only Hungarian and could not understand the soldiers' orders. It was expected that the room be kept in perfect order, with the beds made in precise military style. There were random inspections, and the owner of the best-made bed was rewarded with an extra piece of bread.

Every morning before our bitter coffee, the SS would enter the room and I, as head of the group, would stand to report that there were twenty-two prisoners present.

As usual, we would be counted, told where to stand and what to do. Each of us would be assigned a different task. Some of the girls in the other rooms spoke and wrote fluent German and became secretaries to the German officers. One girl, who seemed kind and spoke gently, was chosen to be a *capo*. As a Jewish commandant, she was required to report bad behavior and disobedience or risk being harshly punished, even killed. Other girls repaired shoes. Some ironed uniforms and shined boots for the SS. The rest of us would be sent to work shifts in various factories surrounding the camp.

The industrial bomb factories were hidden among trees with shrubs and greenery planted on the roofs. The girls in my barrack were assigned to work in a factory operated by Krupp, the largest German industrial company. This particular bomb factory used our slave labor, paying a daily sum to the SS. The owner, Alfried Krupp, was later convicted of crimes against humanity on July 31 of 1948 by the Nuremburg War Tribunal. He served three years in prison and was pardoned.

After making our beds, we would stand before sunrise in lines of five to be counted before being escorted to the gate and then counted again. We would be counted coming and going.

Part of the ammunition plant used prisoners of war from other countries. Most of the prisoner soldiers were from France and fortunate enough to receive daily food packages from the Red Cross. In spite of the language barrier, they would sneak us food, pieces of bread, an apple or even candy. One time I received a cube of instant soup and ate it, thinking it was a piece of candy. I still remember the bitter, salty taste.

Although we were not supposed to talk with the French prisoners, we still did. They had information about the war, and we learned that in the end of 1944 Germany was holding ground. Because there were no watches or clocks, I would often ask, "What time is it?" They taught us to ask it in French, "*Quelle heure est-il?*"

The Germans expected big production from the girls. We worked hard to appease them. One advantage of factory work was that we had an extra change of clothing. The work supervisor gave us uniforms: a jumpsuit and underwear! We were given decent, though meager lunches of soup, small portions of potatoes, and, sometimes, even a little piece of meat served in a clean crockery dish. Occasionally, we would be treated with small portions of sugar and margarine that we would take back to the barrack and save for a Sunday treat, the only day we didn't have to go to the factory.

Once, when we were walking to the factory, a parachutist landed in our midst. We didn't know who he was. Was he there to help us or to learn about the factories? Was he a spy? When the guards caught on to the commotion, they called for help and directed our group back to our barrack. We never found out who that mysterious man was or what had happened to him.

We were resourceful, pulling coarse threads from our blankets to use them as sewing thread. For fabric, we used to steal pieces of gunpowder sacks from the factory and hid them under our dresses. Walking through the exit gates with our arms held tight to our sides, we hoped they would not notice our smuggled goods at the camp entrance. To distract the guards, we would sing marching songs in different languages. I do not remember anyone ever getting caught.

I worked six days a week. On Sunday, I could walk around the camp. The Brano camp had showers, and we were able to wash our dresses. Sunday was also the day we tried to recover our feminine modesty. From the smuggled sacks and blanket threads, we would sew bras and panties. I made a belt to show my waist and express a bit of vanity or, maybe, it was to rescue my human dignity.

Many times when Allies' planes threatened the alarm would sound. We would be marched to the air-raid shelters. The alarm blared, but, fortunately, the camp was never bombed. The Allies must not have known about the bomb factory due to the camouflage of trees and bushes.

There were two eight-hour work shifts a day. I worked the morning one. My job was to scrub yellow particles off the outside surface of the bombs with a small brush as they moved along the assembly line. Special vacuum hoses were used to clean fallen dust from the floor after we cleaned each bomb. The bombs arrived at my station filled with smelly sulfurous liquid. We knew this was dangerous work. Direct contact with the liquid was toxic. We later wondered if we were dealing with something like the murderous mustard gas of World War I. Occasionally, someone would turn blue and faint in the morning. It was scary to see five or six girls, lifeless, sprawled on the floor. I once became sick as well and was taken with the others to the infirmary. A Lithuanian Jewish woman doctor treated us with kindness and told us to try not to be sick. The Germans did not want sick inmates and would quickly do away with those who were not able to work.

The toxic fumes killed a girl from my group. We had no choice but to bury her behind the fence, escorted by an SS soldier. I envied her because she had a sister. We did not know how to say Kaddish, the Jewish mourner's prayer. We just whispered, "Good-bye."

I did not know how to grieve, and it was not allowed. Now I know grief is disorienting and cumulative, and if it is never allowed expression, it torments the soul. I learned how to move on, just one step ahead of the shadow of death.

After a full day's work, each prisoner would receive one ladle of thin soup. I still searched for a piece of potato at the bottom of the bowl. We would also get a small piece of hard dark bread, maybe a two-inch by a four-inch chunk. Sometimes I would save a little bread as I had done with Cipora in Birkenau, hiding it in the mattress to eat for breakfast with my bitter coffee. Once, at work, I found a small roll on the floor near a bathroom and quickly ate it. Hunger pains never left me, and food was the main subject of our conversation. We reminisced about our favorite dishes from home, and our mouths watered.

Occasionally, we would be lucky to find potatoes growing in the ground where we would be sent to dig deep trenches for the Germans to hide from the Allies. We would dig them up as fast as we could and eat them raw before the guards could catch us. Life was so miserable. To this day, I can never throw away a piece of bread or anything edible.

Once I overheard the French factory soldiers talking about how the Germans held on and continued fighting. They were strong. It could be a long time before the war was over. Maybe it would never end. Feeling exhausted and depressed from overwork and starvation, I decided to rebel. I knew it could end my life, but I had lost hope. What's the use? My soul was barking with an uncontrollable rage. One morning I stayed in bed after everyone left and refused to go to work, even though I knew this might be my suicide.

During the first meticulous counting in the morning at the gate, "the pipe guy," the elder good-looking headmaster of Brano noticed that one woman was missing. There were shouts over the loudspeaker, and every room of the barrack was searched until they found me in the top bunk. A female officer yanked me from the bed: "How dare you?" Her black whip cracked on my back, and she thrashed my body from my head to my feet. Bloody, I fell to the ground, humiliated, screaming with pain, hardly able to breathe, gasping for air. She pulled me outside and forced me to remain kneeling in the cold November weather until late afternoon.

Having missed a day of factory work, I was sent to work the second shift that night, even as I suffered from the torture, struggling to walk with every painful step. Somehow I made it through without sleep. The morning after, I worked the regular daytime shift despite my feeble condition. Even though my co-workers felt sorry, they could not help me. They were afraid for themselves.

That evening, at the final count for the day, the tall, handsome assistant to the headmaster walked toward me, his black boots crunching in the gravel. Looking straight at me, he called the number on my dress.

"Step forward, 38,620."

I wet myself in front of everyone, all one thousand girls. I had completely misjudged his character, the handsome blond man with blue eyes, who hadn't appeared to be mean. He beat me savagely with a whip and kicked me with his black boots. Writhing in pain, I fainted. How wrong could I have been about this handsome guy? His outward appearance confused me. Coming around, I wondered, "Am I still alive?"

My beating was a reminder to the other girls of what happened to rebels. In Auschwitz, the punishment would have been a hanging, with my naked body left dangling outside. Only by chance or the will of God was I still alive. I had escaped such brutality for about seven months and then received the full force of it, which would have sent most to the electric fence.

I had learned to survive deep pain and disgrace. Any weakness left within me was gone. From those beatings, I became resilient, more defiant, and resolved to become more rebellious.

To this day I am a rebel.

Whenever I am wronged, I speak up.

When I see others wronged, I defend them.

CHAPTER 13

Never Be At the Back of the Line

January of 1945 was freezing. Germany and the Axis powers were losing the war.

One day, when we arrived back at Camp Brano from work, the group did not go through the gate as usual. Instead, the guards led us to an endless line of prisoners on a march, a late effort to fulfill Hitler's plan to eliminate all the Jews in Europe. Forced forward with whips, we walked for miles, west toward Germany. We walked a nightmare, not knowing where we were or what was ahead. With the Russians close behind, the Nazis marched us onward without pause. Many were dying of the freezing bitter cold, starvation, loss of hope, or bullets, fulfilling Hitler's plan. Our breath would come out like frozen smoke. Those who could no longer walk fell and were buried under the falling snow.

As the march continued, girls from other camps joined the throng. In thin dresses and torn shoes, weak from overwork, cold and hunger, none were prepared for survival. Still painfully aware of my beatings, I was particularly vulnerable. Every difficult step included a crowd of questions: "Where are they taking us? Am I going to die now? What am I to do?" And there were answers: "This is a death march. They intend us to die — every one of us. I want to live! God, please, help me save myself!"

Where was this march heading? We knew that no one was supposed to survive. Prisoners without food or water, clothing or shelter were dying all around us.

German soldiers were tyrants on horsebacks. Anyone who lagged at the back of the line was killed. I never dared to be last or first in line. It was best to stay unnoticed in the middle of a group. I was constantly pushed to keep moving, even when I thought I couldn't take one more step. To this day, in a crowd, I push forward. I feel myself back in the camps.

At nightfall, prisoners were taken to a big, dark barn with hay on the dirt floor. We marchers now included Jews, gypsies, and Poles who had been captured along with male prisoners of war: Russian, French, and British soldiers. Leery of these male strangers, we avoided eye contact with them. We women, grouped together, were relieved to have a roof overhead. I took off my soaking-wet shoes, hoping they would be dry by morning. We gathered straw into piles, and, without blankets, huddled close to one another and slept. Instead of the cold snow, sleep was our cover that night.

By morning, my shoes were frozen solid. I went to one of the Russian prisoners of war and asked in Russian, "Do you have a match to thaw my frozen shoes? I can't put them on."

"Yes. I have a match and even a candle."

He helped me hold my shoes over the low flame. Then I lay on top of them until they softened and I could put them back on, still cold and wet.

"*Schnell, Schnell*," the Germans barked.

We lined up again and marched for another long day.

By evening, the SS men were in front of us. No one was watching our group, the invading Russian army had caught up with us, and the Germans were now looking out only for themselves, leaving us unguarded.

This was our opportunity to sneak away from the march. Some of the Germans retreated to set up defense lines against the Russians. A few Nazis even hid among us.

Three of my friends from Sekernice and I took a chance. Chavi, Peppi and her sister, Sara and I sprinted away to escape, our only opportunity to break away from the group. People scattered in all directions without knowing where they were going. The four of us managed to stay together.

Sara had epilepsy. Luckily, she never had a seizure in front of the German guards, as it would have been her last.

When we came to a village schoolhouse, the Russian soldiers were already there. We hugged and kissed them. We believed they were our saviors.

Relieved, we slept in the local schoolhouse. Were we free now? In the morning, some of us went into the street to beg for food. To our surprise, the first house we found had been abandoned by German owners who had fled the advancing Russians. Warm meat and bread were still on the table. Overwhelmed, we gorged ourselves as only starving people could. We took clothes from the dressers and shoes from the closets. I even took a gold wedding ring, which I later lost. Within a day or two, the Germans had set up their defense and pushed the Russians back.

The village was once again under German control. Some of us hid in a farmhouse held by Russian soldiers. When we went back outside, we were recaptured. My three days of freedom ended, and I was back on the death march. One hundred new girls from different camps had joined us in line.

Thinking back, I still wonder why the SS spent so much energy on this march. Was it just to get rid of the evidence of their atrocities?

The Germans led us to a warehouse that contained remnants of merchandise. An SS officer singled out a small Polish girl to monitor the place while he went to hunt for more escapees.

"Watch so nothing is touched."

The girl trembled in fear at this responsibility. When the officer left, she had no control over us. We moved around. I saw a comb and took it, even though I had no hair. It was something to have, a personal belonging.

When the officer returned and saw that everyone had moved, he took out his revolver and shot her in the eye.

She fell to the ground and screamed. "I can't see."

Seeing this up close, I was sickened. He could have shot me.

He smirked and calmly said, "Don't worry. I will take you to the hospital for treatment."

Not likely. We never found out what became of her.

Continuing the march, we met three sisters I had known in camp Brano. One had been shot in the leg, caught in the crossfire between Germans and Russians, and could not walk. Her sisters were carrying her. Surprisingly, a German gave the two able girls a sled, with which to pull their wounded sister. Later she died of her injuries, and her sisters had to leave her body behind. A heavy, painful sadness overcame me. Although my feet were frozen, numbed by the cold, I still had feeling in my heart.

The basic rule for survival was to keep walking, never to fall behind. I urinated on myself but never stopped moving. Our group grew larger as we marched, collecting more and more prisoners who were also on the run from other camps.

We stopped in a large Polish city Stettin (presently Szczecin, Poland) where we stood in line the whole day while the SS decided what to do with the prisoners. At the end of the day, I got a small piece of bread. The soldiers turned us over to rifle-carrying German civilians, who then became the leaders of the march. We later learned that the SS had moved hundreds of prisoners from Stutthof, north to the Baltic Sea, and shot them, the evidence of their crimes washed away.

The German civilians were less harsh than the soldiers, and the lines became increasingly disorganized. Before dark, the four of us ran away again, hiding in the first safe place we could find – a farmer's shed.

My heart pounded until the rest of the march passed the shack. Though we were hiding, I felt free. In the morning, we continued to another city on our hunt for food. Undetected, we found an abandoned house and slept in its shed.

Hunger drove us to be daring and aggressive. We found a line for rations with other civilians: Germans, Russians, and Poles. Even though our hair was still short, giving away our identities, they still gave us soup and bread.

Hoping to leave the area under German control, we pretended to be Hungarian girls looking for work. We were not stopped. Hungary was Germany's ally during the entire war. By continuing to move from place to place, we managed not to get caught. Invited into a German home, we were believed to be Hungarians because we spoke in Hungarian. Because of our extremely short hair, we were afraid the German soldiers would discover us. They never did.

Moving on, we only spoke Hungarian, even among ourselves. A Polish family that had been displaced from their home by the Nazis took us in. They treated us well and we stayed with them for several weeks. Shortly thereafter, the Russians captured the city.

These soldiers were lustful, always wanting to take women back to their quarters. One day, I went to the water pump by the house, and there stood a Russian soldier. As I came closer, I felt his eyes preying on me. Before I could react, he grabbed my arm in such a way that I was able to slip out of the sweater, leaving it in his hand. I ran back to the house to warn my friends.

That night, as we ate dinner with the Polish family, Russian soldiers stormed into the house.

Looking straight at us and pointing toward the door, they said, "You must come help us prepare our food."

Following their orders, unwillingly, the four of us left in the pitch dark without finishing our supper. There was no alternative but to go with them to a nearby house, where many soldiers were entertaining themselves with smoking, drinking vodka, and singing Russian war songs. The room was filled with smoke. Rifles rested against their chairs.

Politely, one of the soldiers pointed toward the cellar steps, "We need you to peel potatoes." He followed us down the steps to the dim underground room, cold and damp, lit by a small kerosene lamp. A huge sack of potatoes stood in the corner. Handing us knives, he cordially asked us to peel the potatoes. Standing, we peeled the entire sack as quickly as we could, hoping they would let us go as soon as the job was finished. When he left the room, we knew that we were trapped and didn't know what to expect next. There were no windows to escape through.

After several hours, we heard heavy footsteps on the creaking stairs. Four drunken soldiers, armed with their rifles, burst into the cellar, grabbed each of us by the arm and shoved us into a dark corner where four makeshift beds lay on the damp dirt floor. I wondered who would sleep in such a place just as the man pushed me down to the mattress. His gun was aimed at my face. I did not scream or fight back. While the other girls cried, I remained breathless and silent. My heart was pounding.

He dropped down to the mattress next to me and began groping my body under my clothes as he yanked them off. I smelled his weeks-old body odor, the smoke and vodka on his breath. He was so drunk that he fell asleep right away until morning. I was not concerned about rape. All I could think about during the long night was that the gun between us might explode in my face. Bodily insult did not matter. I remembered the German soldier who shot the girl in the eye. Hearing and replaying that scene in my head all night kept me awake, as I shivered from the ordeal and the cold.

Morning finally came. "I am still alive", I thought. Nothing else matters. When he awoke, he tried to rape me. He was impotent.

The shameful ordeal was my secret until almost seven decades later, when after one and a half years of intense work, Menucha squeezed it out of me. I was inspired by the courage of Elizabeth Smart, the Mormon girl who was kidnapped and raped, who bravely spoke publicly about her ordeal. I finally got rid of my long held secret. Disclosure was a relief.

They departed in a hurry at daybreak, leaving us behind. We quickly dressed and listened for their footsteps as they left the house, then jumped up toward the stairs, two of us at a time. No one was left in the house. We ran to the first shed we came to and hid inside until we knew it was safe to run back to the Polish woman's house, the place of our salvation.

The sister who had epilepsy whimpered, "I'm bleeding."

The elderly Polish housewife shielded us. She didn't know we were Jews.

Looking out the windows, we saw the roads were empty. It was time to move on.

We said our goodbyes and left in a hurry to resume our trek without knowing where to go.

We came upon an abandoned car just sitting in the middle of the road. Its owners had fled. Or had they been murdered?

There was a bicycle leaning against a tree. We loaded our bundles onto it and pushed it until a Russian soldier confronted us. His body language showed us he had made up his mind in thinking that we were Germans, and we had no time to convince him otherwise. Like a cornered animal, I sensed imminent danger. I had to think fast. I noticed that he wore a collection of watches from his wrist to his elbow, no doubt confiscated from prisoners and the dead. So I decided to offer him our bike in exchange for our lives. "Take it," I said. As he was carefully studying his new bike, we grabbed our chance and started running, as fast and as far as we could. That was the one time when a bike saved our lives.

Crowds of Germans were running from the invading army in this war zone. Russian soldiers shot the Germans where they stood. Both military and civilians targeted one other, and we were caught in the crossfire. Thankfully, not hit.

As we continued to walk, the four of us came again to the city of Stettin, still under German occupation. There was a work registry and we stood in line disguised as Hungarian girls, dressed in clothes taken from abandoned homes. I signed up as Elka Adler, *Maminka*'s maiden name, because it sounded

German. If I died in Stettin and someone from my family came looking for me, the name Adler would have helped them discover what had happened to Leichu.

The labor office placed us with a German farmer and a peasant woman in Stettin. The four of us girls left in their horse-drawn wagon to go to a nearby farmhouse. Able-bodied men were still off to war and laborers were needed.

We separated when we arrived. Peppi and Sara went with the farmer. Chavi was taken to another farm.

I stayed with the German peasant woman, and she treated me well. It was in this house that I saw a freestanding mangle iron for the first time. She taught me how to use it to press her bedding. My farm job was to feed and care for pigs and chickens. At least, there was food to eat and a nice, clean bed to sleep in. I felt safe with this kind German woman – for the first time since the camps.

One night, a group of German officers and soldiers came to her farmhouse. I think they came to warn the woman of a Russian invasion. The woman told me to prepare food for them. I served scrambled eggs, potato soup, and a salad with bread.

I asked a soldier, "More vegetables? Would you like onions in your salad?"

Mockingly, he looked at me and said, "Am I a Jew to eat onions?"

I contained myself to show no fear, but I had goose bumps. Being blond with green eyes, I looked German enough, but maybe I had given myself away.

When I awoke the next morning, no one was in the house. The soldiers and the farm lady were gone. I was alone. I had no time to think about what to do. The sound of artillery fire was close by. Instinct told me to run outside to look for Peppi, Sara, and Chavi. I found the two sisters on the road, but we couldn't find Chavi. I never saw her again, though I heard that after the war she had found a way back home to Sekernice.

Without knowing where to go, somehow we instinctively found our way, heading eastward, deeper into Poland, hoping to reach Chechia, Prague, and home. For weeks, we trudged along broken roads, through vineyards, over creeks and across fields, sleeping in barns and eating whatever we could find along the way.

Now our enemies were the cold, the war and the crazed, sex-starved Russian soldiers. In this battle zone they were wild animals. At a deserted German military warehouse, I found abandoned clothing: a man's heavy coat to cover my dress, a kerchief for my head and a pair of men's shoes. This disguise as an old woman saved me from depraved men.

Dead bodies littered the ground as we worked our way through Poland in fear of both Russian and German military, mile after endless mile. It haunts me to this day, that to force ourselves onward, we counted bodies. With glazed eyes and open mouths, silent screams of the dead urged us on. Counting, we glanced briefly at what we were escaping, trudging toward our unknown future.

PART III

A New Life

CHAPTER 14

Toward Freedom

January 1945

All of us were still running. After a full day on the road, passing from one Polish farm to the next, we came upon a barn where we could rest for the night. German soldiers had arrived before us and sought shelter in the same barn. Disguised as Hungarian girls wearing dresses, scarves, and women's shoes from our looted bundles, we weren't recognized as Jews. Anyway, no one cared anymore. Everyone was scattering in the chaos. We decided between us if we were asked where we were from, we would say, we were runaway Hungarian girls seeking work from the Germans.

After piling our bundles together in a corner for safekeeping, we mingled among the other refugees and even among the German soldiers. The general summoned his soldiers to one side. Bent, shuffling and dejected, he said to his group, "Germany has surrendered."

We struggled to conceal our relief, joyful inside. A hundred strangers were able to sleep safely through the night.

Nearby was constant shooting, both sides still fighting. While we were no longer oppressed by the Nazis, we were not free from danger. Cautiously cheerful, we thought we had been liberated. Unfortunately, the Russian infantrymen took advantage of all civilian women, including my friends and me.

At first, the Russians were our saviors as we ran from the death march. Then the abuse that Sara, Peppi, and I had suffered at the hands of Russian infantrymen weeks later became common. We kept our distance and spoke only Hungarian to avoid putting ourselves in further danger.

Our single-minded purpose was to reach home in Chust, to reconnect with our loved ones. I yearned to find my surviving sister, Malchi, and my beloved brother, Bencion.

The Russian soldiers were hostile to refugees passing through their Polish checkpoints demanding, "Where are you going? Who are you? Show us your papers."

We had no identification papers. The Russians didn't care where we came from or what horrors we had suffered. Since Peppi and I were blond, we feared we might be mistaken as Germans. We heard that they arrested unsuspecting German women and sent them to Russia as prostitutes.

Desperate, I told the Russian soldiers, "I'm Jewish, not German." To convince them to let us through as Jews, I recited a well-known prayer in Hebrew hoping for one of the soldiers to be a Jew. I think he felt sorry for us. The soldier in charge let us go right away. We never learned if he was Jewish or if he just took pity on us. He gave us new documents so we could continue our long journey.

Walking through the countryside, we came to a deep stream of rushing water and jumped over it like rabbits. At night, we would sleep in abandoned barns and houses. Fearing sexual assault, we would sleep hidden under haystacks. Gentile and Jewish men, taken by the Nazis for slave labor, were also returning to their homes in Poland.

As refugees passing through the city of Lodz, Poland, we registered with the American Jewish Joint Distribution Committee, the "Joint" for short. We learned that Joint posted lists of Survivors' names in public places and even published them in local newspapers. We were grateful that American Jewish organizations were there to help us.

One of our fellow travelers was a young Jewish man from Poland, a little older than I was. As a Holocaust captive, he knew young women could easily become victims. He shielded us from other men, sleeping on the floor next to Peppi, Sara, and me. My brother, Bencion, would have done the same. Looking back at his thoughtfulness, I think it has also been my nature to have compassion for others. While on the run, I held the hand of a little girl for a day until she couldn't keep up and fell behind. Through kindness people survive the worst in life.

Continually searching for food, our group spotted a horse in the field. After slaughtering the animal, the men cooked it over a fire. I ate horsemeat for the first time, savoring its delicious, sweet taste. The young men also caught stray rabbits that scurried through vacant buildings. We had food and we were free. The pangs of hunger subsided, as we became hunters, instead of prey.

To travel from Lodz to Kraków in southern Poland on the way to the Czech border, some of our group snuck onto the top of a railroad coal car. We had company from other refugees who had the same idea. The bouncing rhythm of the train in the open air was so different from our previous caged rides in cattle cars. Fearful of falling off, I held tightly to the side railings. A few unlucky ones, having survived the camps, ironically fell to their deaths.

We were again without food and water, but through that perilous ride, feeling freedom made hunger easier to accept. We traveled for several days atop a coal car as I dreamt of finding my family. We were exhausted from holding on for safety, trying not to fall off.

When we arrived in Krakow, kind locals showed us where to sneak across the Czech border. To avoid being stopped by police at checkpoints, we snuck across the frontier. Onward we walked to the city of Humenné in Slovakia, where we were welcomed by other Jews who had been liberated three months earlier. They generously invited us into their homes as guests. Some of the Jews had been able to retrieve their property back from the neighbors. And, oh, the sweet joy to hear my native Czech language again. So much was understood without the need of explanation. And I was grateful for their hospitality. Filthy from coal soot, I welcomed a warm and private bath, and the dignity of being cared for like a real person. To me, still weak from traipsing for days through war-ravaged fields strewn with gray corpses of men, women and children, this simple bath was a luxury. Now I was more than a number.

I dressed in pants and a white sweater taken from an abandoned home.

The young man I was traveling with complimented me, "You look so different. Now I see a Jewish face." I think he was interested in me, but he kept his distance. People were afraid to attach themselves and be responsible for another. Separation could happen so quickly.

At age nineteen, already mature beyond my years, I knew that now, I was finally strong enough to separate from my friends and be independent. I boarded the train headed for Chust, the city where I had learned to be a wig-maker with Mrs. Shönfeld. On familiar territory, I felt liberated.

✡

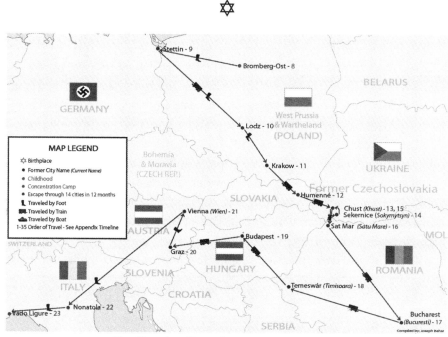

For Complete Map - See Appendix, page 232

After four months on the run from the Death March, I arrived in Chust on March 30 of 1945, on the afternoon before Passover. I spoke both Hungarian and Yiddish, inquiring about the whereabouts of an eatery offering special Passover food. What a surprise to find familiar girls from the camp in Brono who had been liberated more than a month earlier than I, now working as waitresses. Happy to see me, they invited me to stay with them in their quarters in an abandoned home.

The next step was to locate the Shönfeld's home of my apprenticeship days. Somehow, I felt connected to them, to the semblance of their family life. But they were gone. I missed them since the two and a half years that we had been together. I didn't realize how attached I had become. The Jewish owners now lived in the apartment the Shönfelds used to rent. They were fortunate.

Only a few Jewish families were ever able to retrieve their property following the war.

In our frantic departure from the ghetto in Sekernice, Mali had entrusted her next-door neighbor with her jewelry, her sewing machine and some bedding, and I, my one and only treasure, my *Maminka's* ring. I was not so hopeful, but I had to try to find the neighbor.

I recognized his house. Trembling, I knocked on the door. To my immense relief, I recognized the man who opened it, and he remembered me right away. "You've come back!" He invited me in. I was anxious and wondered if he would deny having our things, withhold them from me or say had he sold them.

"Just a minute," he said, as he walked into another room. This kindly Russian Christian neighbor returned with an armload of Mali's towels and sheets, topped, to my delight, by the tablecloth *Maminka* had embroidered so long ago. I took it from the pile but it was my mother's ring I yearned for the most.

With a twinkle in his eye, the gentleman opened his hand. "I believe this is yours." There it was, *Maminka's* gold ring, circled with the small rubies.

Overwhelmed and tearful, I grabbed it and held it to my lips.

"Thank you, thank you!"

This physical link to my long-gone mother and my home in Brustury was one of those recollections that had sustained my hope in the concentration camps. I was reunited with what was left of my family with these two heirlooms. The Nazis had taken away my name and dignity, but they couldn't steal my memories or my hope. From then on I would always wear the ring.

On a half-hour train ride from Sekernice back to Chust, I bumped into an elderly man, a very close friend of my father from Brustury. He felt like my own family. I ran to hug him. Recognizing me, he had thrilling news to share, "Your father's sister, Aunt Ruchel Leah Bash, has survived, and she's living in Bucharest." I was so happy I could barely speak.

He encouraged me, "Why don't you go and visit her?"

I knew about her from my father, but we had never met. We were separated by the Romanian border. Drawn to any family I could locate, I was determined to find her.

My trip to Bucharest was interrupted with a stop in Sat Mar, Romania (presently Satu Mare, Romania). I heard from other girls who had been at

Camp Brono that we could convalesce in a Satmar Jewish hospital. With me still weak from the death camps, the kindness of good meals, a comfortable bed, and medical care was soothing to my soul. I didn't suffer boils, frozen hands or feet or coughing unlike some of the other girls. Though I was comparatively healthy, the trauma of my time in captivity and torture took its toll. I suffered from excruciating nightmares, anxiety, weight loss, and loneliness. Uncertainty about my future haunted me continually day and night. Though I had no tears, dry sadness clung to me.

Through the convalescent hospital, I reconnected with myself, my independence, my physical strength, and dared to dream of my future. I found the Steinmetz family from Brustury, along with their seven children, who now lived in a house in Sat Mar. Our families had been close friends, and we went to school together as young children. The Steinmetz's were the only Jewish family in the whole of Carpathia to have escaped deportation, sheltered by Christians in underground bunkers for a huge sum of money. They had each other. Ratzie Steinmetz, my childhood friend, was able to rescue a photo album with a fifth grade school picture. She kept it in the bunker where they were hidden. There in the group, I saw myself at ten years old – innocent, happy, unaware of what was to come. This is the only photo of my childhood in Brustury. Much later, Ratzie made copies for the few of us she found alive.

School Photograph (Leah 2nd row, right end); also on book cover

After two weeks of rest and recuperation, warming myself in a quiet garden between nourishing meals, I felt pampered. Meeting other Survivors and not being under the pressure of the Nazis, I was beginning to heal. I was now contemplating how to start over. Someone came to talk to me about my reentry into regular life, offering to help me find any surviving relatives or friends. I think he was a psychiatrist from the Satmar Jewish hospital.

In our pajamas, Leah and I sit at the computer and work late into the night. Leah confides in me as her new best friend, the gratitude she has for her life, and the relief she feels from sharing her pent-up privacies through *Soul-Writing*. We both benefit from her recovery through our mutual connection. She's becoming healthier and happier as she reveals deep, depressed thoughts buried for all those years. The computer screen gives light to the piles of marked-up drafts on my desk, a testimony to hundreds of hours of atrocious stories.

Eddie sits at the other computer playing solitaire, pretending not to hear our conversation. "Writing a book is as hard as having a baby," he blurts.

"Yeah, you just have to keep pushing," Leah shoots back.

We laugh at this comic relief. I hand Leah a chocolate and kiss her cheek.

Absently, she leans toward the school photo, names everyone she points to and matter-of-factly states, "Most of us are no longer here."

I'm at a loss for words. My outrage seethes. This little woman sitting next to me, comfortable in her aqua bathrobe and slippers, is overcoming a past of unimaginable horrors, yet able to relive her nightmares so that children and grandchildren will never forget her legacy of bravery and resolve.

"Life is a test," she says. "Every day brings something new. Let's go further, time is short," she directs. *Soul-Writing* benefits both of us. With patience and repetition, I continue to rescue more from her invaluable memory. She directs me again, "Let's go on further now."

Leaving the hospital with new strength, I hitched a train ride to Bucharest to find Aunt Ruchel Leah Basch. The twenty-four hour trip was free for refugees. From my worn bundle that contained my every earthly possession, I wore the ugly striped dress from the concentration camp to identify myself as a Survivor. The striped uniform was a token of my being alive. It was with me through the most difficult time of my life. It had become like a security blanket that had kept me alive. Yet, for many years, I would never buy anything with stripes.

Traveling from Satmar to Bucharest, I was relieved to be free and excited about meeting Aunt Ruchel Leah. I chatted with others who were also planning for a new life, worried about how to start over. We were all looking for someone from our own family. I dozed off and time passed quickly.

We arrived in Bucharest, a big bustling city. I hated for people to have pity on me when they saw me wearing that striped camp dress uniform. I would have rather been like a regular person, but the dress bought me a free ride.

With Ruchel Leah's address in hand, directed by kind strangers, I arrived near my aunt's apartment by streetcar. Approaching Ruchel's door, I was nervous, but hopeful to be accepted by a new part of my family.

I knocked and the door was opened a crack, "Who is it?"

"I'm Shlomo Cik's daughter, Leichu," I held my breath.

The door flew open and I was enveloped in hugs and kisses.

Ruchel gasped, screamed. "Hersch! Come! My niece! Back from Auschwitz! My brother's daughter!"

Pulling me into her home, she set my ragged bundle aside and returned to gaze into my eyes and caress my tired face. Such family reunions were a gift of the liberation still underway as Allied Forces continued to sweep north and east to meet the Russian armies.

Elated, she exclaimed, "Welcome to our family! You are at home here with us."

Their quarters were one room with a small kitchen. She was so welcoming to someone from her family who was alive, that she gave her bed to me and set up another bed for herself in the kitchen. I now shared Ruchel's bed with her daughter, Goldie.

It was April of 1945 in Bucharest, when I was among the first in our family to join Aunt Ruchel Leah. In their home, I also met my cousin Hershey Felberbaum, Ettu's brother, for the first time. When we were together in

Auschwitz, I gave Ettu the sleeves from my sweater to keep her from freezing. That part of the family was from the ghetto in Sighet, Romania (presently Sighetu Marmatiei, Romania). I was from the Sekernice ghetto.

The Felberbaum family had been herded to the Sighet ghetto. They rode the cattle car to Auschwitz along with the future Nobel Prize winning author, Elie Wiesel, who later wrote of his Holocaust survival in Auschwitz.

From that day on, my first cousin, Ettu Felberbaum, played an important part in my life. Ettu's fate was still unknown, but many life-enhancing surprises were ahead as Hershey and I lined up together in our daily visit to the American Joint. There, Survivors received a cash allotment to help them begin new lives. While waiting our turn, we asked others in line about any family who might have escaped the ovens. World War II had completely destroyed our lives, and everyone longed to reconnect with lost relatives. I would have given anything to have had a sibling next to me in the camps.

At the end of each day, I went back to my aunt Ruchel's house for supper and to sleep the night. Returning to the Joint early in the morning, I would find my place in line. Everyone knew who was in front of whom. There was no such thing as cutting in, and no one ever lost their place in line. It took several days to receive our cash distributions.

Wherever I went, my question was the same, "Do you know anything about the Cik family from Brustury?" Having temporarily lost God, I only had hope to keep me alive. That fire for life, discovered in Auschwitz, still burned within me like a torch.

One day in line, I miraculously spotted my dear little camp sister, Cipora. We had been separated in Camp Stutthof for almost a year, without the chance of saying good-bye. Jumping up and down like small children, we hugged and kissed each other and cried. It was a miracle she had survived, since she was not very strong. Now she had gained weight and was happy. Both of us wore real clothing and our short hair was growing back. We were flourishing young women once again and felt good about ourselves.

I trembled when Cipora told me a rumor she had heard.

I shouted, "My sister Malchi? Alive? In Budapest?"

Rumors birthed reunions between lost souls. Sometimes one must wait for miracles to openly reveal themselves. Both of us had been spared. Malchi was too far away for me to reach her immediately. I began planning how we could be together again.

The Nazis had taken Malchi on the last transport from Budapest to Auschwitz. She was soon on a death march and, eventually, taken by cattle car to Austria. After being liberated by the Russians, she returned to Budapest to live with her Aunt Ruchel Lebovic and Uncle Herschel, who had returned to their pre-war apartment. Malchi later married Herschel, her first cousin. As a young married couple, they went to Germany and were held in a German DP camp for displaced persons until they would receive their visas to America.

Chatting in line at the Joint one morning, Hershey was astounded to learn that Ettu had not only survived Auschwitz, but was also freed by the Russian soldiers. She had found her way to Aunt Tzili in Temeswár, Romania (presently Timisoara, Romania). This was the same loving Aunt Tzili who had cared for our family after *Maminka* passed away. In his excitement and disbelief, Hershey left the line immediately to catch the next train to Temeswar – without his allotment. Ettu was far more important to him than the money. To find a loved one after liberation from the labor camps was like being reborn.

I chased after him, "Hershey, Hershey! Wait up. I have something for you." I had my allotment and wanted to share it with him, but I knew he would be too proud to take cash from me, his young cousin. Determined to give it to him, I put some bills in a cigarette box I found lying on the ground. As he boarded the train, I handed him the box through the window.

"Hershey, don't throw away the box. Look inside."

As train chugged away, Hershey discovered the rolled-up bills. Laughing, he waved good-bye.

While still in Bucharest, I registered for identification papers at the Czech Embassy, and was thrilled to be handed a passport, stamped in big red letters: *Lenka Cik, 14/3/1925, Brustury, Czechoslovakia*. My name on an official document - proof of my existence! The embassy even provided me with underwear and bed clothing to supplement my scant wardrobe, including my striped camp dress. Small acts of kindness warmed many hearts during those times. Slowly, the healing began.

I was anxious to see Aunt Tzili. My childhood love for her was still strong. Eager to reconnect with her, Ettu and Hershey, I rode the train from Bucharest to Temeswár. Hershey had done the same thing and was now living with Aunt

Tzili and Ettu. Upon my arrival, Tzili's five-year-old son Mendy greeted me outside their small two-room apartment on his red tricycle, surely another sign of better days to come. I was embraced as new family. Ettu changed my name from Leichu to "Lily," sounding more Hungarian to suit the locality.

Strangely, life took another turn the very next morning.

CHAPTER 15

Escaping to Israel

Breathing the warm air in Temeswár, Romania, in June of 1945, Ettu confessed that she and Hershey were now part of a secret Zionist underground organization, the Aliyah Bet, set up to smuggle Jews into Palestine. The smuggling was necessary because Great Britain had a mandate to control Palestine and chose not to allow entry of new Jewish immigrants. At my pleading, Ettu agreed to ask their leader, Yuri, if I could join the group. Should they agree to take me, I would have to decide on the spot whether to accompany them or not. There would be no time to think it over. Ettu would have to convince the Zionists that, as her first cousin, Leichu, now "Lily," belonged with their Hungarian and Romanian group.

I was desperate to flee Europe for Palestine, *Eretz Yisroel,* the land of Israel, promised by God to Abraham in the Torah as our forever home where Jews lived for thousands of years. At the end of World War II, Russian communist troops took over my last hometown of Chust. I heard that Jews there were not allowed the freedom to travel, and I could not bear the thought of such restriction, feeling trapped again. Free from the Nazis, I could not take any more military control. Being in Israel meant I would no longer feel persecuted for being a Jew. A yearning for feeling safe burnt inside me. Surely, Israel would be my salvation.

To my relief, I was accepted by the underground group, allowed to leave with them early the following morning on the train for Budapest. They spoke mostly Romanian, which was a new language for me. I begged the tall, handsome young leader from Budapest, Yuri, for permission to search in Budapest for my sister, Malchi, whom I hadn't seen for some time. Years later I learned she had been in a Budapest ghetto before she was taken by a cattle car to Auschwitz, also survived a death march and was liberated by the Russians. She somehow made it back to Budapest and was now living with our Aunt Ruchel Lebovic and her family.

Our secret group would be in the city for only two days. He allowed me a short two and a half hours to find my way through the busy capital of Hungary. I remembered Malchi's address from when I used to write her letters before Auschwitz. After taking several streetcars with her address in my hand, I found my beloved sister in the late afternoon.

Malchi didn't know I was coming. She did not even know I was alive. I climbed three flights of stairs to find her apartment. Trembling, I knocked on the brown door and heard the lock clicking from the inside. Malchi opened the door and gasped. We hurled ourselves into each other's arms, sobbing. We couldn't speak. For the first time since I left Chust, I allowed myself to weep fully, no longer alone with my pain of dry tears.

Even though the Aliyah Bet had warned me to keep the escape a secret, I had to tell my sister I was going to Israel. Thoughtfully, Malchi took off her small round Omega watch and buckled it onto my wrist. I wore it for many years as a memento of our reunion. We had to separate again. At least I knew she was alive.

Returning by streetcar, I reached the group just as they were leaving. A few more minutes spent with Malchi, and I would have been left behind.

Thirty of us traveled to the Austrian border on a normal passenger train. During the trip I clung to Hershey and Ettu as a child would cling to her parents. They protected me. Ettu, a teacher, had my respect for her intelligence and maturity. She became my role model. Because she knew of the deaths of so many babies and children in Auschwitz, she never wanted to have children of her own, a decision she would later regret. She went on to have a rich professional life in Paris as a French teacher and interpreter. The others in our Aliyah group were strangers to me.

We crossed several different zones of occupied Austria, and at every border we feared being caught by the authorities. At the city of Graz, we walked to safe lodgings with clean beds, running water, electricity, and the luxury of an indoor toilet down the hall. We ate in non-kosher eateries. Those meals were against my religious beliefs, but this was 1945, and I was escaping World War II. Without that food, my mission to reach Israel couldn't continue.

The head of the group, Yuri, was extremely vigilant about us not being discovered by the locals. The leaders meticulously searched our belongings for any evidence of our identity. It hurt to see my passport and camp dress burning with the others, yet Yuri had earned my trust. Again, I was a nobody, though this was for a noble purpose. I knew who I was, with dreams for my future.

I told myself, "Calm down, nothing is easy, things don't usually go your way — you are safe with these people." Under the cover of darkness, we wandered the roads at night through villages for several weeks. Exhausted, we slept in abandoned barns before the sun rose. I didn't know where we were and knew not to ask. Maybe the leaders had maps and a timetable to follow. Hidden during the day in barns, our guides taught us beginning Hebrew and Jewish history. To inspire us as Zionists, they taught us the national anthem of Israel, *HaTikva*, "The Hope."

From the borders of Austria, we stumbled through ink-black nights toward the capital city of Vienna. Each of us hauled a knapsack. Our routine wasn't always consistent. The first night we slept in an open field near a noisy river. Early next morning, we waded across the river. I floated my heavy wet backpack in front of me, keeping my left arm above the water to protect Malchi's watch. The stronger boys swam while pushing their rucksacks through the water with their heads. Upon reaching the opposite bank, we laid out our soaking wet clothing from the rucksacks to dry in the sun on hot rocks. Resting on the grass, we dried off before moving on.

The boys snuck onto nearby farms to dig potatoes and also managed to steal eggs from roaming chickens' nests. Milking the cows into rusty cans they found in the fields, we had enough food to fill our stomachs. Fresh milk and eggs were more delicious than even from back home. It was fun to make a campfire and to cook in the milk cans. We were adventurous young people, all of us in our late teens and early twenties, united in our goal to get to Israel. Those times were happy. To pass the time, we sang, danced, and acted in our own made up plays while still vigilant of our surroundings.

Upon reaching a British military camp near Vienna, we were accepted as war refugees. We were assigned to an army barrack and given canned food.

Our hosts didn't know we were headed for Israel on a secret mission. For the first time in my life, I saw a black man. It was strange for me, having only read about black people from my eighth-grade textbooks that described different races. I was ignorant about the comparison of Jews of the Holocaust to that of what people of color had suffered in nations seen as free. I stared at this soldier curiously. Later, I saw many black American soldiers in Austria who also helped us.

The guides knew how to obtain ration cards for food. With those cards, we could eat in a tavern with ample food. There I enjoyed my first taste of SPAM. I had no idea what that English word meant. It tasted good, salty, and cold. Straight from the can, it satisfied my hunger. I later learned it was ham, a food forbidden to Jews. I felt guilty that I had eaten pork. But food was still in short supply after the war, so we ate whatever we could find. Once they served a thin green soup made of cucumbers. As a prisoner, I had only known soup made of potatoes or beans, with dirt broth.

Most of our group spoke Romanian, but lucky for me, Hungarian as well. We communicated, but our world views differed drastically. They did not observe Jewish laws and the customs of my upbringing, yet I knew I had to adapt to their rules. Many of them seemed more sophisticated and more clever than me. I was just a country girl! Maybe they had grown up at home with their parents and were not taken to the camps. I was uncomfortable with their custom of being intimate without being married. I didn't allow myself to connect with anyone. One of the girls became pregnant and had to have a scraping. This couple later wedded. What kept us all together was that we were Zionists on a mission to get to our homeland. But I felt strange among them.

I, who wanted so deeply to be independent, now found myself part of another group, here in Vienna, learning again that sticking together for a common goal was the best way to survive. This I learned in Auschwitz: fill your belly with anything if you want to go on living. We hid our knapsacks in a shack so no one would be able to identify us as refugees on the run. Hoping to keep the few things we had, the group left two of us on guard duty at the shack while others were eating or sleeping.

We snuck our changes of clothing up the back stairway of the American military barrack and slept on a hard wooden floor with a blanket as a mattress. They didn't know who we were or where we were headed. Every day, I helped wash the floor to keep it immaculate. I was assigned to work with a girl who spoke only Romanian. We got the job done by using sign language and a big mop.

Soon it was time to leave Austria. None of us knew how or when we would reach Palestine. Our leaders had a prior arrangement with a secret Jewish Brigade. The Aliyah Bet informed us it was time to go to Italy.

The hike through and across the Italian border was strenuous. We climbed our way up the hills, then over high mountains, carrying our heavy backpacks. We scrambled down uneven and difficult paths. If someone tripped and fell, he got up and kept on moving. I felt strong, I didn't fall. Being free, we laughed and joked along our way. It was a happy journey. Being liberated and not afraid of the Germans anymore, we were free to laugh and joke like normal teenagers.

The war was over, but gunshots were still heard from all directions. The Austrians guarded their property from trespassers of other countries, like us. We risked being shot or captured by local police. I feared what would happen if we were discovered.

Upon arrival to Italy, our group joined Jewish soldiers from Palestine. They were members of the Jewish Brigade that had served with the British, fighting the Germans. Their secret mission was to bring Jewish refugees to Israel.

Our leader took us to Nonantola in northern Italy. Only our guides knew this next step to our destination. As we walked through southern Europe, all of us had to trust our fellow Jewish Zionists.

CHAPTER 16

From the Alps to the Opera

August 1945 – January 1946

The Israeli Brigade soldiers set up training camps in Italy for refugees who wanted to immigrate to Israel. I waited for the next step in the village of Nonantola, in the northern Emilia-Romagna region. During our six-month stay, they took us to visit other groups stationed in Reggio Emilia, where I made a new friend, Sara Rotbart from Poland. We became close friends, speaking Yiddish, reminiscing about our lives before the camps. Other refugee groups were in Florence and Bologna. This was a peaceful and healing respite.

Hershey, Ettu, and I, along with the rest of our group, lived in a stunning villa in Nonantola, a well-kept two-story house on beautiful grounds with bronze and marble statues. I wondered who used to live there. I had never seen anything like it. We slept in beds, dormitory style, in one large room on the second floor. Our days were spent in classes, learning Hebrew, English, and drawing. We had motivating lectures on how to live in Israel, and I couldn't wait to get there. During drawing lessons, I made a sketch of a guard with a dog in Auschwitz behind the electric fence escorting the prisoners to work.

Leah remembers Auschwitz in 1944. These people threw me the sweater over the fence.
2013 – Pencil Sketch

We were given chores. I was delegated to laundry duty. In Nonantola, I was introduced to modern life through their self-service laundry. My job was to help wash, dry, and mend clothing. Working there would be good training for my new life in Israel.

Ettu and Hershey were assigned kitchen work. They helped prepare good food, and we ate in a large dining room. It was the first time I ate pasta with raisins and sugar mixed with margarine by *Ceres*, supplied to us by the Jewish American brigade.

Friday nights, in honor of Shabbat, tables would be covered with white cloths. After dinner, there would be a party with fruit juice and cookies. We used to sing songs and socialize. Here I was among friends in a clean place and with enough food to continue regaining my health and self-respect. Every day I looked forward to seeing my new best friend, Sara Rotbart.

My stay was more like going to school, with a lot of free time. Our group was taken on local tours, including the opera in Padova. Here I was, a Czech country girl who grew up in a house without electricity, attending the opera in Italy. The music I knew from home was mainly Czechoslovakian folk songs. Yet the opera reminded me of the classical music I heard at Grandfather's house in Brustury. My eyes and ears were straining to capture the dignified architecture of this grand Italian opera house with the beautiful singing accompanied by an orchestra. The performance ended with all of us standing, clapping and cheering — all kinds of people in the audience. Who were these people?

Looking around, I saw ladies with sparkling gowns and jewels. We were a contrast, wearing our everyday clothes. At nineteen years of age, I had never seen such luxury. The lofty beauty dazzled me. This music had the power to bring together many kinds of people. To think that just one year ago, the Nazis had tried to cut off my life in the concentration camps. I would have missed this moment of splendor and glory. It was hard to rationalize this opulence with the brutality and bestiality of death camp horror. Was this like heaven? Who could I thank for this wonderful opera? Perhaps, it was the Jewish Joint.

During our stay at the villa in northern Italy, in a country I could not have imagined, I was relieved to be treated with respect and have plentiful food. All of this happened post-war. As I continued to recuperate, my confidence grew little by little and my senses became open to another world. In Venice, we were taken on tours through meandering waterway inlets on small boats. It was fun to see outdoor vendors selling jewelry, dresses, shoes, and scarves. I'd never seen street sellers before, but I had no money.

While touring by bus, we stopped at many different eateries along the way, whetting our appetite for a larger variety of home-cooked foods. Touring kept us very busy, distracting our minds from the horrors we had lived.

The Joint gave me dresses, pants, and a custom-tailored winter coat. I could not have gone into a store to buy ready-made clothing without money.

Schooling continued as Jewish soldiers trained us how to escape a threat in an emergency. I learned to climb a roped wall and to camouflage myself on the ground near bushes.

It was a cold evening on January 7, 1946, when I was abruptly awakened in the middle of the night by our guides. Jewish soldiers were waiting outside for us in idling military trucks. I dressed in the dark, grabbed my bundle and jumped into a truck. Secretly and quietly, we were taken to a port where a small ship, *Enzo Sereni*, took on passengers headed for Haifa, Palestine. The cargo ship had been rented from a Jewish Italian merchant. I later found out that 908 new adult settlers were crammed onto that modest vessel. No one complained, as this day toward freedom was finally here.

The early morning light found me boarding the ship. I climbed down a ladder to the lower deck, where we would sleep in hammocks, three layers high. We were as tight as a flock of birds following their leader.

Feeling vulnerable because of all the young men, I did not sleep well at night. There was no supervision or separation in the sleeping quarters. No longer confined, many went up on the deck to stretch out and fall sleep in the fresh sea air. Stars illuminated the ship's course toward our paradise in Israel. I was free, but on guard to protect myself from men's uncontrolled desire.

1945 Enzo Sereni detained in port of Haifa, Israel

After a meager breakfast of coffee and bread, I returned to my hammock, while others played cards or made up simple games to pass the time. Some people became seasick and vomited wherever they were. Buckets of sea water were used to clean the vomit away. I was never sick. It was a dangerous voyage. If a plane was heard passing overhead, we ran below deck, afraid to be seen by the British Air Patrol. They searched the waters for fleeing Jewish refugees trying to sneak into Palestine. How would we get in?

After almost two weeks on rolling the seas, someone shouted, "I can see land!" We rushed to the deck to witness this miracle as the ship approached the shores of Haifa. Dancing with joy, we began singing Israel's *HaTikva*. Coming closer to the shore, I saw no mountains and very few trees, a flat landscape and white rooftops, so different from the peaked roofs in Europe, with snow-covered mountains, trees, and rivers. The warm sun was welcoming, but this new land appeared uninviting — dry, barren, and brown.

Our excitement was short-lived. British aircraft hovered overhead, while their ships surrounded the *Enzo Sereni*, forcing her toward the port. Afraid of being captured, younger boys jumped into the sea to escape. On January 17, 1946, we docked in Haifa, ten days after our departure from Italy. The British Navy boarded the *Enzo,* escorting her and swiftly herding us into lines again, military lines. We disembarked to buses with motors running, disappointed as our new hope was interrupted. We were not as afraid of the British soldiers as we had been of the Nazis, but we had to follow their orders.

1946 Coming off Enzo Sereni to waiting buses in Haifa

From the port of Haifa, the British soldiers took us on a short ride to Atlit, a detention camp, guarded by watchtowers that were surrounded by a wire and wooden fence. This wire enclosure was not tall, secure or electrified, but it was a reminder of the concentration camps with a tall watchtower. Where are we? Every hope seemed to be dashed. What a downfall. It was set up as a detention center to capture Jews found illegally entering Palestine, because the British favored the Arab position of keeping the Middle East Arabian. As a Holocaust Survivor, I was reminded of Brano. We were enclosed and always being watched by the soldiers. Once again, I was being led to showers and stripped naked. Only this time they were real showers with soap and water. We were being fumigated. We were not tortured. No one died in these showers.

1946 Lenka and Sara behind the fence at Camp Atlit, Haifa, Israel

Once again, I lived in close quarters, but this time I was fed three ample meals a day. These were weeks of rest, with us washing our clothes at the pumps and eating. Bored, we roamed around the sandy grounds the entire day, waiting for someone from the outside to claim us. I knew my cousins, the Adlers, were somewhere in Israel, but how would we find each other? They did not know I survived. How would they know to look for me? I knew no one else. Would they come for me?

Years before, Britain had approved of the Zionist concept of a Jewish homeland in Palestine. This was agreed to in the Balfour Declaration of November

1917, before the end of World War I, making a place for Jews to live. The idea of a Jewish homeland was in response to the problem of European anti-Semitism. I felt I would be safe in Palestine, the only place I could go and be with my people.

Palestine had been ruled by the Ottoman Empire until the end of World War I in 1918. Control of Palestine was given to the British under a mandate, put into effect in September of 1923. A quota was allowed for both Jewish and Arab immigration to Palestine, until the beginning of World War II in 1939. With the British military in control, Jewish refugees were barred from legal entry into Palestine. The quotas did not end until Israel's Declaration of Independence on May 14, 1948.

Jews argued that they had a historical right to the land from biblical times. God had freed us from slavery in Egypt and then led us to the promised land of Palestine, Israel. Jews had been living there for more than 3,000 years.

Of equal importance was the fact that six million Jews had been killed by Hitler in the Holocaust. Most nations had refused to accept the Jewish refugees who had pleaded to escape the killing regime. For Zionists, a Jewish State in Palestine had become the only place where any Jew could find refuge from persecution.

The Palestinian Arabs based their claims to the land on the fact that they had occupied it for more than 1,000 years. The British government's pro-Arab policy provided almost no enforcement of Arab immigration quotas, while being very strict with the quotas for the Jewish immigrants.

As we now know, the debate about a Jewish homeland in Palestine has gone on for almost 100 years and is still threatening world peace.

CHAPTER 17

For Love of Zion

January 1946

I said to my friend Sara in Yiddish, "We're finally in Israel, but really not free."

Sara fumed, "Nothing goes our way."

I was saved from the death camps yet still under pressure being told what to do, where to sleep, where to wash up, and where to eat. After three weeks, the British decided to give me my freedom. Young immigrants were not afraid of the British because they took care of us.

Zionist organizations arranged living places for the refugees. Some new comers were claimed by their families, while others were sent to collective farms as settlers. Ettu went to her uncle in Tel Aviv, while Hershey went to Kibbutz Maagan, near Yam Kinneret, the Sea of Galilee. They sent me and 38 others to Kibbutz Gesher, near Maagan, on the Jordan River. Sara came to the same kibbutz, while the rest of my group, Polish boys and girls, were the people I didn't know. The Polish language they spoke was close to Czech, so I was able to understand most of what they were saying.

I finally felt safe in Israel. There was time to think. Who am I? Am I the same person I used to be? The last three years of my life had been filled with anti-Semitism, mass murder, war, death, grief, and my own starvation. That was enough to unbalance any person.

Nothing in life is meaningless. I've heard that everything happens for a reason. I survived the war, although I never understood the meaning of so much death and madness. By nineteen years old, most of my education had come from real life.

Kibbutz Gesher was a new establishment, founded by a group of Sabras, native Israelis, who only spoke Hebrew. This was the first time I heard conversational Hebrew. Seventy idealistic young adults had formed a kibbutz settlement. This socialist community was different from anything I had ever known. As guests, we were required to live by their rules. Everything was shared, even the bathrooms and showers, just like the camps, yet, so pleasantly different.

Members cooked in a big kitchen, and we ate together, seated on benches at long tables in the large family-style dining room. The kitchen served 120 kibbutzniks for breakfast, lunch, teatime, and dinner. Meals were the time to become acquainted with one another. There was a young Polish man, who had also been in the camps, but he wasn't the one for me because he wasn't educated. I became acquainted with Asher from Romania, but he, too, was just a friend. We were comfortable speaking Yiddish together. I made many new girlfriends, all Survivors like myself. We talked and sang together on the lawn during our free time. Yet we heard people referring to us with the slang word *sabon,* or soap – to belittle Holocaust Survivors, because of Nazis' rumors that soap was made from fat boiled from the bodies. I pretended I didn't hear it, but I felt degraded. We were not normal. We were damaged from the war, yet our minds were free to dream of the future. I hoped to be married one day and have a family, to create what was stolen from me.

There were two cooks working in the non-kosher kitchen. Girls from our group of Survivors worked as waitresses. This dining room was large enough to be used as a meeting hall, theater, and the polling place for annual elections to accept new members. Membership in the kibbutz was not automatic, but rather by election of kibbutz members.

Our work schedules and other announcements were posted on the cafeteria wall. Beside daily work assignments, there were pictures of us at work. It was our responsibility to know when and where to show up for our daily assignments. The wall was our information center with news about Israel, and the whole world. Mealtimes were also used for gossip about members' romances. Many new relationships began at this wall.

I was no longer worried about my next meal, suffering hunger, being naked or ashamed. In this Promised Land, it was a new life, a new beginning. Yet we knew that our experiences in the Holocaust were not open for discussion. There was no sympathy for Survivors from fellow kibbutzniks. The society encouraged stoic suppression by never talking about the Holocaust itself. I don't think they knew what to say. I didn't have the courage to talk about it, either. If I did, I don't think they would have believed me or even understood.

Survivors weren't given jobs requiring greater responsibility or sensitivity such as childcare or office work. Rather, we were assigned to hard physical labor. Young and healthy, we labored at many different jobs: gardening, farming, raising animals, and even breaking up rocks in a stone quarry. We rode to work at the quarry on a tractor, aware that we were not given more important jobs. This attitude did not enhance my self-esteem.

1946 Going to work at the stone quarry

Washing, mending and ironing our clothes was done in the laundry room. Nametags were sewn into all our belongings and distributed to our cupboards. We slept in a small wooden structure with one bedroom. I was assigned a room with two Sabras who spoke only Hebrew. I knew they felt sorry for me, and I felt inferior. Sara was assigned to a different room, yet we remained close friends. When it became stifling hot, we moved our cots outside and slept under the stars and mosquito netting.

One of the most distinctive features of this communal living arrangement was childcare. The kids slept in dormitories away from their parents and were raised by Kibbutz caregivers. Families spent limited time together after a long workday. Marriage was not a requirement for bearing children.

Our supervisor, Edith, said, "Men need women." We were encouraged to have a "free sex" life, which was not for me. I lived according to my own values and Jewish law, as taught by my traditional family in Brustury.

This was a socialist farming community where everyone worked for the benefit of all. Jewish religious customs were not a priority in this kibbutz. If members had to work on Shabbat, they would get another day off. These practices were foreign to me. Many members of the group had university education, but as Zionists, they had chosen the kibbutz way of life.

Military training was mandatory for everyone. The Jewish population, living in Palestine under British rule, was anxious to add more land to the territory. Under the cover of darkness, trained kibbutzniks pitched tents on unclaimed territory. These shelters, erected overnight, established the right of property ownership. Although the British had a mandate to control Palestine, Turkish law still applied to territorial transactions. Not many among us knew of this clandestine activity. There were parcels of earth owned by no one, "no man's land." How did I know? One of the girls in my bunkroom told me about going out one night on a courageous expedition to claim land for Israel. The mission could have ended her life.

1946 Kibbutz Gesher military training
Leah is now 20 years old

Becoming more confident, I learned to stand up for myself in this collective, but democratic environment. One day during free time, four of us, two boys and two girls, decided to go for a swim in the Jordan River behind our kibbutz. We did not know this waterway as the locals did. Some places were shallow and inviting. My close friend, Asher, went into the shallow water. The river suddenly became a deep, swirling whirlpool. The eddy currents caught him.

His hands were waving and splashing as he screamed, "Help . . . help me!"

And then silence as he slipped away . . . he was gone. The Jordan River had swallowed him.

None of us knew how to swim in the deep, turbulent waters. We hollered and cried. Just moments before, all of us were laughing and joking. It happened so fast. We couldn't save him.

The next morning his body was recovered. At his funeral, someone gave me greens to place on his grave.

Soon after the funeral, the authorities were notified and police investigated. In a British courthouse, I had to place my hand on their Bible, swearing to tell the truth.

I testified, "There was no lovers' quarrel. Asher did not commit suicide. The three of us had nothing to do with the accident."

I knew if we hadn't gone to the river, he wouldn't have drowned. Different from death in the camps, I felt this was somehow my fault. It was heartbreaking to lose another friend. I had accumulated so much grief that had never been mourned. Sobbing, I poured out my sorrow to Sara.

"So much has been stolen from us, and now we've lost another close friend. Asher left his mother behind in Romania. None of our mothers are even living."

Sara and I grieved together. There was the

1946 My best friend from Italy, Sara Rotbart, left

time to feel my deep sorrow. In the camps, I never had a chance to mourn. Now every death scraped still raw wounds. We, Survivors, have a culture of our own, knowing painful suffering from hunger and grief that has no words. Only we can understand one another.

Kibbutz security was essential, with armed members guarding the fenced perimeter at night. Arab men came to conduct business during the day, friendly to our faces. We had to be wary, cautious with these neighbors. We even had classes in basic Arabic. To defend ourselves from potential Arab intruders, counselors taught us how to use military weapons such as rifles, pistols, and hand grenades. I still remember the directions for using the grenade: open, ignite, throw.

One time, lost in sad thoughts, I wandered alone into a vacant field. When the counselor realized my absence, she sent someone on horseback to find me.

He scolded me, "Are you out of your mind? Going away alone is dangerous."

I was out of my mind, alone with my sorrow.

When the Arabs came to do business at the kibbutz, there was one who had his eye on me. I was blond and full-figured. He wanted to buy me as a wife. My friends teased me, but the kibbutz protected me.

In the mornings I worked in the vegetable garden, picking tomatoes, cucumbers, and green beans. We worked a half-day in the hot fields, drinking warm tea to stay hydrated. The kibbutz leaders explained to me that if I had cold drinks, my body would lose water faster. Following our afternoon break during the hottest time of the day, we had teatime, freshly baked warm bread with jam and halva before we went back to the fields as the temperature was dropping. We worked until sundown. I gained weight eating an abundance of soft, warm bread, denied to me for so long. When we returned and showered, a nice cooked supper was waiting for us in the dining room.

My early years in Brustury had taught me how to live with nature. Once again, vitality filled my body, alive as the ripe vegetables I was harvesting.

In the multipurpose recreation room, my education began again – with books, newspapers, and magazines. One of the greatest things in my life has always been books. I loved to read. We had half-day study groups as required by the Jewish agency, the Haganah that sent us to the kibbutz. We were expected to speak only Hebrew. I struggled with this new tongue, as did most other newcomers, who often used sign language to be understood. Coming from different parts of Europe, we spoke our native tongues in private. Intensive classes, all in Hebrew, offered Jewish history, civil law, and Zionism. To relax, we played cards, domino, and learned the strategies of the war game – chess. I was making more friends, as I felt accepted in this young pioneering group. I developed a special friendship with one of my bunkmates, a Sabra who was also our Hebrew grammar teacher. I was fortunate that she taught me privately in our room at night.

In 1946, there was fighting between the Jewish resistance group, the Haganah, and the British military. Within and around Palestine were millions of Arabs who were against the idea of a Jewish state. The point of conflict was who would own and control the land.

It was important to know how to use military equipment. I felt powerful learning how to use weapons. Our guns were never fired during practice because ammunition was so scarce. We developed the skills needed to protect the kibbutz from assault. Where did the Israelis get these arms? Some of the guns and explosives were stolen from the British military warehouses. Some bullets were manufactured in secret underground factories that operated day and night, right under British noses. War materials were supplemented with guns secretly brought in from Zionist groups in America and Chechia. This information was unknown to me during my year at the kibbutz.

Military training led me on long mountain hikes in heavy heat without water. On my hip I carried a canteen, but I was not supposed to drink from it. On reaching the destination, I was ordered to pour the water on the dirt. Training to go without water for long periods, under trying circumstances, further toughened me.

This exercise was not like the starvation and abuse in Auschwitz. That camp was for death. The training in the Jordan Valley was preparation for life, a new kind of team survival. While extremely tired, I no longer had to stand alone.

Looking back at this experience, I see how different it was from Europe. The socialist- based kibbutz preached and practiced equality between men and women. We were treated alike and expected to do similar work, women being trained the same as men — to kill in combat. My traditional Jewish up-bringing as a girl had not prepared me for this perspective in my new country. Where I was from, girls were not allowed to talk to boys, let alone ride their bikes.

Some members worked for other kibbutz communities to earn additional income for our kibbutz. I was sent to another Kibbutz for the summer, a resort for tourists, where I, alone, washed dishes every day, all day. In my boredom, I began smoking a lot of free cigarettes. I slept with other women in the corner of a hot canvas tent. Workers were both girls and boys. There was no privacy. I was lonesome. When I returned to Kibbutz Gesher at the end of tourist sea-son, many people had left my kibbutz. I was surprised when my best friend, Sara, went to Tel Aviv to live with her cousins.

There was enough free time to look for family members who had come to Palestine before the war. I searched for relatives by placing an ad in the local newspaper. It was like a miracle when dear Cousin Chaya saw my ad and immediately came to visit me.

Excitedly, she said, "Oh, God. You're here. You're safe . . . all grown up."

I cried in joy at this reconnection with my past. She still cared about me.

She was the first relative I found in Israel. It was the same Chaya who had sat with five- year-old Leichu when they took away my mother's body. Fortunately, she had been able to leave Czechoslovakia for Palestine before the war in 1937.

My cousin Chaya now lived in an established non-religious kibbutz with her husband and their two young children. She didn't like the collective life-style either. Concerned about my way of living, she spoke to her brother, Yitzhak Adler, who invited me to live with him and his wife, Ruchel, in the village of Pardes Katz, near Tel Aviv.

Once again, I left the only home I knew with few belongings. A little over a year had passed since I had arrived at Kibbutz Gesher. The kibbutz leaders were unhappy when I told them at the last minute, "I am leaving today to live with my first cousins."

Irritated and disappointed, the counselor said, "Had you told us earlier, we would have persuaded you to stay."

I followed others who had left before me, like my best friend Sara. Not everyone was suited to cooperative kibbutz life. Members of the kibbutz had to accept the fact that they could not have anything of their own except personal items. Their lifestyle was shared, and I, with an independent streak, was anxious to leave. My friends helped me secure my state-issued iron bed on top of the bus. We hugged and said good-bye. I never went back to visit.

March 1947, Pardes Katz (near Tel Aviv)

I didn't know what to expect from my cousins, Yitzhak and Ruchel Adler. They were in their early thirties with two little children. I had just turned 21.

The bus stopped on the dusty road. We recognized each other immediately and embraced affectionately. Yitzhak had an Adler face. Here was the warmth of being home with real family.

My cousins worked hard in a knitting factory, not far from their small apartment. Ruchel was the head designer. They paid me good wages to care for their children, my first adult post-camp earnings. With years of experience raising my stepsiblings in Brustury, it was easy for me to oversee the daily lives of Ayala, a girl of six, and Ramie, their infant boy.

I was like a daughter to Ruchel, even though she was just ten years older. I accepted her as the mother I would like to have known. She taught me how to dress and behave, to be more refined and bought me new clothes with shoes to match. One dress was brown and well tailored. Being a designer, she knew quality, fashion, and color. She bought me a lime-green sporty knit dress that she had designed herself in the factory. It matched the color of my eyes and made me feel special. Living in the Adlers' home was loving and comfortable. I was important to someone and began to feel even better about myself.

After the camps were liberated, Survivors became aware that the world at large could not understand the reality of the horrors we had experienced. Almost no one asked me questions or wanted to hear my stories. How could I act like an ordinary person when I had just emerged from hell? We had the sickening feeling that we were not wanted. Survivors needed food, housing, and jobs from a new country still establishing itself. We felt there was always a bridge between the proud old settlers and the new, frightened newcomers in Palestine. I didn't feel like one of them.

I pretended all was well, following my father's advice to put on a face, as *Tatuka* had taught me when I was little. This was my way of assimilating into my new life, to hide things that would diminish me in the eyes of others. We would never let on that we were Survivors, but people probably knew anyway. Survivors most often married among themselves.

Ruchel introduced me to a private library run by German Jews, where I chose a book in German entitled, *Trilogy of a Mother*. This was the first book I read after liberation and it reminded me of my mother's love. Reading provided much-needed solitude. To this day, I'm an avid reader. Books have been the best thing in my life, providing escape, comfort, and inexpensive entertainment.

After her long day at work, Ruchel would teach me how to cook, observing kosher laws. She introduced me to many female friends, who welcomed me. With delicate sensitivity, she helped me assimilate among her peers and I felt very comfortable with these women as my new friends.

The concentration camps had robbed me of my youth and my Jewish lifestyle. Through Ruchel, I returned to the traditional life as a Jewish young lady. Whatever faith I had lost due to the Nazi terror, was regained in Israel, living with the Adler family. Circumstances of the camps cut me off from Jewish roots, and she gently brought me back to them. Belonging is believing and trusting others. I had always made choices on the spur of the moment, according to my intuition, trusting my head over my heart, without support. Now I had Ruchel as my mentor and I trusted her. I had her love, recognition for who I could become and acceptance for what I was.

One Shabbat day I planned to meet my friends at the bus station to go to Tel Aviv. I began to iron my blouse to prepare for the trip.

"Not in my house, you don't," she said. "You can't iron on Shabbat."

I did not rebel and wore something else, but I did ride the bus that one time. With Ruchel as my role model, it was easy to return to the ways of my parent's home.

May 1947

Caring for the Adler children, I met a friend of the family, Menachem Roth. I had then turned 22 in March. In those days, birthdays were not acknowledged with parties or celebrations.

I was home alone at Ruchel's house when a man wearing shorts and sandals knocked on the door. He was there to deliver a fresh chicken.

Smiling, he said, "I'm an acquaintance of the Adlers." He handed me a package wrapped in brown paper. "This is their order."

"How did you get here?" I asked.

"I rode my bicycle. It's over there, leaning against the wall."

I recognized his Slovak accent.

"Where are you from?"

With a smile, he straightened up. "I'm Menachem Roth from Czechoslovakia, in Slovakia...and you?" This gentleman was a little taller than me and had brown wavy hair, nicely combed.

"I'm the Adlers' cousin, Leah, from Brustury, Czechoslovakia...in Carpathia."

Not only did he speak Czech, he was nice looking and seemed mature, somewhat older than my twenty-two years. A shiver came over me. He was sure of himself in a worldly way. We spoke in Czech as my Hebrew was still at a beginner's level.

He began telling me why he was a delivery guy. "I am studying for my teacher exams, so I work for a few hours a week for the butcher."

He asked, "Where are you from in Carpathia?"

"I was born in Brustury and lived in Chust."

Small talk continued, but the camps and the Holocaust weren't mentioned.

I never wanted anyone to take pity on me. The burden was mine alone. I never spoke of it. If you weren't there, you could never understand.

Skipping over most of my history, I explained my leaving Kibbutz Gesher to help the Adlers with their children and to better my life.

We stood a long time by the door, fidgeting as we chatted. I liked that he had worked in a religious kibbutz, Kfar Etzion, when he first came to Israel before the war. I was actually amazed he had also lived in a kibbutz.

When Ramie began to cry, I asked Menachem to come in. I picked up the baby. My new friend asked, "May I come back and see you another time? I must continue my deliveries."

I gave him the answer he wanted, "Please do. Come when Ruchel and Yitzhak are here so I'll have free time."

The next time he visited, we took a bus to Tel Aviv, walked on the beach, and enjoyed tea and chocolate ice cream at a cafe by the ocean. He had nice table manners, and that mattered to me. Most of all, he was kind and attentive.

Menachem explained, "As a college graduate with a teaching certificate, I taught Jewish studies and botany for two years in Czechoslovakia. Now I'm studying to take a Hebrew teacher's examination."

I was impressed.

At first we were just friends, meeting several times a week. I introduced Menachem to my best friend, Sara, but they didn't like each other, so Sara and I visited in the evenings after Ruchel came home from work. My life was easy, and I could do whatever I wanted. Over time, Menachem and I learned more about each other. Menachem's parents had passed away of natural causes in 1938, before he left Slovakia. He escaped from Hitler with the aid of the Jewish underground, the *Haganah*.

In pre-war Europe, a college-trained teacher had a dignified life. Having taught in Czechoslovakian public schools gave him a certain sophistication that attracted me. Menachem also played the violin and the wooden shepherd's flute. He gave private music lessons on both instruments.

After we went out a few times, he put his arm around my waist and kissed me. No one saw. This awakened new feelings within me.

We continued to date, going to garden restaurants with live music. We talked and had tea and our favorite chocolate ice cream. I paid for myself. It was not considered proper to accept a man's generosity without a commitment. Anyway, I knew that his money had to go for tuition and living expenses. As we became more comfortable together, I asked him to teach me Hebrew. I wanted a deeper understanding of the language. He agreed to tutor me.

Ruchel said, "Leah, why don't you take a vacation?"

I told Menachem that I could take time off from my job. Soon we planned to visit Natanya together, south of Haifa. We both had places with friends where we could stay. I stayed with my cousin, and Menachem with a married friend. While there, we celebrated the Jewish holiday of *Shavuot*, the time when the Jews received the Torah from God at Mt. Sinai. It was also the anniversary of my mother's death and, because we were now close, I asked Menachem to say Kaddish, the traditional mourner's prayer, for her. It was significant for me to share this. I told him what I remembered about *Maminka*.

After our trip, I was surprised when Menachem gave me a three-page handwritten letter in Czech.

"Read this in my presence," he said, "because I express myself better in writing than speaking face-to-face."

I objected, "No. I insist you read it to me in person."

"I'm having some doubts. We are different because of our education backgrounds."

With thoughts flashing through my mind, I was thinking that Menachem didn't want me because I was a Survivor. I knew we were thought to be "damaged goods." It was even rumored that Survivors couldn't bear children.

I listened through my tears as he continued saying that he was uncertain about our future. He had completed teachers' college, while I was an unschooled refugee from the camps. It was a rejection that made me angry. I was so in love and had found the person I wanted to marry, but Menachem couldn't make a decision. When I was with Menachem, it was easy to stop feeling sorry for myself. Was Menachem unsure of me and my background or was he unsure of himself? I trusted him and felt secure and protected. I thought he was falling in love with me, but he was cautious.

Using my voice as my weapon, with my hands in the air, I screamed, "How can you disappoint me like this? I don't want to see you anymore." I pretended to walk away.

I felt his hand on my shoulder as he turned me around, "I am not ready to commit . . . yet." Looking at me with sad blue eyes, he pleaded, "Please give me more time. Wait for me."

Even with his soft kiss, I wasn't sure. There were other men interested in me. Sadly, I wanted Menachem. I loved him. Eight years older than me, he was nurturing like a father and reminded me of a gentle and inspiring grade-school teacher in Brustury, Mr. Faltynek. His reserved charisma attracted me, yet I had to prove I was a normal woman. He knew I was dating two other men. He was probably jealous.

Within a few days, he learned that a young man from the kibbutz was interested in me. He came back to Ruchel's house to talk. Sitting on the porch, hesitantly, stroking my hand, he whispered, "Let's start over."

Meeting Menachem was the best thing that ever happened to me. I was sure of myself and sure of my decision. I was confident.

He shared a room with a friend in Bnei Brak, a city near Tel Aviv, while continuing his studies. He didn't know how to cook and didn't have money to spare, so he ate cheap bread and chocolate during the week. Observant

Jews do not handle money on Shabbat, so Menachem prepaid for his Shabbat meals at a local restaurant.

To earn a living, Menachem continued to deliver chicken for the butcher, making good use of his bicycle. He also painted flowers on blouses and scarves and sold them to a clothing vendor in Tel Aviv. He was artistic in many ways. Like other students without parents, he worked hard and was thrifty. I was the same.

"When he becomes a Torah Studies instructor, we will be married," I told my friend Sara.

Menachem was offered a position in Hadera. Because of this job, we became engaged. He moved into a residential hotel where he lived until we were married. I went to visit him at his school and was proud when he introduced me as his future wife. We were happy and in love. When I received his mother's gold ring with a three-diamond clover, I knew that our engagement was for real. I still wear the ring. Later came a second gift, a beautiful gold bracelet.

I called him Latzi, as his mother had. I was his Leichuka. He sent love letters written on both sides of crinkly thin stationery from Hadera. He spoke about life's obstacles, and how we would overcome them together.

1947 Leah and Menachem are engaged

CHAPTER 18

The Scholar's Wife

October 25, 1947

As any other girl, I hoped to have an extraordinary wedding. My future marriage to Menachem was scheduled so as not to interfere with his teaching job. I counted the days. Our wedding would take place after Shabbat, Saturday night, on October 25, 1947, in the garden of the chief rabbi of Tel Aviv.

We had no parents to help pay for our wedding, so the cost had to be minimal. We had very little money for expenses. Menachem did not have a suit to wear, and we couldn't buy one in a store. At that time, there was no such thing as ready-made in Israel. We chose gray material at the fabric shop and a tailor there made a beautiful suit with a matching hat, one he could also wear after the wedding on Shabbat and for other special occasions.

I *had* to have a white dress, even if it was not a real wedding gown like I remembered from Brustury. A friend lent me a short white dress, two sizes too big. It was a daytime dress that could be worn for anything. It was white, and I was grateful to have it. Just like the simple red winter dress that I wore to my brother's summer wedding, my white wedding dress reminded me that I needed to be happy with what I could get.

Our parents were not alive to accompany us to the wedding canopy. Even though we were happy to marry, our hearts were sadly quiet while our souls sweated tears of courage and hope. We remembered our deceased family members and symbolically invited them to be present. We were two orphans dancing with memories. Shadows of sorrow accompanied our joy, and I no longer felt impoverished. I was so proud. I felt as though Menachem had put a crown on my head.

Ruchel walked with me under the canopy, as my *Maminka* would have, had she lived. Menachem's only living brother, Vilko, and his wife, blessed us with their presence. A few first cousins were also there to witness our nuptials, and there were the ten men required to say the seven traditional wedding blessings.

My sister Malchi, my only surviving sibling, and her husband Harry, were unable to attend, as they were still living in a German DP refugee camp, waiting to immigrate to America.

We couldn't afford a photographer to take pictures during the ceremony or musicians. We scraped up enough to pay for a small outdoor reception - juice and cookies for our thirty guests. After the reception, we walked leisurely down the street, hand in hand, to a photographer's studio. Our original wedding photo captured us above the waist only, to hide my baggy dress. A year later, I borrowed another dress that fit so that a proper full-length portrait could be taken.

October 25, 1947, My First Happiness (Original wedding photo)

Yitzhak and Ruchel invited us and our few guests to a wedding meal in their home. Everybody brought gifts of absolute necessities for the kitchen or bath. Ruchel gave us a fine set of china for six, and Cousin Chaya, who took care of me when *Maminka* died, gave us some bath towels. We owned nothing, so I was grateful for all these presents. Malchi sent a beautiful set of Salinger flatware as well as the top of a used Singer sewing machine. Later, when we could afford it, I bought the bottom foot treadle and a cabinet. When complete, I used the machine for many years. Even though we were poor, we were satisfied with what we had. I treasured everything we owned. Normal life seemed within my grasp.

Our honeymoon lasted only one day – Sunday. My husband had to return to Hadera to teach on Monday. They did not allow extra vacation time. Here I was, a married woman living alone.

I moved into his old apartment in Bnei Brak, while he continued to live in the hotel in Hadera. Every day my beloved Menachem wrote me letters, the next closest thing to hearing his voice. Back in 1947, there were few public telephones in Israel.

It was hard to rent an apartment in Hadera, because of the shortage of housing. We saved up and prepaid a year's rent before we could move in. Our one room was inside a nice villa. Again we saved and bought a bed with a mattress, a dresser, and an armoire, along with a table and four chairs. There was a tiny attached kitchen the size of a closet that only had a sink with running water and a counter, but without a stove or an icebox. The country was poor and living conditions were basic. We could not leave a towel or toothbrush in the bathroom down the hall that we shared with the owners. We shopped every day and cooked over a kerosene burner in the closet-kitchen. Carrying home bags of groceries, I would be welcomed by a yard of blooming flowers that I could see out the window over the sink.

We lived there for two years. While Menachem taught in public school, I taught kindergarten in a religious school. During the afternoon, Menachem rode his bicycle to yet another school nearby, where he taught Hebrew to dark Jewish children from Yemen. I was reminded of the first time I saw black soldiers in Austria, but this was the first I knew of dark-skinned Jews.

On May 14, 1948, Israel declared its independence as the State of Israel, just hours before the end of the British mandate to control Palestine.

Immediately, U.S. President Harry S. Truman recognized the new State of Israel.

All the Jewish native-born Israelis and immigrants like me were celebrating in the streets. I had never seen anything so exhilarating. I was present at the birth of a new nation, my State of Israel, just as the Bible had prophesized. I saw a true miracle with my own eyes.

Our celebration was short-lived. Arab armies attacked Israel the very next day.

CHAPTER 19

Israel's War of Independence

On May 15, 1948, the day after Prime Minister David Ben Gurion declared Israel's statehood, a war broke out immediately as five neighboring Arab countries attacked, trying to block the establishment of the new Jewish state. That was a bloody war. They failed. At that time, it was rumored that Israel had only one wooden tank that was moved from place to place, making a lot of noise to create the image of a powerful army. Israel won the war.

1948 Leah as a kindergarten teacher

As a teacher, Menachem was exempt from combat duty. Nevertheless, he was part of the military reserves and reported for service many times during the conflict. I never knew exactly what he did. Women under twenty-five without children were also required to register for the army. As a kindergarten teacher, I was allowed to finish the school term.

After the school year finished, I was sent to serve in Pardes Chana, a small military city near our home in Hadera. Because of my religious background, I supervised the soldiers' kitchen, making sure their food was kosher.

A month later, observant women like me, who were deferred from the military, would be given civilian jobs. When I returned home, I was re-assigned to the Israeli Red Cross in July of 1949, now known as *Red Star of David*, my duty for the war. I cared for soldiers, cleaning and rewrapping their wounds. Some of the injured screamed in pain. In an effort to distract them, I talked gently in a motherly voice.

"I'll be finished with your dressing soon. You'll heal nicely." I had no idea what I was talking about.

In between bandaging, I would answer emergency phone calls.

An anxious caller shouted, "My wife is about to give birth. I need help. Please send the ambulance." There was only one in Hedera.

The driver and I picked up the mother-to-be and took her to the closest hospital in Hadera. As I rode in the back, holding her hand, she was breathing heavily, like the woman on the train to Auschwitz. Here in Israel, this young woman would be able to keep her baby. She knew nothing about Auschwitz.

Back at the first-aid station, big trucks were constantly arriving with injured troops. I helped the doctors and nurses as they cared for broken bodies. It stirred up memories of the concentration camps, traumatizing me once again. The War of Independence, lasting over nine months, left 6,000 Israelis dead and 30,000 wounded. This was an enormous loss for a small country of less than a million people.

Being away from Menachem in the second year of our marriage, serving my country with the Red Cross, I missed his gentle touch and loving words. As a Survivor, I tried not to react to things that I could not change, telling myself, "This will pass, and Menachem and I will soon be together".

For the September of 1949 school year, Menachem was offered a better teaching position in the city of Bat Yam, near Tel Aviv. He rented a one-room apartment. I stayed behind in Hadera, caring for the wounded for another month. After joining Menachem in Bat Yam, I got a wig-making job in Tel Aviv. I always worked, not only for bread, but also for security.

One day, after the bus ride to Tel Aviv, I was walking to my job on the main road of Allenby Street, when I heard a familiar voice behind me. I spun around and screeched, "Cipora!"

Other walkers stopped and stared. We made such a scene. People gathered around us as we cried and hugged and kissed...my Cipora was in my arms. Finding my little camp sister again from my past was like being reborn. We'd last been separated in Bucharest, waiting in line for money from the Joint, not knowing if we'd ever meet again.

Now we continued to see one another often. Cipora came to visit us in Bat Yam on Shabbat. Menachem's good friend always came to visit for lunch. We arranged for them to meet at our Shabbat table. They got along right away and were married within six months. We had become each other's family.

Cipora reminded me of the time when we were first separated in Stutthof, when I was transferred to work in Camp Brano and she was left behind. Looking small and frail, she had been sent with a hometown friend to a barrack near the crematoria, along with other small children who were scheduled to be gassed. Realizing there would be no probability of survival, they took a chance and together ran back to their barrack in Stutthof, where they found their beds were not yet occupied by someone else. Undetected by the guards, they were held there for another two months. Cipora was able to bathe daily, found warm clothes and, with more food, developed rosy cheeks. They were chosen to go to another working camp. By taking this brazen risk, she had survived.

Menachem and I saved enough money to put down a deposit on a new house being built in a part of a religious settlement on the outskirts of Bat Yam. Meanwhile, feeling more secure, we decided to start a family. When I started throwing up every morning, I knew we were going to have a baby. My sister began to send me packages of maternity clothes. We weren't going to be in our new house until after the baby would be born.

From the hilly desert of the Ramat Yam area, wind gusts created mini sand dunes in unexpected places, clogging the only road leading to the settlement. We waited more than a year for our one-story house to be finished. It was a two-bedroom, one bath with a separate toilet room, a foyer with a window, and a smallish combination living room/dining room area. When we came to see it the first time, I was amazed it was ours. Even with no furniture, I sat in the middle of the floor and said, "I don't want to leave." It wouldn't be finished for another year.

Menachem was not satisfied with me being a simple housewife. Being a Torah scholar, he wanted his partner to know the Hebrew language well enough to understand the Torah. For the rest of our lives together, every Shabbat afternoon, we used to study the Torah and commentary: husband

- the teacher, and wife – the willing student. During my pregnancy, these lessons opened a new understanding of life for me. Menachem explained the meaning of our prayers, the Torah and Jewish history. This collaboration helped us form a deeper partnership. Proud of my learning, he told our rabbi, "My Leah understands everything you discuss in your sermons."

As we were waiting for the house to be finished, still in the little apartment, the baby came. When I was ready to give birth, we walked from our one room apartment in Bat Yam, for over an hour, to the Dagony hospital in Jaffa. When I had a contraction, we stopped. I leaned on Menachem until it was over. Supposedly, walking exercise would make my delivery easier. It didn't. This older hospital had no elevator. I climbed four flights of stairs to share a six-bed ward with other women also giving birth. The staff sent Menachem home for the night. Nurses and the doctor impatiently waited for the next push from the screaming women. The howling from other mothers, both Jewish and Arab, scared me. I joined their chorus of excruciating pain for the next six hours. Giving birth was so hard that I decided I would never have another baby.

I was both relieved and overwhelmed when my little daughter was finally handed to me: soft, pink, and beautiful, with a full head of dark, straight hair – the image of Menachem. It was Tuesday, July 24 of 1951, and I was as happy as I had ever been. God gave me this new life. This baby would re-establish the family I had lost. There was hope now for future generations of Jewish children. Hitler's aim was to exterminate the Jewish people. Every Jewish baby born is a slap on Hitler's face.

After only three days, the staff decided I should leave the hospital. As I was holding my baby girl, my bed was pushed into the corridor toward the stairs. I could barely walk because of my stitches. Even though it was Shabbat, I was expected to leave. Menachem was in the synagogue for our baby's naming ceremony. She was named Elka, after my beloved *Maminka*. Secretly, he found a student who knew how to get a taxi for medical reasons, even though it was still Shabbat when riding was forbidden. A female cab driver picked me up with my new baby, and I arrived home. A short time later, Menachem came running from the synagogue to see our baby. We were now a real family and could hardly wait for our new home to be finished.

Later, we officially changed our daughter's name from Elka to Elia, a Hebrew name formed by the combination of two names of God. Menachem adored Elia. When she was nearly a year old, he took her to the synagogue with him every Shabbat so I could sleep in. Everyone fawned over this sweet child, especially her *abba*. He called her his little Elinka, even after she was married and had children of her own. As a baby, I dressed her like a doll, my very own baby, in clothes sent to me by my sister Malchi, who was now living in Miami, Florida.

I was a good mom, just not too warm with hugging and kissing. I had no role model. We were strict parents because we didn't want our children to be spoiled, but rather to be strong, and able to stand up on their own, not to be dependent on others. In the camps, those who were spoiled dropped like flies. However, unlike when Menachem and I grew up, our children had birthday parties.

Cloth diapers were rationed, and we never had enough. I washed them by hand and sterilized the diapers in an electric boiler before hanging them outside to dry in the fresh air, and

**Leah, Elia and Menachem
in front of the kitchen shed.**

then I ironed them. From 1949 through 1954, Israel was a poor country, with rationing of everything, both food and clothing. Menachem scrimped from his wages to buy me beer to increase my milk supply and the chocolates that he knew I loved.

Before bathing the baby in our small one room apartment, I had to warm up the room with a *petilla,* a small, primitive kerosene wick, that was also used for cooking. One day I was bathing Elia in a small tub set on a chair. I accidentally overturned the lamp. Burning kerosene spilled on the floor, and my long house robe caught fire. I ripped it off, quickly threw the baby on the bed, before putting a wet towel on top of the flame to extinguish the rest of the fire. I told Menachem about my mishap when he came home. Relieved,

Menachem said, "Thank God you saved our little Elinka...thank God, you're both OK."

The three of us lived in this one room without a kitchen. We were resourceful and bought a used wooden shipping container that had transported furniture for new *Olim*, immigrants, from Czechoslovakia. I also bought a used crib and carriage from the same family. We placed the container in the landowner's yard next to the house and, improvising, I used it for a kitchen. It was a very strongly built crate. To put a container in someone else's yard was *chutzpah*, nerve, but we did what we needed to do. We cooked in this shed on a small wick, like a lantern on a stand without a dome.

We washed dishes in the yard with a hose, as we had no water in the container where I cooked. We only had running water in the bathroom down the hall, where we could not wash dishes. We bought a small icebox. Every day I stood in line down the street to buy more ice. Just like food and diapers, ice was rationed. There was not much to eat. The black market provided a little more, but we had to pay extra.

Menachem hid from his students inside the shed when we washed our dishes. It was not considered dignified for a teacher to be seen wearing shorts and washing dishes out by the pump. He felt uncomfortable, embarrassed if a student saw him.

Our new home in the settlement block, a *Shikun* in Hebrew, was completed in 1952, when Elia was a year old. We moved our furniture and other things, and now used the large "kitchen" container as a storage shed in our new yard. The three of us were so happy to live in our comfortable house with electricity, running water, an indoor kitchen, toilet, and a bathing room with a shower. We were able to buy a bathtub a year later, along with the doors for the bedroom, the closet, and the kitchen. It was a real home where we lived happily for the next eight years.

This new settlement was built in a desert-like area. There was sand everywhere. And now Menachem and I had to have a garden of flowers and green trees. He worked very hard to carry buckets of soil from a nearby oasis for planting. This was a continuous project that took months of labor, with Menachem hauling heavy pails of dirt after work. He couldn't use a wheelbarrow in the sand. We had both been brought up in Czechoslovakia, where we loved green vegetation. Now we could have what we wanted for our home. After three years, we had plenty of plums for jam, red and green grapes, and beautiful flowers. Chickens and geese roamed our little garden. We kept their food in the shed, along with gardening tools. Here it felt like Brustury, warm and pleasant. We created much of what I had lost.

While Menachem taught in Bat Yam, I would stay home with Elia and make wigs that I would send back to the manufacturer in Tel Aviv. For entertainment, we would take turns babysitting with close friends when we'd go to Tel Aviv for music performances. Our favorite was going to the opera. We'd also attend concerts and live theater. On Shabbat, we'd have friends from the synagogue for lunch and share many Shabbat meals. Menachem would teach bar mitzvah boys, and we would be included in their private family celebrations. Twice, Menachem and I took a one-week paid vacation to a resort hotel, while Cipora cared for Elia. Our life was full and comfortable.

Nothing was ever mentioned about the Holocaust between Menachem and I. With Cipora, Sara, and other Survivors, we finally spoke freely about the Holocaust for the first time. We learned that we were all suppressed and suffering through our memories of inhumanity at the vile hands of the Nazis. Our sorrow remained private among the three of us. We appreciated our life now more than anyone could possibly understand.

I missed my sister terribly, my only living sibling. Malchi lived over the ocean, far away in Miami.

CHAPTER 20

An Immigrant Again

Spring 1956

Malchi and I were desperate to see each other. She lived far away in Florida and we had no telephone. Letters would not satisfy us. She wrote, asking me to visit her, even offering to pay half the ship fare to New York. Menachem understood that it was my only surviving sister, whom I hadn't seen for nearly eleven years. The last time I saw her was in Budapest, when she blessed me with the gift of her wristwatch as we said good-bye with a quick hug.

The United States required visitors to enter with a passport and a visa. Israel required a birth certificate to issue a passport. For most Survivors like me, proving identity was an ongoing crisis. Luckily, my marriage certificate contained my legal name, Leah Cik Roth. For Israel, this was enough to issue a passport. Menachem couldn't join us because of his work, but he encouraged me, "If you can make the arrangements, please go with my blessing." As soon as I received Malchi's written invitation, I took it to the American embassy to apply for a visitor's visa.

Two days before we left, Elia came down with the chicken pox. She was four and a half years old. "Medically, she can go," said our doctor. "She is no longer contagious."

My close friend in Bat Yam, Edit, who had been in the camps for three years, had sewn two new outfits for me. I was elegant in a royal blue dress with a drop waist and pleated skirt, and I bought new shoes and a hat to match. Elia was dressed in a pink princess dress.

In May, Elia and I sailed first class from Haifa to New York on the new Israeli ship, *Zion*. It was hard for Menachem to say good-bye to us. When a lady in our shared room reported that Elia had chicken pox, the ship's doctor confined us to our own cabin. During our few fancy meals in the main dining room before this discovery, the maître d', also a survivor, befriended us because he was fond of cute little Elia. He had lived in Israel, too. He spoiled her with special big red apples – a treat we couldn't afford in Israel. A couple of weeks after leaving Haifa, the ship gave us souvenirs and other goodies, just before entering the New York Harbor.

From a distance, I could see the big statue of the green lady holding a flaming torch – the Statue of Liberty. Someone explained that on its base was a poem written by a prominent Jewish poet, Emma Lazarus. I didn't completely understand the words, but I knew it meant freedom.

Menachem's cousin, Frieda Diamond, met our ship. We stayed with her in New York for three fun-filled days. Frieda treated us to a ballet at Radio City Music Hall. We visited Central Park and Macy's department store. In my journal, I recorded the first time when I saw a "talking picture box" at their house. It looked like a radio with a moving black-and-white picture. It was a television.

Cousin Frieda took us to visit the Statue of Liberty that welcomed us upon our arrival. After climbing the stairs to the top, I could see the immense city of New York. This huge green lady meant liberty, and I felt freedom in the air.

The flight to Miami was my first plane ride. The only planes I had seen previously were bombers, but this was a plane for pleasure. It was a thrilling experience taking off through the clouds and hard to believe we rode in a machine that could fly.

Upon landing at the airport in Miami, we saw Malchi was waiting with her two children and a bouquet of flowers. To my surprise, there was also a newspaper reporter from the *Miami Herald*, with a camera hanging around his neck. He took pictures of us, two sisters meeting again after eleven years. "Please, tell me how you and your sister became separated during the war." This kind of notoriety was a new experience for me. Our story seemed significant when an article appeared on the front page of the newspaper the next day. I felt like a celebrity. I mattered.

For three months I was visiting as a tourist. Malchi found me a job that I couldn't turn down. It was well-paying work on the second floor of the Miami Seybold Building – making men's toupees. It was a fancy place of business in the downtown near Burdines Department Store (now Macy's). My boss was a young gentile man, a German. The owner was a successful American businesswoman. This was an unexpected opportunity. Even though we spoke in German, I never mentioned the war.

The Miami Herald

Thursday, May 10, 1936   Most Complete Local News Report   Section C

All That's Left of Family of 12

Sisters Meet Here After Surviving Nazi Horror

Leah and sister, Malchi

At the time, minimum wage was twenty-five cents an hour. I earned a dollar fifty an hour. My Menachem back in Bat Yam, wondered what I did all day. I told him that we were visiting places in Miami, parks, and museums. I could not tell him the truth. I had to keep my job a secret out of respect for Malchi's husband, Harry. He was a prideful man, embarrassed that his sister-in-law was visiting as a tourist, yet working every day. To him it was shameful but I needed the money. I was torn about keeping my job a secret from Menachem.

While in Miami, I reconnected with "Miss Suri" Mermelstein, my fashionable cousin from Koshelie. She touched my heart with a story about my brother Bencion's bravery in Auschwitz-Birkenau.

"The SS ordered him to work at the Birkenau crematorium," Suri said. "I was in Block C, across from Bencion. A tall fence divided the areas between men and women. He was able to write a note, wrap it around a small stone, and toss it over to me. The message was about his devastating experience of removing bodies from the gas chamber and putting them into the crematorium to be burned. He'd come upon his own wife's body with her arms around their baby and the body of their eldest lying close by. He put their bodies onto the cart along with the others, while silently reciting memorial prayers."

Bencion was an unwilling undertaker; himself eventually fed to the flames. I'm sure he asked God, *why?*

Suri's story was a reminder that in the camps, all prisoners had the same status – living, but soon to be dead.

Later, Bencion wrote Miss Suri another note about the jewelry, including Maminka's pearls that he had hidden inside the basement wall, three feet from the steps, five feet high, behind the plaster.

Hiding valuables was a legacy of hope that someone in the family would survive and come back.

After the war, Bencion's sister-in-law was able to return to Ganich, not far from Brustury. She did find the jewelry hidden in the wall and kept it all. I wanted Maminka's pearls, but she never gave them to me.

Having survived Auschwitz, Malchi and I were left with the responsibility of carrying on our family name. We cherished our three months together in Miami, from Memorial Day to Labor Day. But we never talked about the Holocaust.

Menachem wrote to me every day that he was lonesome by himself in Israel. He promised we would never again be separated. I realized how much I missed him and that Elia missed her *abba*. I anxiously waited for the mailman after work every day.

A teacup set

We left Miami for Israel on Labor Day of 1956 and boarded the *Zion* from New York. Two days later, we celebrated Rosh Hashanah, our Jewish New Year, on the ship. When we anchored in Naples, Italy, Elia and I were invited by new friends from the ship to enjoy an evening of outdoor theater. We saw a glorious performance of the Ice Capades with a live orchestra. I so missed Menachem, knowing how much he would have enjoyed that spectacle. The next day we toured the city and I bought a crate of delicious apples, a luxury in Israel. Only the wealthy could buy this expensive fruit. For a souvenir, I splurged on a set of teacups. I still have a few of them.

Before *Zion* arrived in Haifa, the maître d' of the dining room asked me for a favor. "I know you can't give me a big tip," he said. "Just put this five-dollar bill on the table on the last day and others will follow your lead."

It worked. I was glad he received substantial gratuities.

Menachem took a long bus ride from Bat Yam to meet our ship returning to Haifa. The first thing out of Elia's mouth was, "Abba, buy me *Coca-Cola*." He didn't even know what *Coca-Cola* meant.

Elia started the first grade in September. A year later, we were blessed with the arrival of a beautiful baby boy, born August 25, 1957. He looked just like a little Menachem. The circumcision took place in the hospital. Since I had no one to help me prepare a celebration at home, my doctor allowed me to stay in the hospital for eight days until the procedure. We named our baby Moshe Shlomo, after our fathers. Now with both a daughter and a son, our family was complete. Always planning ahead, I never thought we'd be able to afford proper schooling for a third child.

Son Moshe is 1 year old

As our children were growing up, I would explain to them how things were done in my father's house before the war, how matzos were made, about cleaning for Passover, and the traditions of other holidays. I never talked about the Holocaust. I hid it from the children so they wouldn't feel inferior to their friends, and Menachem never asked. He must have picked up on bits and pieces of my history through stories in the newspaper and on the radio, but we never discussed it. In those days, the media rarely mentioned the Holocaust.

I shared etiquette and table manners with the children. "Manners matter. They make us sensitive to others," I told them. "Never enter a line in front of someone. Be patient. They have a right to be there, too." This was hard advice for me to practice. Lines reminded me of the rapid walking in the death march, during which I pushed ahead for safety to the middle of the pack. It's still instinctive for me to impatiently push ahead through a crowd. "Push ahead. Push ahead." Many things in daily life remind me of the depravity of my youth. To this day, as I drive down Interstate 95 in Miami, the Tower of Barry University looming over the traffic, reminds me of the watchtower in Auschwitz.

When I was visiting Miami, Malchi tried to persuade me to stay in America, even suggesting that Menachem join us at the end of the school year. Though back in Israel, I began thinking it would be better for the children to grow up near family. I missed my sister. It took me the next two years to convince Menachem to leave Israel. As a Zionist, he never wanted to go away from his homeland, the country that saved him from the Holocaust.

From my pressuring, he eventually relented, thinking maybe it would be better for our children to grow up with their cousins in America. Because we weren't sure that our move would actually be good for us, Menachem arranged for a one-year leave of absence without pay from his teaching job in Bat Yam.

We decided to "try out" America. Menachem was verbally offered a job at a private Jewish school in Miami.

We began to liquidate our belongings through word-of-mouth. Eventually, our house sold through an advertisement in the newspaper.

Cipora was so angry that we left Israel that she didn't answer our letters for two years. As a patriot, she couldn't accept the idea of us leaving. After she visited Auschwitz with a group to try to deal with her experience during the war, she wrote a long letter to us, explaining her feelings of frustration and abandonment.

We moved to the United States in September of 1959 with our children – Moshe, two years old, and Elia, who was then eight.

We sailed for more than two weeks on a Greek ship, *Olympus*, from Haifa to New York. All our books, along with household items, accompanied us in a wooden trunk. I packed everything myself, including dishes, a treasured soup tureen given to us by my cousin Ruchel Adler, and Menachem's precious violin.

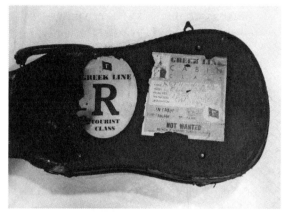

Violin Case with the ship's identification stamp

The tureen was white with a domed top and sprinkled with spring flowers. Elia still uses it to decorate her kitchen in Monsey, New York.

Moshe holds tender memories of the tunes that his father once played on the violin. The case is still marked with the ship's identification stamp.

The Soup Tureen

On the ship they served us kosher meals. The four of us slept in one cabin in bunk beds, and ate in a fancy dining room. Like us, most of the passengers were new immigrants to America. I ran into one of my best childhood friends – Rozi, from Brustury. As we watched our children play on deck, we reminisced about the lovely village of our youth. We never mentioned the Holocaust. We only spoke of our dreams for America.

Elia was inquisitive, running up and down the stairs, exploring the large ship with her new friends. I often feared she was lost, but we always found one another in time for the next meal. She was having the time of her life.

My two-year-old baby Moshe had a hard time adjusting to ship food, as there were no special meals for babies. As a walking toddler, he had to be kept occupied during his waking hours, which was a challenge.

Having come from a simple village life, I was astounded as I watched the staff wash and wax the wooden floors. It was a surprise to watch the careful care given to the shiny brass railings on the staircases. So much attention was given to make group dining an elegant experience. The windows were decorated with curtains tied back with tassels, and the table was elegant with many beautiful dishes. Waiters, wearing dark suits, white shirts, and black bow ties, served our lovely meals. Thinking back, I remembered sipping soup from a metal bowl with twelve other girls, freezing in camp Birkenau.

From Haifa, our first stop was Istanbul, Turkey, where we walked to a synagogue. On the way, a shoeshine boy heard us speaking Hebrew and surprised us by reciting a Hebrew blessing. The boy accompanied us, happy to connect with other Jews.

The journey continued until we entered the New York harbor, this time as legal immigrants. The Statue of Liberty welcomed me, a new resident, once again. We received our green cards just before docking in Brooklyn in mid-September of 1959. The passengers queued in separate lines — one for tourists and the other for legal immigrants. At last I was documented, allowed to live and work in the United States. The crisp air was cooling my warm tears.

Soon it was time for Menachem's and baby Moshe's first plane ride – from New York to Miami, into our uncertain future. Menachem looked down to the earth, feeling as though the plane was suspended in the clouds.

We settled in Malchi and Harry's home on Northwest 10th Street in Miami, surrounded with tall mango and avocado trees. Malchi took Menachem to his job at the Hebrew Academy. When the school administrator of the private day school realized that Menachem could not speak English, he rescinded his offer. My husband came home shocked at this rejection, not understanding how a private religious school would go back on their word. With his reputation as a highly regarded Hebrew, Science and Music educator in Israel, it was a slap in the face. He was completely humiliated. "Trying out" America was no longer an option, as we had sold everything and sent the money to my sister. My brother-in-law "borrowed" our money to build their new house.

My husband never let me forget what he sacrificed for our children and me. I felt forever guilty imposing my plan for our family against his resistance. Menachem had lost his secure employment and, even worse, the prestige he had earned in Israel.

Eventually, another private school offered Menachem a full-time position teaching advanced Hebrew, but for much less pay. He also taught the wooden shepherd's flute. In order for Menachem to travel to this teaching job, we bought an old car with a rusted floor for one hundred dollars. He used a plank of wood to cover the holes in the floor. He could take driving lessons in his own car and now drive to work.

I looked around for a toupee making job and was hired immediately. I took the city bus to work while Elia was in school. Malchi helped care for the children until I would come home. In the evenings, Menachem enjoyed learning English at the Dade Community College.

After two years, we understood that Miami could not provide teaching opportunities to keep my husband fully employed. Menachem was invited to teach in Rochester, New York. A longtime friend, who was a principal at a Jewish day school, invited Menachem to teach there. He was impressed with Menachem's qualifications. My husband took the position immediately. I was left behind with the two children to pack our meager belongings. Within weeks, we joined Menachem in Rochester. My husband taught at the Hillel Day School in the mornings and at the Hillel High School in the afternoons.

Once we settled in our rental home in Rochester, I was privileged to continue my education. I studied college-level Hebrew, Torah pedagogy, and Jewish history. Eventually, we recouped our financial stability as professionals. I was able to work as a well-paid wig and toupee maker, using the skills Mrs. Shönfeld had taught me. A New York wig factory contracted me to make men's toupees, sending me the supplies in the mail. In the afternoons, I taught at a public Hebrew school through a synagogue.

As typical immigrants, we lived a frugal modest life. With both of us working full-time, we were finally earning a decent living that allowed us to accumulate savings. After a year, we were able to afford the luxury of a vacation to Brooklyn, New York.

This is when my past came back to meet me.

CHAPTER 21

Reunion with Mrs. Shönfeld

While visiting Brooklyn on vacation with the children during the hot summer of 1963, I heard that Mrs. Shönfeld, my wig-making mentor, was living alone in nearby Williamsburg.

She and her daughter had also suffered through Auschwitz. She survived by saying she was younger then forty. After the war, her son Shmuli had found them near Prague in Czechoslovakia. Her husband Morris and their other son Yakov had been murdered by the SS in Auschwitz.

I immediately phoned her, not knowing what to expect. Laughing with excitement, she insisted we get together right away. Menachem was curious to meet someone who had known me before the war. We dressed in our best clothes for the short train ride. I wanted Mrs. Shönfeld to see who I had become.

Overjoyed to see us, she received me like her own daughter. With tears, she embraced my twelve-year-old Elia. "You look just like your mother when she lived with us." We all felt like relatives. Because Elia had never known grandparents, she hoped that Mrs. Shönfeld would be like the grandmother she never knew. This was her first experience with an older person, as the previous generation of both our families had perished in the Holocaust.

After a warm handshake, Menachem chatted with Mrs. Shönfeld, but very little because of the language barrier. Mrs. Shönfeld only spoke Yiddish and Hungarian. Menachem spoke many languages, but he didn't speak

Yiddish well. He was embarrassed, so he remained an observer for most of our visit, smiling to be polite. He seemed to understand what we said to one another without contributing to the conversation.

Mrs. Shönfeld was still elegant and impressively good-looking, but a changed woman. Even though we became good friends, I never felt close enough to call her by her first name. Memories of the past were understood between us without words. I had found a person who shared my young life. Avoiding talk about the war, we enjoyed a pleasant conversation about our children and our current lives.

I did not forget what she had taught me in her house. She had given me a trade that served me well my entire life. Now we were both financially successful. She, too, was working as a wig-maker for a New York firm to support herself.

While we couldn't change the past, we were able to embrace our present. Life itself was our precious gift. Suffering changes a person, and our past conflicts no longer mattered. With our social classes equalized, we were now able to become friends. Eight years later, Mrs. Shönfeld even came to Moshe's bar mitzvah. That time both she and Menachem spoke fluent English, able to engage in easy conversation. However, she had not become the grandmother Elia had hoped for. Elia and Moshe had friends who had grandparents but were hesitant to ask us why they didn't have grandparents. By then, they knew something about the Holocaust and were reluctant to bring up that hidden and forbidden subject that could hurt me, yet they felt a void in their lives.

Mrs. Shönfeld lived several hours away. She had her own grandchildren from her daughter Shaindy and her son Shmuli. She dealt with her sorrow in her own way.

CHAPTER 22

Healing Family Bitterness

While we were still on our first vacation, my cousin Joe Adler came to visit us in Brooklyn and brought us to his home in Monsey. During our visit, he introduced Menachem to the principal of the Hebrew Institute in Rockland County, Monsey, New York.

They hired him immediately.

Anxious to promote Menachem's career, we moved to a religious community in Monsey, New York, where private Jewish education for our children was superior, but more expensive. Menachem finally had regained his respect.

For the first year, we lived in another rental until our brand new three-bedroom home on 3 Rita Avenue was completed. With our savings, we were able to buy our new house for twenty-two thousand dollars, with a six thousand dollar down payment. The bank loaned us the rest for thirty years at six percent interest. This repayment mended old family wounds. Now we were a close family again and visited each other often.

Greenery, trees, and flowers in the yard reminded us of the homes of our youths. Near a synagogue, we made new friends and the children were happy in their schools. Menachem worked at the same school for the next twenty-seven years.

Luckily for me, I was never afraid of hard work and took on three jobs. I worked on wigs in the morning and late at night for a factory in New York. I had private clients who would come to my home for custom toupees. I also taught afternoon Hebrew school three times a week.

In 1964, at age 39, I was proud to complete my GED in English. The following year, Menachem and I finally obtained U.S. citizenship during a beautiful ceremony in New York City in an impressive public building. There we were, waving American flags with hundreds of others, representing many races and countries, while listening to our new national anthem. My family was dressed up, befitting the importance of that day. Finally, we were naturalized citizens. Now we had voting rights. Children automatically became U.S. citizens with their parents. Now we had a dual citizenship — U.S. and Israeli.

I had a new close friend who became sick, and I volunteered to help her with cooking and shopping. They lent me their car for transportation. She suggested that I would be a good nurse, helping sick people. When she improved, I did apply for a job at a nursing home close by. During that third job as an aid to both Jewish and Christian patients, I experienced my first American anti-Semitism. Other co-workers resented me. I was white and Jewish. They would never come to my aid to lift a patient or finish the assignment. They were jealous that I got Shabbat off from work. I was traumatized when I noticed that my patient, very tall Hans, had an "SS" tattooed under his left armpit. No one else knew that it meant he was a Nazi. I was afraid to say anything. I knew they wouldn't believe me anyway, because it didn't matter to anyone. No one knew I was a Survivor or even what that meant. I didn't discuss that incident with Menachem, because I never discussed anything German with him or about the camps. But it shook me up. Once I said something to him, but I was so disturbed that I can't remember what it was or what he answered back. I've blocked it from my memory. Hans spoke to me in German and I think he knew that I knew that he was a Nazi. He tried to befriend me because I spoke to him in his language. Bedridden, he was probably lonely. One day he commented that my white boots were too tight and could compromise my circulation. I just told him they were comfortable and walked away. He was moved to another ward when he became weaker.

Sometimes, on special holidays, I would bring fourth grade children from the Hebrew school to sing for the nursing home patients in the dining room. They would be accompanied with my tape recorder of Menachem singing Chanukah songs. The workers would sneak a peek and enjoy listening from the back of the lunchroom to my choir, sometimes with their patients in wheelchairs. I think they were surprised that I brought the children during the day in addition to working alongside them at night.

On holidays and Mother's Day, I would bring home a patient for a couple of hours, give her a home cooked meal with a sweet sponge cake. My guest was so happy for this interlude away from the nursing home.

I used to come home from my nursing job at eleven at night, but sometimes I worked a double shift for double pay. Worried about my health, my son Moshe complained that I worked too hard. But we were able to built a new life for our family and buy our new home with a yard, with bushes, flowers, and tomatoes. I even bought beautiful new furniture, afforded summer camp for Moshe and Elia, and secured our children's further education.

I was fired from the nursing home because a patient in my care took a fall. I felt awful. Now I had more time during the day and unemployment benefits, so I took English classes at the community college in Monsey.

Our property on Rita Avenue suddenly rose in value due to its proximity to the Vizhnitzer Rebbe and the synagogue. People knocked on my door, asking if our home was for sale. When someone offered me a ridiculous high price of one-hundred-and-fifty-thousand dollars, we sold it to buy a bigger three-level, two-car garage house on a larger property in a newer section of town.

Menachem was drawn to the idea of taking up painting again. He had painted flowers on blouses before our wedding in Tel Aviv and taught painting at school in Bat Yam. He thought he would enjoy watercolors as a new hobby from the free Adult Education classes offered by the city. I bought supplies for him: twenty tubes of paint, ten brushes, and special watercolor paper. He took two classes before he announced that that teacher wasn't for him. He quit. I couldn't waste the supplies, so I decided to take his place in the class and I loved it. I always wanted to try new things. It gave me a new perspective.

After many sessions, I brought a fist full of lovely iris flowers from my garden to the teacher. "This is wonderful. Today we'll learn to paint iris flowers," she said. I was proud the whole class was painting my iris flowers. I had no idea about the meaning of iris. As I later learned, each flower had three petals that represented faith, valor, and wisdom. I had no idea that they symbolically represented my life story. I've since painted many iris watercolors for my family and friends as gifts.

Menachem and I had finally developed a true partnership and a normal American life, honoring and appreciating one another and our whole family in a new way in our new country. We lived an ordinary American life in Monsey, New York. The children went to school and college. They had beautiful weddings, created their families of our beloved grandchildren and great-grandchildren.

Menachem finished out his teaching years, and in 1987, we sold our house for two hundred and fifty thousand dollars and moved back to Miami, Florida, for retirement in a lovely community with other retired Jews, many also Holocaust Survivors.

In 1990, I broke my silence about my life in the Holocaust and gave my testimony to the Spielberg project, as did many

Menachem Roth, the Torah scholar, botany teacher, and musician, with son Moshe

other Survivors of the Shoah. Now Menachem and the children knew much about my life. It was a relief to all of us. Now we could talk. Grandchildren writing essays in school about the Holocaust began asking questions. It was a tremendous relief of a lifelong burden in my heart.

The worst day of my life was the day I became a widow on October 31st, 2002. Three days later, Menachem's body was brought to Israel to be buried there. Menachem's death opened a wound deeper than any I could have realized. Now I fully grieved.

Many stones on his grave in Israel attest to his remembrance by others to this day, eleven years later.

Grave of Menachem Ben Moishe Roth. "Taught babies and scholars… a gentle voice in prayer and song….".

✡

My father often said, "Things happen for a reason. Hills don't come together, people do."

A couple of years ago, in 2011, while leaving the synagogue after High Holiday services, I had a accidental encounter with a tall, good-looking man in the foyer. He inquired, as many do when they hear my accent, "Where are you from?"

"From Carpathia . . . in Czechoslovakia . . . now Hungary."

"But from where?"

"You wouldn't know it . . . from Brustury and Chust," I said.

Wrinkling his brow, he stepped closer "My father was born in Chust."

Stunned, I asked, "What's your name?"

With squinting eyes, he leaned toward me as if expecting a surprise.

"Morris Shönfeld," he softly said. "My father is Shmuli."

I felt myself turn white at this unexpected discovery. I knew Morris's father, Mrs. Shönfeld's son, even before his bar mitzvah.

"I lived with your grandmother and grandfather as an apprentice when I was a teenager, more than seventy years ago. I cleaned their floors and slept in the same bed with your aunt who was my age."

A cascade of memories flooded through me upon hearing that name from my childhood, instantly transporting me back to Chust, into Mrs. Shönfeld's home.

"Did you ever go back to Chust?" the Shönfelds' grandson asked.

"Yes, in 1945, at the end of the war, after the death march. I wanted to see if the Shönfelds had returned. Regretfully, only the owners of their rented apartment were there."

Morris Shönfeld was excited to tell me his family's story. "My father went back and found his mother's candelabra and his father's Kiddush cup, which had been buried in the garden behind the house, just before they were forced into the ghetto by the Hungarian guards."

He paused and took a breath as he remembered, "My father told me that when he was a boy, there was also a young girl, Leichu, living with them."

"That was me! I was fifteen then," I said.

The young Mr. Shönfeld said he could not wait to tell his father of our serendipitous meeting. I never heard from him or his father again.

The past is gone. My life is a miracle. With gratitude to God, I'm still here to remember and to tell what happened to me during the Holocaust of World War II.

PART IV

Perpetuation

CHAPTER 23

I Have Spoken

2013

Our time here is short. We are dying out. I'm *von tuf vomun*, the last person alive who knows my immediate family history from my precious village of Brustury. My first cousin, Joseph Lebovic, who is four years younger than me, is also from Brustury. He has his own story, different than mine. His entire family survived in Budapest, masquerading as Christians with families who protected their children for payment. His parents were separated during the war from their three children.

I experienced horrible threats to my dignity and to my life. I survived the gas chamber, four Nazi concentration camps, and a death march. I was liberated by Russian soldiers when they took over Germany. I escaped on foot through the Austrian mountains to Italy and on a ship to freedom in Palestine, now Israel. I married and had my family. Because I was liberated, I can tell my story now. Liberation doesn't mean just liberation from the camps. It means being freed from the prison in my soul.

I never wanted pity, only to be loved. After the war, my past chased me as I struggled to stay present. I pretended to be an ordinary person, even though I felt impaired. My smile was only on my lips, not in my heart. I spared our children my story; I never mentioned my past. They knew I suffered, but didn't know the inside of it.

Young people are often not interested in their heritage until their parents are gone, when there is no one left to ask. My children, my grandchildren and great-grandchildren need to have a Holocaust consciousness. They need to know that our relatives were murdered because we were Jews. My obligation is to tell what happened. My time is running out. Only my sister Malchi and I survived the war. All of the rest of my immediate family died — my father, two sisters, and six brothers. Now only I remain. My legacy must be a holy inheritance for my family.

Children and grandchildren sense unspoken truths. My children were married with their own families before they saw my first video testimony for Steven Spielberg's Shoah Foundation. Finally, Survivors were being encouraged to speak up. The Foundation spread the word: "The time is late." Slowly, Survivors came out of their shells and began documenting their testimonies. This is when I became comfortable speaking at gatherings for Holocaust awareness.

My children are not comfortable asking me questions about my experiences in the Holocaust. But now I'm telling everything to complete strangers, to the whole world. Menucha encouraged me to open up.

Successive generations must pass on the legacy of the Holocaust so that it shall never be forgotten. It is the most documented genocide in history. Reading books is not enough. One must hear about the Holocaust firsthand, while we are still around; dialogue about the causes of hate and anti-Semitism; honor our similarities and appreciate our differences, rather than make believe with a veiled attempt to put up with one another. This history must not be repeated against any population. *Never again!*

I began writing at the age of 83, so enthusiastic about telling my story that I bought a computer, not knowing how to use it. It was hard for me to understand the manual, so my son Moshe in New Jersey gave me computer lessons over the phone. I used my pointer fingers to find the keys as I tried to follow his instructions. Many times I would forget to click *save* and lose the whole thing. Then I would start all over again.

In the beginning, I listed only main events and family names, with a few short stories about my life, with many things left out. Learning so young to hold in my feelings, I had a hard time opening up to tell my whole story. Yet I am not a victim. Mainly, I wanted my children to know how many in our family were killed, that they shall not be forgotten.

My daughter Elia was the first to read what I so proudly wrote. "Ima, what you've written is not English. An English-speaking person will not understand your expressions."

I argued, "I don't want to change anything. I write just like I speak, and I spell phonetically, and with an accent. I want my story to be in my own words."

My daughter wanted to rewrite my story, but I pushed her aside. I could never reveal hidden secret things to her.

Moshe spent many hours correcting what he thought I meant to say.

Then my new friend, dear Menucha, appeared in my life and began to help me organize my thoughts. Asking questions, she patiently encouraged me to recall the memories I had spent a lifetime of energy suppressing. She guided our conversation with her method of *Soul-Writing*. Her quiet listening gave me emotional space and time, the courage to remember. While all the threads of my story are organized and skillfully woven, crafted by Menucha into a tapestry of my remembrances, it's still my life story. I worked alongside her on every word. Every sentence and event had to be defended and approved by both of us.

When we began to write, I was not completely open. I held back. Some things were too shameful. Painful demons lurked over my shoulder yet I began to understand it was somehow healing to reveal the inside details I had hidden for so long, even from myself.

"I'm an ordinary person," I said. "Who would want to know my story?"

Menucha gently replied, "For it to be relevant, you must tell the whole truth as you remember it. I will help you. You are living history. We must fulfill your dream to hold your story in a book." She encouraged me, "Together we can do this. I am here for you." We admire one another and have developed an unbreakable bond. No more secrets.

My husband Menachem had so often reminded me, "While the past matters, we must live today and plan for the future." Born in Slovakia, he escaped Europe in 1938 before the war. Somehow he reached Israel. He didn't experience the camps and never asked about my suffering. I think he couldn't take it.

And that's what I did. I lived for today and tried to bury my past. I never thought I could share my story with anyone.

Little by little, after a year and a half, I finally had the guts to tell Menucha the most embarrassing things, stories I had never told to a soul. Hidden emotions poured out like a running faucet.

My long-held secrets were like parasites that sucked and chewed at my insides. Memories of being chased came to the surface. Nightmares screamed in my dreams. The torments of violent, sickening events were facts I had suppressed for decades. Menucha and I both wiped our tears. It was a relief to finally loosen the shackles, to tell someone who really cared and listened for hundreds of hours, accepting — never judging.

The pain of telling affected me. It forced me to reveal my degradation. You can't heal what you deny. Terror digs deep into your soul.

While time may soften the pain, nothing erases naked shame, the abuse that was inked on my heart like an ugly tattoo. The SS Nazis treated Jews as if they were less than crawling worms.

Telling began to consume me as I continued to remember more and more. Something inside of me began to change. I am proud that I can now give a voice to those memories unspoken. I am no longer a prisoner of my past, concerned about feeling inadequate or being judged. I can now finally share my story with my own children.

Seeing my words and feelings on paper frees me. Like a balance sheet, I have become accountable in a new way. Most of my youth was stolen from me, not easy or happy, but today I am grateful to have lived. With fewer heartaches and nightmares, I am no longer threatened.

New generations – children, grandchildren, and great-grandchildren – have given me new beginnings, my final revenge. I am the winner, yet I still miss the love I could have had from my parents and grandparents.

I may not laugh or smile as other people, because it doesn't come from inside my heart. It's only on the surface. But when I don't dwell on the past, I can be happy for a while. If I let myself wallow in my history, it will destroy me from inside. Accepting what happened is to live with it every day. It's always in me yet I must live for today, toward my future. Time goes away and never comes back. I allow everyday happenings to distract me from ruminating about my past. Interacting with people interrupts my sad thoughts. I try not to isolate myself from others. Helping others in need, like visiting the sick, helps me feel stronger and makes me a better person.

As an activist, I participate in Holocaust Education workshops. I speak to groups of South Florida high school students about my experiences during the war. University students want to meet with me and ask questions to understand how the battle against anti-Semitism continues. I tell them it begins with hate.

I want to pass down my zest for life and my resolve to endure the shadows of the Holocaust.

"When you have to stand up, do it right away. Being practical, I have no patience to waste a moment. Time goes – tomorrow comes quickly and yesterday doesn't come back. Don't wait to take a stand against despicable evils around you."

I'm as proud as my father would have been to witness our children and grandchildren following the Torah way of life.

I tell the young people, "Be strong and don't let others misguide you. Your voice is your defense. Stand up for goodness." You don't know the strength you have inside until you need to fight for your life. Holding grudges hurts you by keeping you angry and depressed. We are not born Survivors. Survivors emerge from dire circumstances. I survived.

CHAPTER 24

My Eyes Looking Back At Me

Leah and I arrive at the Holocaust Memorial in Miami Beach, Florida, inspired by a local artist and architect, Kenneth Treister. Our eyes are drawn to an imposing bronze sculpture of an outstretched arm, seven stories tall, engraved with number A13898. "A" represents Auschwitz. I was there. Covered with over 100 life-size sculptures of emaciated human beings, it's a frightening monument depicting Hitler's evil. The open hand shrieks for help. Victims grab toward heaven's protection, the divine intervention that never came.

Leah says, "My number, A38620, was sewn onto my dress. I was on their list to be exterminated, so I wasn't tattooed."

Miami Beach
Holocaust Memorial
Credit: Jeff Weisberg and Albert Barg

Next to the arm is a bronze statue of an embarrassed, naked mother clutching her wailing baby, tight to her bosom. I'm horrified and heartbroken when Leah tells me, "The SS told young mothers to clasp their baby close so that they could kill them both with a single bullet."

Standing in the presence of a living miracle, I suppress my outrage at the monstrous evil that human beings are capable of. We cry.

Leah points to her family names engraved among thousands on the curved massive black granite wall. "They have no graves. This is the only place I can honor them." She reads Psalms, sacred prayers for transcendent comfort as she remembers her beloved murdered family.

Leah Roth discusses her archival photo with Alan Freeman

Leah Roth prays for her murdered family

In the quiet sanctuary of remembrance, Leah is absorbed through a restless veil, a permanent camp shroud that Survivors must wear. Her strong body stiffens with the weight of the invisible. She relives the horrors, transported back as if it's happening right now.

"Hitler did not win – I survived." Nearly inaudible, I hear her whisper, "Exhausting cries from my nightmares haunt me to this day."

I follow Leah to the Dome of Contemplation, a circular area symbolizing a gas chamber. Imprints of lines on the walls symbolize scratch marks left by desperate, suffocating victims. The stained-glass window in the ceiling casts a six-pointed yellow Jewish star on the floor, a Magen David. It's inscribed with *Jude,* the German word for Jew. This dome is a replica of that where the Nazis planted Zyklon B pellets that gassed millions and almost murdered Leah.

Zyklon B *Giftgasi (Giftgas)*

**Leah Roth prays in the
Dome of Contemplation**

With lips quivering, she looks down to her tattered, treasured prayer book and once again recites Kaddish, an affirmation of God's name. Praying comforts her.

With pride, she walks up to the etched photograph of an archival image on another wall. Pointing to the engraving, Leah says, "This is me." I see a young Leichu standing there in her winter coat, in the center of the downtrodden crowd, soon to be exiled onto the cattle cars bound for Auschwitz.

"My Eyes Looking Back at Me"
**Permission from sculptor, architect, artist, author Kenneth Treister,
A Sculpture of Love and Anguish, S.p.i. Books "Resettlement to the East," page 103**

"Years ago, I stood here with Elia, as she stared at this photo for a long time, examining the details. Pointing, Elia cried out, *'Ima . . . this is you . . . your face!'*"

"I recognized myself in this pack of prisoners prodded like animals."

She presses her finger over a Jewish guard's face, as if to erase him. I was speechless, recognizing a younger Leichu.

She pronounces, "I now notice . . . look Menucha . . . I'm not looking down. I'm looking out . . . defiant."

Pausing, she reflects, "I see my eyes, my own eyes, looking back at me."

CHAPTER 25

Healing

"Create a halo of silence and they will tell you their story."
Menucha Meinstein

Most afternoons, we sit in my kitchen sipping coffee. Leah is on the edge of her chair as usual, knitting colorful scarves with ruffles. I imagine the detail and patience she once needed to weave single strands of hair into wig caps. Even though she strains, her eyesight, as well as her insight, is still remarkable.

I ask her questions to encourage conversation. Cast out at an early age, she was never asked how she felt about anything. But now she is able to express herself, finally exposing her repressed pain. Reminiscing opens her up, encouraging her to give meaning and understanding to her experiences. I ask questions and take notes. "How did you feel when that happened?" Sometimes she can't explain anything to me. At other times, when she remembers, she can elaborate for days with greater detail.

Leah has a great deal to tell about falling to her knees in defeat and rising up proudly in victory. Like an archaeological dig, a "tell," the mound rebuilt over ruins, she has rebuilt her life. We excavate through the labyrinth of recollections, dusting off each fragment. Not knowing where it will fit, we examine and connect random stories the way one would piece together an ancient broken dish. We record what we find as more facts are unearthed. Survivors built a new life over the stratum of ashes. She has finally chosen to share this transformation, her revenge against Hitler's hateful madness, anti-Semitism, and the attempted genocide of our people.

As Leah's soul-scribe, I wonder what preserving this one Survivor's history will mean. Each story is a precious but painful legacy rescued for us to experience as if we were there, to bear witness, remember, and honor the victims.

Many Survivors have chosen not to tell about their near-death escapes, especially to their children. "I spared my family. I wanted them to grow up normal," says Leah.

Many Survivors are reluctant to share, but their anguish is visible to others. Some block the details, keeping them locked inside. Their secrets die with them. Leah has finally chosen to share. "Time is short," she says.

I ask, "What did you have to do to stay alive?"

"No one can understand how numb we were unless they were there in the camps," Leah frequently repeats. She tries to explain what happened and how she coped by pushing herself. "Somehow, sometime, I might be free." How she felt is more difficult. *Not* to feel was her subconscious way of coping, of hanging on to hope.

She explains, "It's still not easy to reveal personal memories and risk being judged."

Probing her memory is like watching surgery performed without anesthesia. It's agonizing. I want to protect her, but she insists, "Let's go further. We have to get through it." It's always about finishing.

As a virtual witness, I'm in angst as I join Leah's struggle, becoming her voice. In sharing and writing with me, Leah breaks through her stoic shell, dredges up memories, revealing her torment.

Reminiscences bleed out as she remembers them, in no particular order. Seeing them written on paper seems to give her comfort. "I should only live long enough to see my story published."

"I never told these inner things to anyone before," she whispers. "Let's have another cup of coffee."

My mission has been to encourage Leah to remember, to help her dig through the ruins of her buried past, examine events and try to make sense by documenting them. Her words whisper her truths. Every story redefines her life, now uncovered and understood through her adult awareness.

I have been privileged to accompany her on this excruciating and very private journey.

Translating through a braid of eight languages, she finds words to tell the secrets she has never revealed before. Leah remembers each event in the language in which it occurred. It takes time to find the English equivalents. Leah's school education ended after the eighth grade in her little mountain village of Brustury. Her education was with Menachem's dialogue, direction and teaching. Years later, she went to college in a new country, in another new language. With strong natural intelligence, she's able to recall colorful minutiae from her early life.

I find my view of her changed from our first meeting in her apartment. Rather than the martyr I anticipated, I now know her to be an adaptable and ingenious woman.

Absently wiping a spill of coffee from the table, she continues to remember sharing her long-held privacies. Telling and disclosing is her healing. Over time I see her move from tight inner stress to relaxation. We laugh often and more spontaneously. Leah is becoming more self-accepting as she recognizes how well she has coped through her prolonged grim past. She possesses inherent matter-of-fact guts and bravery, honed from a very tender age. I am in awe of her resilience, her stubborn and tenacious hardiness through a turbulent life. Leah somehow found a way to justify the juxtaposition of the atrocities of war with her longing for a secure life.

"I'm afraid of very little, except I hope not to be sick. Things you cannot change you should not complain about," Leah says. "Let it go. Hide it below where nobody sees. Go past it. Life has to go on."

Train whistles, big dogs, swastikas, the sound of knocking black boots, and especially, sleeping in rooms with closed doors, bring back horrid memories. Now I understand why she instinctively sits uncomfortably on the edge of her chair. She is ready to flee.

Leah has lived her dream of an ordinary life as a married woman raising a family, despite an interrupted youth. Leah has a story. Leah is her story.

CHAPTER 26

Activism

"Turn from evil and do good, seek peace and pursue it."
Psalm 34

March 2012

High school students pile off belching yellow school buses at the Miami Airport Convention Center. The morning air is hot and humid. In their designer jeans and sneakers, fancy tops and skirts, fashionable jewelry, belts and bags, the girls' faces are fresh with makeup and lip gloss. Some are giggling, while others have a dreary look of anticipated boredom. It is 8:15 in the morning as they stream through double doors into air-conditioned space at the center. Today is *Student Awareness Day*, an invitational day-long Holocaust education symposium.

Students are from public, private, and parochial schools. The Florida Department of Education mandates the study of the history of six million European Jews annihilated during World War II. The students will spend the day learning the disastrous effects of hatred and prejudice straight from the voices of Holocaust Survivors, a few elders still here to bear witness.

"Young people need to hear directly from Survivors how we were forced to develop skills of endurance or perish. The time remaining to question us gets shorter with each passing day," Leah states.

As students enter the lobby, they are handed their Learning Resource packet. Teens are assigned to tables with other students they have never met, separated from their friends. The convention room is filled to capacity with a thousand students seated at round tables of twelve.

"My table is facilitated by Menucha. As a Holocaust Survivor, I am a guest invited to speak to the students. We awkwardly become acquainted while we wait for the others to be seated. I'm thinking, I wonder if they see me as just a little old lady with a strong voice and an accent. They will soon learn I represent the history they have studied and will now witness on the gigantic movie screens."

The moderator announces that Survivors may leave the room during the film. I choose to stay because it proves again, "I was there." Seeing the film helps me better relate to the children's questions. I watch their faces as the lights are lowered and the documentary begins: *Children Remember the Holocaust.*

As archival footage unfolds, the students are hypnotized by the hatred and genocide of Hitler, his German citizens, and their accomplices. Teens are visibly moved as they bear witness to the story many deny. They begin to squirm trying unsuccessfully to hold back tears as they see evidence of the appalling slaughter. They are discreet, wiping their eyes when they see the killing fields: bullet-ridden bodies piled in open graves, children clinging to toys as they are torn from the grasp of their horrified parents, bodies thrown into garbage trucks and hauled to pits that other Jews were forced to dig, pits where their families will decay en masse.

The horrors of the Holocaust continue to explode on the screen. Young voices intensely narrate Hitler's carnage and terror. The film splices show happy, young innocence, separated and butchered by shooting, gassing and other horrific means, often leaving only one Survivor, most of the time, no one. The victims had done nothing wrong except they were born Jews, or had Jewish ancestry. Every intermarriage joins Hitler's success, putting a feather in his cap, assisting him in his plan.

A small number of Jews were able to flee the ghetto roundups by hiding in attics, escaping deep into forests, hiding in holes dug underground or living in sewers and other inhumane conditions. Some were able to pass as Christians.

Others weren't so lucky. A young student responds with a poem she had written to express her outrage.

Why Will I Remember?

I am a Jewish girl
I am an only girl
I go to school
I have food and clothes
I have friends
They are nice to me
I have a lot of cousins
I have brown eyes and black hair
My birthday is today
I'm now 5 years old
I'm happy
On my birthday I hear noises
Loud ones
I hear people screaming and shouting
I hear gunshots going off

Then all is quiet
All I hear are the cars on the street
I run to my mother
I'm scared
I'm frightened
My mother gives me a hug
"It's okay, we will leave.
Remember, You Are a Jew"
I cry

We start to pack things so we can escape
I pack a warm sweater
One shirt and one skirt
We go outside
It's cold
I'm hungry
I'm scared
We run
I see soldiers
the mean bad ones
I tell my parents what I see
We start to run
Faster and faster
The soldiers are fast but we are faster
My father picks me up
We run
We see a big rock
We hide behind it
We wait

They come
They find us
They take their guns out and shoot
My mother is gone
I cry

They come
They find us
They take their guns out and shoot
My mother is gone
I cry

Boom!
They shoot
Again
My father is gone
I'm too crushed to cry
I feel like there is a big empty hole in me
Next is me

I run
Faster and faster each second
I see the hollow bark of a tree
I climb in
They look
They see me
I cry out
Shema Yisroel Hashem Elokanu
Hashem Echad

I'm gone
I will remember
People young and old
Babies to Adults
Innocent were they

Gone
6 million souls
Killed

I will remember
We will remember
Thank God every day
We are living
We continue our lives
Like nothing happened
But long ago
People lived life in fear

We must remember
I will remember
We will remember □

Tzivia Druin, age 12

The documentary continues. "I am made speechless by a vague recognition of my brother Bencion standing in a striped uniform. He was one of the men who shoveled corpses onto stretchers to be burned in the ovens. Was this image really Bencion? It went by so quickly. I wasn't sure."

Later I was able to obtain a video of *Children Remember the Holocaust* and carefully watched it to find the photo I saw at the Student Awareness Day. We pause at the frame I thought might be my beloved brother, Bencion. I stare at his image for a long while, speechless. My visual memory of Auschwitz comes back in full color to torture me once again. It's as if I am in a nightmare. Unable to move, I imagine I see Bencion's *eyes looking back at me* – a "sad, aching heart." Is it Bencion? His eyes seem so hollow, my protector. But I am filled with my memory of the last time I saw him, when he took me to the row-boat that would take me across the river to the train station, when we kissed good-bye and embraced one last time.

1937 My Brother Bencion.   Prisoner in Auschwitz 1944
Czech Defender

Bencion Cik, 1917-1944

Numbed in memory, I escape to my bed for the comfort of a nap. When I awaken, I take a shower as if I could wash away all those decades.

The teens think they are informed about the Holocaust. They've learned it is one thing to read history books and engage in class discussions; it is another thing, a riveting experience, to sit at a table with a Survivor while watching a documentary narrated in children's voices describing their terror and suffering. Innocent Survivors describe their childhood memories of hunger, emaciation and anguish, images they can never forget. Today's Survivors live quiet lives of pride and dignity. No one can understand this time in Europe's history with total comprehension unless they were there. A few of us are still here today. We are aging out.

The group at my table represents different schools, races, and nationalities. Discussion follows the video and centers around each person's questions and responses. Menucha invites them to address me directly. At first, they are shy and hesitant. I encourage them. "Never forget what you saw. It really happened," I say. "Hitler enlisted others to kill us. As a coward, he took his own life after he lost the war. He took the easy way out."

The students politely ask thoughtful, innocent questions.

> *"How could you endure such inhumanity and still be around to talk about it?"*
>
> *"How did you survive?"*
>
> *"Why didn't large groups gather together to rebel?"*
>
> *"When did you know you had lost all control?"*
>
> *"How old were you when you were captured for the ghetto?"*
>
> *"How was your life in the ghetto?"*
>
> *"Were you with any of your family?"*
>
> *"We have a lot in common. I also came from a country with a dictator."*
>
> *"How did you know where to go after liberation?"*
>
> *"Can you ever forgive the Nazis?"*
>
> *"Do you still believe in God?"*

I tell them, "Yes I do. It's personal for everyone. You cannot walk in anyone's shoes. Everyone has their own path. I can just share my experiences with you."

I thoughtfully answer their questions with statements that might open their minds.

"Can you believe this happened only seventy years ago, from 1933 to1945, during your grandparents' era? Germany was a scientific and technologically advanced culture. Music, arts, and higher education thrived."

Education or intelligence does not ensure humanity.

Most kids think this could not happen in America. I question, "Are you sure? Don't create for yourselves an illusion of a false sense of security. Everything is not fine. Be aware of where you are. The world is not just here for you. Look around. Don't fall in where I was. Not everything is roses."

Students respond to Leah's testimony in their own way.

All I Am

A wounded man
Is it all I am
Just weakness
Or am I just speechless
Red splattered
Black hovering
White soaring
And the circle keeps moving
Is it just darkness
Or is it because I feel homeless
The painter tries to paint
To blend the red into black
And black into white
But they don't converge
What does emerge
Is the wounded man
That's all I am

Riki Druin, age 17

In the late 1980s, I became aware that other Survivors were being encouraged to speak up. Why did I transform from keeping my Holocaust secrets to becoming an activist against hatred? Now I know it is my obligation to declare the truth, to give my testimony to others. It is my greatest revenge. There's a proverb that says, "If you know, don't hold it to yourself. It is your duty to teach it to others."

I ask them to ponder on the question: Where does prejudice comes from?

- parents
- religion
- peers
- school
- the street
- a political viewpoint
- a lack of intellectual evaluation.

For the most part, these children today have not experienced war or the civil rights movement. They are naive.

I remind them that there were social and economic problems in Germany. Adolf Hitler led people to believe Jews were the cause of their troubles. Those anti-Semitic judgments have occurred too often in human history. Even though German society was highly educated, they were barbaric. Hate and prejudice grow stronger during financial downturns. Prejudice incites violence. Hitler was evil. He did his best to promote senseless hatred through persecution and genocide. I am a living proof that he failed.

Many adult German citizens, ordinary people with jobs and families, chose to turn their heads, coerced into believing they could do nothing to stop what Hitler enforced: to create the Master Aryan race by extermination of every Jew. The vast majority of Germans approved and joined in or acquiesced. It's easy to be a conformist. To be tolerant and follow the crowd is ignorance. Many Germans alive today who were children during World War II, and their children now struggle with guilt for the deeds of their parents and grandparents.

They believed what Hitler was screaming in his tyrannical speeches. He had been planning his takeover, the Final Solution, for years, leaving a stain on the German people for eternity. A loud, charismatic speaker, he charmed his country into listening and acting without thinking.

Edmund Burke said, "For evil to flourish, it only requires good men to do nothing." Where were the good people? Some were hiding their righteous deeds of trying to save the Jews, lest they be murdered as dissidents.

Seemingly decent people did not stand up for those who could not help themselves. To do so was most likely certain death for the dissenter. People were ruled by fear for their own lives. As cowards, most chose silence. It took courage to speak up and resist. Many people are unaware that neo-Nazis, white supremacists, anti-Semites, Holocaust deniers, homophobes, the Ku Klux Klan, and the Muslim Brotherhood are heavily recruiting the youth right here in America through rock music, television, and pamphlets in schools and colleges. I explain to the students that we live in a society in which intolerance, coarseness, and violence are being tolerated as they become more prevalent. Young people are needy for love and attention and often become aggressive and violent in order to belong to something bigger than them.

This was poignantly expressed by Angela King, a former skinhead member. After a three year stint in jail, Angela realized this extreme violent and bigoted lifestyle was not for her. She went on to earn an M.A. in Social Sciences and now works with a not-for-profit organization, *Life After Hate* that denounces violent extremism. Angela speaks to audiences worldwide, promoting kindness and love and inspiring young people to honor individual rights and to appreciate our differences.

Angela King, former skinhead, with Leah at Student Awareness Day 2014

She states her view that "the best way to achieve a society free of discrimination is for people to take responsibility for their own actions. Hate promises oppression.

You always have a choice," she tells them. She knows because she made the choice to change her life and her destiny: Angela is an educator of peace.

To wrap up the morning, I remind the students that there is a difference between listening and hearing. Sometimes we hear and don't pay attention. Sometimes words scream evil from hurtful intention. In the camps, no one was better than anyone else. Standing naked and shorn, everyone was equal, no matter their heritage, their former wealth or accomplishments. We were all destined for death.

Sometimes you may risk your life when you take a chance to promote justice. Not everyone is your friend. Sometimes people feel more powerful when they demean another person.

My life has been a test. I've tried to get the answers right. I am accountable for my actions – to my God and to society.

During lunch, our discussion continues. Preoccupied with private thoughts, the students appear to eat absently and swallow without tasting. I feel tension building.

Motivational speakers throughout the day emphasize the power of individual choice to speak up against hatred, bullying, and prejudice.

I advise, "Pay attention when in conversation. Hold back your response before answering. Think. Evaluate."

What is the underlying intention of a person's message? Is their control and influence intended to be hurtful or to be strengthening and empowering?

Conscience understands right from wrong.

The Bottom Line

R*aise* your awareness about the dangers of bigotry by studying the effects of prejudice, hate, and oppression on Survivors of the Holocaust.

E*nhance* your understanding and appreciation of diversity.

L*earn* you can face any hardship in life.

I*ndifference* is the greatest sin.

G*row* through your suffering.

I*solate* yourself from apathy toward evil.

O*ptimize* goodness, one-on-one.

Never be a bystander.

The day ends with an emotional candle-lighting ceremony. The facilitators light a *yartzeit candle*, a memorial tribute, in memory of the six million. Holding the candle, participants are asked to speak about what the conference has meant to them. Even students who have been quiet during the day speak with surprising clarity and intention, resolving now to be more aware of their own prejudices and actions toward others.

They make a public pledge to resist apathy and take a stand. One student proclaims, "I will not be silent. All of us belong to the human race."

Plato said it best: **"The price of apathy toward public affairs is to be ruled by evil men."**

I have learned that to write a memoir is to compose a commentary about the times in which one has lived, what influenced that person to become who they are and what they have enjoyed. I survived horrors. I have also experienced deep fulfillment and pride in my life through the love of my family and close friends.

Students learn that I now feel worthy and have dignity. I was once a victim. Now I am a victor. My story is my legacy, my epitaph. I hope that from my story, young people today can learn to overcome obstacles that may seem insurmountable. I know it is possible to create a future of dignity, self-worth, and contribution. I am one of many who have done it.

My motto is: "Life must move forward, no matter how painful it may have been. It is possible to create a better future and to triumph over evil if your desire is strong."

In conclusion, I appeal to each and every one of you, those present here and future readers, "Stand up and keep your power. One person can make a difference. Be there when you are most needed. To do nothing is to *give power* to the oppressor. You are never alone. The sages say, *"Whoever saves a life is considered to have saved the entire world."*

The solution lies in what you personally *do* to counteract prejudice and intimidation of others, by confronting your own prejudices and speaking up. Apathy and indifference condemns the innocent and gives power to injustice.

I've learned that when I respect others, they usually respect me back. I say, "Allow others their place in line. They also have a right to be there."

Whom do you stand up to? *What* do you stand up for? If *you* don't wage war against apathy and indifference, who will?

Do you take things for granted at home? Consider taking them with gratitude.

You have more potential and strength than you know. Rely on yourself. Do for yourself. I learned early on that I was on my own – no one was behind me to push me forward.

I am inspired by the words of Hillel, who said, *"If I am not for myself, who will be? And when I am only for myself, what am I? And if not now, when?"*

CHAPTER 27

Salve On An Open Wound

Dr. Miriam Klein Kassenoff with Crystel Dunn and Alissa Stein
The University of Miami Teacher's Institute, Summer 2014

Menucha and I attended the 2014 Holocaust Teacher's Institute at the University of Miami, hosted by Founder and Director, Dr. Miriam Klein Kassenoff. She is also a Survivor from Czechoslovakia. We were inspired by many presentations from noted historians, educators, journalists, and artists.

Arnold Mittelman, Founding President
National Jewish Theater Foundation /
Director of NJTF Holocaust Theater
International Initiative

Dr. Michael Berenbaum,
Award winning Holocaust
historian, author, lecturer,
teacher, historical consultant.

Through a twist of fate, one of the guests introduced was the German Consul General in Florida, Jüergen Borsch. I was astonished. I wondered why Miriam would invite a German to speak. What positive contribution could a German possibly have to make at this conference for teachers about the Holocaust? I shivered, as he was about to speak.

With the Consul's eyes cast down, this post-war born young man, humbly asked to be forgiven for the Nazi war crimes of his people. With my own ears, I heard the Consul state:

> *"Every upright and honest German today feels the inherited guilt for the unspeakable atrocities the Nazis did. We all feel shame and remorse. We grieve the countless victims, honor the few Survivors, and ask you to forgive those not involved - and never forget. The most important message for the future is to never forget! We accept and stand to our historic responsibility and for the guilt. Today Germany is a free democratic, hospitable, and open society. And we see it as a sign of great trust in the modern German society that in these days, we host the fastest growing Jewish community in the world. We stand united with everyone.... and speak out against all kinds of disrespect, racism, anti-Semitism, hatred, and injustice. It is our historic obligation to tell the*

truth, to keep up the memory, and to educate our children
in this sense. I promise that we teach our children to teach
their children, and they, in turn, teach their children, the
story of the Holocaust."

My heart was weeping inside as he spoke. I felt he was speaking directly
to me.

I was moved when Borsch gave a spontaneous, heartfelt plea of regret
for the crimes of the Nazis and their henchmen. I have never personally experienced this kind of apology from a German. I've always been fearful of
Germans since my first encounter with Dr. Mengele in Auschwitz, my beating, the gas chamber, and the Death March.

He did not offer excuses. He could have said that German citizens were
under pressure to conform and couldn't help themselves or that they didn't
know what was happening.

His authentic words made an intense impact on me, startling the deepest
layer of my emotions. Something moved in me. I felt close to the Consul, *a*
German. I was surprised at the insight and awareness I had at that moment.
As he acknowledged the demonic behavior of his people in front of a live audience, I saw that Jürgen Borsch was a man
of genuine high moral character. It was a
confession, a plea for reconciliation that
jolted me. Frozen in my chair, I heard ap-
plause for him.

During the break in the program,
I approached the Consul to shake his
hand. Tears welled up in his eyes. He was
human. As we hugged, I blurted, "I can
never forget what the Nazis did to me
and my family, yet we must be friends
from now on. We must go forward."

He looked straight into my eyes and
said, "I know about your suffering and
I'm truly sorry." I choked up, speachless.
Two past enemies now face to face, hand
in hand, one to one.

Jürgen Borsch and Leah Roth 2014

By his personal public statement, I sensed the Consul was bettering himself as a human being, and that's why I could befriend him.

The famous psychiatrist Avraham J. Twersky, M.D. says, "Dramatic changes in feelings can occur when there is a direct relationship."

When Menucha and I began writing my memoir, I generalized that all Germans were responsible for the genocide; all Germans were bad people. I used to resent every German and shouldered this burden of hostility for decades. I even hated to hear the German language that my husband spoke. After processing the Consul's words, I was surprised that I felt a tremendous relief. His words were like a gift, beautifully wrapped with his courage and a bow of sincerity.

My heart acknowledges that many Germans born after the war, today's Germans of moral conscience are guilt ridden, shamed by the actions of their forbearers. After hearing Borsch speak, I have recognized that today's German children are not responsible for their elders' actions or inactions and many suffer as they grapple with knowledge of the deeds and misdeeds by their parents and grandparents. It is hard for the children and grandchildren of the perpetrators to know what their elders and their country were capable of doing to the Jews.

Children are born innocent, yet hatred can be instilled beginning from birth, by modeling attitudes and behaviors of their parents. Only education at home and at school can teach all our children that hatred between human beings is never right. Hatred breeds evil and inhumanity. Hatred will never lead to peace.

I can finally stop blaming those who were not responsible. My perception shifted. I can no longer hold my prejudice tight, especially for those who were not yet born. I thank Consul Jüergen Borsch for opening my mind.

At no time did I ever think I could cross this bridge toward unity. No matter how much I wrote, this burden burned the core of my soul. I can't forget the suffering of our Jewish people through the ages. However, I've realized that what a person doesn't acknowledge cannot begin to be healed. The emotional pain imprinted on my heart will never leave me, but it does not have to dominate. Life goes on, and our children must live in unity in a democratic way.

For peace, I accept a personal obligation to build bridges, by speaking *OneToOne* for a changed tomorrow. I must help repair our world, one person to another, eye to eye, with my handshake, my hug, and my words through my intention to mend bridges.

I was living with hard resentment from my lifelong ordeal. In overwatered plants, the roots rot. I was hurting only myself, angry with self-pity. It's time to let go, to free myself from the chains of blame. Letting go is freedom.

As a child of God, I must stretch myself to judge each person on their individual merit. Letting go is not forgetting. Our children and our children's children must remember — NEVER FORGET.

Leah Roth Summer 2014

CHAPTER 28

Moving On With Strength

Leah and I have celebrated life events; an 87th birthday party in 2012, her first birthday party ever. My friends became her new friends. She has only one close friend left in Miami. The rest have died. Guests brought gifts, "a bead and a blessing" to the luncheon in my home. The beads were made into a colorful necklace. Blessings written to Leah are set among photos in her album. She smiled like a sunbeam as the whole apartment was decorated with yellow balloons and blossoms.

2012 Leah's first birthday party with Menucha

Together, we attended her granddaughter's wedding in Monsey, New York, where she danced the joyous hora with delicious abandon. I saw her truly happy. Catching her breath, she remembered, "If I didn't survive, none of this would happen. It reminds me of Cipora's birthday in Israel, when her daughter told me, 'If it weren't for you, we would not be here to celebrate my mother's birthday.'"

We traveled to Washington, D.C., April 28, 2013, for a tribute weekend commemorating the 20th Anniversary of the Holocaust Memorial. We heard President Clinton and Elie Wiesel speak. Leah was an honored guest, one of 870 other Survivors who were accompanied by their families. Through the museum database, she found recently released German records detailing her as a prisoner in the camps. Viewing her papers for the first time, she was stunned at how precisely the SS detailed her physical description.

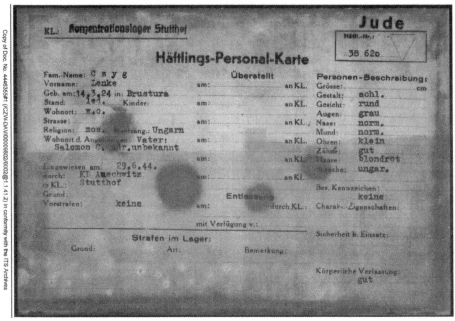

German documentation of Leah's transfer from Auschwitz to Stutthof, June 29, 1944
Notice her birthday is incorrectly written as 1924, making her a year older.

In December 2013, I was privileged to visit Israel with Menucha and Eddie. It was a surprise to meet contemporary Israeli culture face-to-face through the children of the Youth Israeli Philharmonic Orchestra in Jerusalem. After a rehearsal, I was graciously invited to speak to them about the Holocaust. They were truly interested in my story and asked insightful questions both in English and Hebrew. We were special guests at their 40th Anniversary Gala Concert of the Jerusalem Music Center in the Crown Symphony Hall. We were ceremoniously greeted by Hed Sella, Director of the Jerusalem Music Center, and Yorum Kligman, the administrator. Israel has grown so much since its statehood in 1948, when there were less than a million people. Now we have over six million Israeli citizens. We're getting to know a few at a time.

On a tour arranged by the Jerusalem National Fund, led by Ariel Kotler and Yedidya Harush, we roamed the grounds of my Detention Camp, Atlit, now preserved as a major Heritage Site in Israel. I was the first Survivor that Ariel and Yedidya had taken on a tour. They were amazed when I remembered the first names of my group from the ship on a life size photo. Upon seeing the watchtower, I was transported back to nearly seventy years ago when, as a young girl of twenty, I was an "illegal immigrant," stripped naked to be disinfected in the showers. This time no one died. It was eerie to be back to where I was held for several boring weeks in sandy fields until I was assigned to Kibbutz Gesher. There were few trees on this vast barren landscape and little water.

Water shortage is a dry fact in this desert area. We saw how many public schools are studying water conservation through the Green Horizons program Liaison, Karmit Arbel Rumbak, another program of Jerusalem National Fund, teaching children how to conserve and reuse rain water from the roof of their school. Now Israel is flourishing. City landscapes are full of tall buildings, and new highways and bridges are crowded with speeding traffic. Red-and-white Magen David Adom ambulances are always on alert. We toured the command center with Jonathan Feldstein, Israel Representative. I am proud that I have dual Israeli-US citizenship.

When we visited Ayala in Tel Aviv, the little six-year-old girl I cared for in Pardes Katz, with her brother, Ramie at my cousin Adler's house, I remembered the relief I felt to be "back home." They gently brought me back to my Jewish roots. Ayala still feels emotionally attached to me as I were her second mother. We've always stayed in close contact.

Ayala and Leah 2013, Tel Aviv, Israel

As we left a restaurant in Hadera with Ariel Kotler and Yedidya Harush, our Jerusalem National Fund guides, a woman my age stopped me as she recognized me from 1948 when Menachem and I lived there. We were all in awe of this accidental meeting. Wherever I go, I usually identify someone I have known, even after all these years.

To be reunited with Cipora Gottlieb in Tel Aviv, my little camp sister from Auschwitz, was another heartwarming reunion. With Cipora I could reminisce and count my blessings. Now, nearly seven decades older, we are both blessed with beautiful children, grandchildren, and great-grandchildren.

Leah and her "little camp sister" Cipora
Tel Aviv, Israel 2014

I was proud when she told Menucha she was grateful that I gave her a bite of bread when she was very hungry, just before she fainted. We talked about how we stood shivering in line at the counting, afraid every minute, but now grateful for our lives of family and freedom. Our bodies were weak. Our spirit was strong. *Hitler failed. WE WON!*

APPENDICES

Life Map

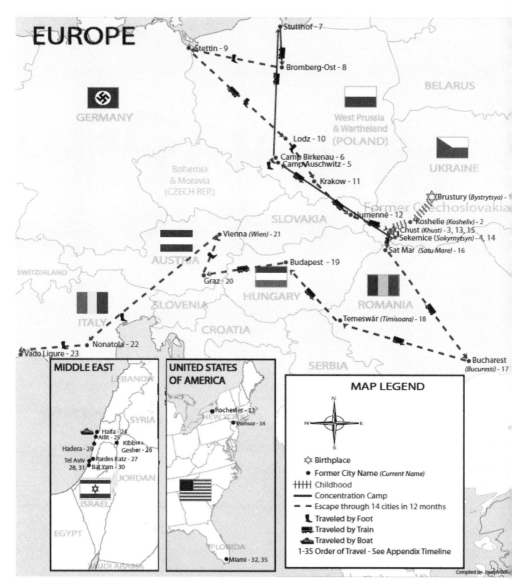

Go to MyEyesLookingBackAtMe.com for a larger view of this map.

Life Timeline

1. March 14, 1925 Lenka Cik, Born — **Brustury, Czechoslovakia,** in Carpathia (presently Bystrytsya, Ukraine)
2. August 1939-August 1940 — **Koshelie, Czechoslovakia,** became Hungary 1940, presently Ukraine
3. August 1940-July 1943 — **Chust, Czechoslovakia,** became Hungary 1940, presently Khust, Ukraine
4. July 1943-April 15, 1944 — **Sekernice, Czechoslovakia,** became Hungary 1940, presently Sokyrnytsyn, Ukraine
5. April 1944 — **Camp Auschwitz, Poland**
6. June 29, 1944 — Walk to **Camp Birkenau, Poland,** sub-camp of **Auschwitz**
7. July 15, 1944 **Camp Stutthof, Poland,** by open train (east of Gdansk, Poland)
8. **Camp Bromberg-Ost, Poland,** by open train
   January 1945-1946 — escaped through six countries and 14 cities in 12 months
9. **Stettin, Germany,** walking
10. **Lodz, Poland,** walking and coal train hitchhiking
11. **Krakow, Poland,** walking across the border to
12. **Humenné, Slovak,** by hitchhiking train
13. Train to **Chust,** now Hungary(1940) (presently Khust, Ukraine)
14. Train to **Sekernice, Hungary** (presently Sokyrnytsyn)
15. Train back to **Chust, Hungary** (presently Khust, Ukraine)
16. Train to **Sat Mar, Romania** (presently Satu Mare)
17. Train to **Bucharest, Romania** (presently Bucuresti)
18. Train to **Temeswár, Romania** (presently Timisoara, Romania)
19. Train to **Budapest, Hungary**
20. Train to **Graz, Austria**
21. Walked to **Vienna, Austria,** then through the Alps (presently Wien, Austria)
22. Walked to **Nanantola, Italy**
23. Walked to **Vado Ligure, Italy**
24. January 7, 1946 — Sailed from Italy for two weeks on ship, *Enzo Sereni,* to **Haifa, Israel**
25. January 17, 1946 — Arrived in Haifa, Israel, to transfer camp **Atlit, Israel**
26. February 1946 — *Kibbutz Gesher*, near **Tiberius, Israel**
27. May 1946 — Left kibbutz for cousins' home in **Pardes Katz** and then **Tel Aviv, Israel**
28. October 25, 1947 — Got married to Menachem Roth in **Tel Aviv, Israel**
29. Lived in **Hadera, Israel**
30. Lived in **Bat Yam, Israel;** daughter Elia was born 6-24-51; son Moshe was born 8-25-57
31. Lived in **Tel Aviv, Israel**
32. September 1959 — Moved to **Miami, Florida**
33. September 1961 — Moved to **Rochester, New York**
34. August 1963 — Moved to **Monsey, New York**
35. July 1987 — Moved back to **Miami, Florida**

Reading Group Guide

Questions and Topics for Discussion:

1. What most impressed you about Leah's story?

2. How has knowledge of the Holocaust influenced your opinion about stereotyping?

3. Have there ever been concentration camps in the U.S?

4. Do you think a Holocaust could happen again?

5. What Holocaust-like events are happening in today's world?

6. How is mass grief (like a natural disaster) different from individual grief (loss of a loved one)?

7. How is profiling happening today?

8. How does hazing and intimidating promote prejudice and intolerance?

9. Have you ever belittled someone or been belittled by another person? How did you feel about it?

10. How can you contribute to reducing discrimination among your friends?

11. How do you personally contribute to tolerance in your own family, your community?

12. Do you have friends of different ethnicities and/or races? Describe the similarities and contrasts in the cultures of your friends. What conclusions can you draw from your evaluation?

13. Discuss different types of prejudices that exist in our society today?

14. How did Leah deal with the alienation of being an outsider throughout her life?

15. When, how, and why did Leah feel powerless, vs. when, how, and why she felt she could live a powerful life?

16. Have you ever been blamed for something you did not do?

17. How have you failed to take responsibility for your own action, blaming someone or something else?

18. How does love, hope, faith (familial, romantic, collegial and between friends), influence the course of events in this memoir?

19. Discuss experiences in your own life that compare to Leah's.

20. Discuss the meaning of alienation and exile.

21. What characteristics of Leah's personality served her in her young life during the war, in her marriage, and in her widowhood?

22. Discuss Leah's experiences that compare to those in your own life.

23. Discuss characteristics of Leah's personality that sustained her.

24. What were Leah's various lifetime sources of resilience and eventual healing?

25. What does the following quotation by Edmund Burke mean to you?

"All that is necessary for the triumph of evil
is that good men do nothing."

(Attributed to Edmund Burke (1729-97)
Irish philosopher, author and statesman.)

Mendel Chaim Cik footnote from page 77

Mendel went to Israel and became a policeman, rising to the rank of commander. He took an Israeli name, Menachem Zafir.

Fifteen years after his arrival, Menachem Zafir was an interrogator prior to the trial of Adolph Eichmann in Israel, March 1961. At the trial, Zafir's team of police protected the documents used by Eichmann's prosecutors.

Eichmann was a German Nazi SS Lieutenant Colonel, head of the Gestapo's section for Jewish affairs, responsible for detailed extermination plans, the "architect" of the Final Solution. He sent all Hungarian Jews to their deaths. Eichmann had been hiding in Argentina where he had fled using a false name. There he was arrested by the Israeli Security Service in 1960. Brought to trial in Jerusalem, he was found guilty on June 1, 1962, of fifteen war crimes against Jewish people and humanity. He was hung and then cremated, his ashes spread at sea beyond Israel's territorial waters.

Eichmann's highly publicized trial raised Holocaust awareness throughout the world. It opened the door for people to begin dialoguing about the Shoah [Holocaust]. Some Survivors began to speak freely and publicly about their capture and suffering at the whim of the Nazis. Many Survivors could now justify their prolonged grieving for their murdered family members to others.

I personally felt grateful for this revenge, because it was Eichmann who commanded the Hungarian military to take my parents from Karpatorus to the killing fields. Under Eichmann's order, I was also among those taken from the ghetto in Sekernice to Auschwitz, along with hundreds of thousands of Hungarian Jews.

Commander Zafir expressed his feelings as both a victim and an interrogator of Eichmann in a video interview, as [later] viewed by his daughter, Naomi:

"'Did you see him?' the interviewer asked.

Dad answers, 'Yes twice. Every two weeks Eichmann was brought before a judge to extend his remand. On two occasions, together with two other officers, I went to see that monster.'

The interviewer asked, 'What did you feel?'

Dad is uncertain for a moment and has to think how to formulate his feelings. He then responds: 'mixed feelings. On one hand, he aroused difficult feelings within me, and re-awoke the memory of the dark past. On the other hand, I had a feeling of satisfaction. Here I am, that 'little Jew' who the Germans and Hungarians trod over, tortured, and humiliated — standing opposite the same beast that condemned my family and all European Jewry to death, and now I and colleagues are in charge of him, and interrogate him. He is submissive and addresses us differentially, using the word, 'Sir.'"

[From the Book, "I Am Mendel" by Naomi Koral, daughter of Menachem Zafir; Printed in Israel 2005, publications.marketing@yadvashem.org.il]

Love Letters

From Daughter, Elia Filhart

Growing up in Israel as a young child I did not feel anything out of the ordinary. I never realized that my mother had gone through horrible times in her life. I had not an inkling that my family was any different than any other family in the neighborhood. The same was in school. I was like all of the other children in my grade. Yes, my mother had an accent, but many of the parents had accents. These were the beginning years of the State of Israel and people moved there from many different countries around the world. My parents who were starting their lives without any help from family members lived a frugal life, but I received everything that I needed and never felt deprived of anything. Around the time that I was 12 years old and living in America, we studied about the Holocaust in school. I had known that my mother went through the concentration camps; however, since she never spoke about it, I did not think that she was affected by it very much.

Every once in a while I would learn something about life in pre-war Europe or about our family. I guess there was a sense that this subject was very sensitive, sort of taboo, and I did not want to ask too much about it. I remember being sorry for myself that my American friends had bigger extended families than we did and that they had grandparents that would visit them and shower them with gifts. I wasn't too verbal about my emotions in order not to hurt my mother's feelings. The one thing that I would envision is having a bigger family of my own and that my children would have grandparents.

When the Spielberg foundation came around, my mother opened up about her life. I felt both elated and sad. I was elated that now I was able to get a picture of my mother's past, and sad that this past was so horrible. We still never sat and had conversations about this subject. Then the pages came that Mom wrote, that gave me more of an insight into her life. I was upset that she did not want me to help her write her life story; however, now having read the book, I understand my mother's mindset.

What I realize now is how much suffering my mother went through and what a strong personality she has had for raising my brother and me as normal children. I was given many extracurricular activities such as music (piano and flute) and art lessons and sent to sleep away summer camps. Both my parents raised me to be an independent person and always trusted my decisions, even though they did not always agree with them. I am grateful for the way that I was raised and praise both my parents, my mother who had gone through the Holocaust, and my father who did not, but had most of his family perish.

I love you Ima,
Elia

From Son, S. Moshe Roth, OD

My earliest holocaust-related memory is awakening to my mother's shouting and crying out in the middle of the night. Even as a young child, I knew there was an underlying history but I could not appreciate the enormity until I was considerably older. Even on Saturday afternoons, when we took a mid-day nap, it was not unusual for my mother to awaken to her own loud vocalizations from haunting memories, situations that were never discussed. It was understood without words that there were demons of the past that continued to haunt and possess her.

As a young child, I was fascinated by "army" shows on TV and everything military. A friend gave me a combat uniform with a tommy gun that made sounds that closely emulated those in real life. My tommy gun set had a helmet and two plastic grenades. I played with plastic toy soldiers, tanks, and figurines. Those toys shot rockets and missiles. Perhaps, my fascination had its roots in my mother's history.

Anyone that remained alive after "the camps" had a story of fortuitously fleeing or jumping from one line to another. Obviously, it was these fateful and life-determining choices that made the difference between those who ultimately survived and those who did not. An inner voice told the individual that somehow, or for some reason, they made choices to follow their instinct to make way from one line to another. Those that made a poor and fateful choice were fatalities. Unlike Darwin's philosophy of survival of the fittest, it was survival of the fortuitous.

My father had the foresight to leave Europe despite having to leave his family, parents, and a grandmother. It, no doubt, was a difficult decision, but one with vision. He saw the writing on the wall in Europe and the impending birth of a state that he so much wanted to be part of. He went from darkness to light, from persecution to freedom and self-destiny. My father was one of a few who pursued and achieved an academic degree in Europe to attain a prestigious teaching position. In Israel, he followed his love for teaching and attained esteemed certification. He was always so proud of all his students. His love for Israel made it very difficult for him to leave for the US in order to please my mother. She wanted to be near her only remaining sibling Malchi in Miami.

Other children in my class had grandparents, and some of them even had grandparents with accents. There was a point when I realized that having grandparents was more normal than not having them. All children are self-absorbed, the center of their universe, unaware that there is a lineage that precedes them. The present is reality. I was unaware at the time of the horrors my mother endured.

More often than not, my parents' friends also had accents with the commonality of being immigrants. I recall my parents' inner need to be self-supporting with their relentless work ethic. Father always had at least two different teaching jobs, both morning and afternoon. In addition, he would often teach bar mitzvah lessons. Mother used the skills she learned as a wig-maker at a young age, working hours on end 'in the back' at Peter's salon where she made hair pieces for men. She also worked as a nurse's aide at a number of nursing homes. Now I realize it went to pay, in part, for my high school and college tuition.

My father had a passion for both teaching and music. He taught me and my friend how to play the violin. Another passion was cultivating flowers and vegetables. I fondly remember building the succah together, and I carry on that tradition with my girls. Once he took me and my neighbor to the Chasidic Vizhnitz enclave behind our home to watch them bake matzoh before Pesach. I recall watching the men roll the dough on the table, the Vizhnitzer Rebbe coming to us and rather than embracing and welcoming us, saying, "*Kinderlach, shteh by de tier."* This meant, "Children, stand near the door." Essentially, you can stay around, but don't get in the way because it may contaminate the matzos.

My mother ran beside me when teaching me how to ride my red-orange bicycle. Ultimately, I decided to try it on my own, and I remember that very first bike ride without her around. To this day, I vividly recall the elation of being able to ride my bike by myself and precisely where I chose to stop my bicycle. In retrospect, this symbolized "giving the skills" but ultimately I had to do it on my own.

We are all products of the times we are born, the circumstances in which we grew up, and the order of birth among siblings. I had an intimate tie to the state of Israel that was inculcated both at home and in school. I made art projects and posters with biblical and Talmudic themes. They were artistic representations from our own inspiration and interpretations of what I envisioned them to mean, from what resonated within me.

My father told me stories that seemed to simply flow from biblical sources of Talmud and prophets. I had difficulty trying to emulate the same ease with my own daughters and needed to rely on books to help me 'tell the story'.

In retrospect, so much of my childhood centered on unspoken recollections and values from both my parents. Wounds and scars persisted and were incorporated into our individual persona. We in the US are a conglomerate of those that came in search of a better life, recalling the positives, unable to erase many of the negatives as we searched for a better future.

I am forever in debt to my parents, Their sacrifices for me, their endurance and hard work so that my life would be easier and better than theirs. They took much pride in me and my sister.

Thank you, Ima and Abba.

Surprise Letter to Granddaughter, Margalit Roth

*Given to my granddaughter, Margalit, age 17, on arrival
at Auschwitz during her 2011 Heritage Tour to Poland.*

March 27, 2011

My dear sweet granddaughter, Margo,

I was told you would receive this "surprise" letter as you are standing in Auschwitz Concentration Camp as an observer. You are standing where I stood – naked.

I am so impressed, my child, that you found it necessary and important to go on this trip, to see for yourself what those beasts did to my whole family and me. You are now seventeen. I was nineteen when I stood where you are standing, but without clothes or hair. They are not to be forgiven. We must never forget what they did to us.

I was in Birkenau in the Section A Barrack, stripped of everything: my clothing, my hair, and my self-respect. I was even stripped of my name, and it was replaced with a number 38,620. In the big room near the crematorium, we were standing nude and helpless, like sheep going to the slaughterhouse.

Hashem (God) had changed The Plan. "Man proposes and God disposes." The Germans needed workers, cheap hands to use for hard work. The Nazis and their accomplices chose people who were strong enough to work for them. We were ages 14 to 30. They tortured us.

All the others, those with small children and all older people, were gassed the same day they arrived.

When you see the suitcases and big piles of shoes and eyeglasses, believe they are real. This is not a museum from the olden times of torture chambers. It really happened when I was in the camps sixty-five years ago.

I am spending a lot of time with my computer, especially since I now have the Internet. I am content with what I have. I feel fine. I have new friends. I exercise and swim and play cards.

I am happy to hear you visited your cousin Simi and her family in Natanya.

Pesach is around the corner, so to speak. I am happy you will come home from school for Pesach vacation so we can spend time together.

My dear child, I love you dearly and will see you soon.

Love,
Your Savta (grandmother)

Margalit was attending a girl's seminary in Israel during her gap year between high school and college. Following her trip to Poland, in memory of the Holocaust, she reported to her classmates.

During my year studying at seminary in Israel, I took a trip to Poland with the Heritage organization to learn more about the Holocaust in person. Auschwitz Birkenau was the last stop on my trip. It certainly had the biggest impact on me because I knew my Savta had been there many years before.

As I first entered the camp, the many stories that Savta had told me after Spielberg's video were spinning through my head. It was hard to believe that I was actually there, walking on the same ground where she and her family walked, while trying to survive their every step.

After touring the camp and learning so much about what happened there, I had an even greater appreciation for my Savta and what she endured. It is clear that Survivors must have had a very strong will to live and belief in Hashem.

We made our way to Barrack A, the section of barracks where my Savta had been. We had a closing ceremony in a bunker there and I lit a candle for all of her relatives who had passed away during the war. This was a very emotional time for me.

There was a depressed feeling in the air, as everyone mourned their relatives who had been murdered. However, I also felt a strong appreciation for my Savta, as I knew that if not for her and her strong spirit, I would not be standing there on that day.

My Savta was our age during the war. She couldn't call her mom when she was homesick. She didn't even know where her parents were. I could never imagine doing most of the things she did. I envy her courage, bravery, and passion for Judaism. She was always the model in our family.

She taught me to be determined and to never take for granted what I have. To this day, she will not waste anything because she still remembers when she didn't have anything extra to waste.

I am so grateful to have her in my life; I learn something new from her every day.

In Leah's Words to Menucha

We became so close, Menucha and I. There are no secrets between us, a friendship I never ever could imagine in my life. She inspired me to freely express my feelings. She would twist her questions until I came out with an answer. Then she'd ask again, "How did it feel?" When we finished, I felt satisfied to see my story written down. I'm so proud I could tell it. I have never done this before, this experience of writing a book.

Menucha made me alive and it is unbelievable someone cares so much about me. She makes sure my medical needs are taken care of. She wants to know how I follow through on the doctor's recommendations. Even though I am aging, I feel healthy, because of what Menucha does for me. She brings me tea before I get up from the bed. She makes sure I eat a breakfast of oatmeal for fiber and bananas for potassium. Now I feel like every day is a special day.

I am especially blessed in how she encourages me to be dressed perfect, hair combed, lipstick and blush on, nails polished. She *kvells* with pride when we're together in public. She brought me back to life. I adore Menucha.

We even went to Israel together and Washington D.C. We go to many activities: trips, synagogue, Torah classes, concerts, movies, the press club, and shopping. She encourages me to speak up and share my story. Menucha makes me proud. I'm not able to thank her enough for what she does for me, and to her husband, Eddie, for welcoming me, advising me, and accepting me in their home and their daily lives. Many times I have felt like an intruder for taking away their privacy. I know that my presence has separated their private time together, as we work such long hours. Even more, if Menucha becomes exasperated with my stubbornness, Eddie defends me.

May Hashem help Menucha and Eddie to have long and healthy lives, with continuing nachas from their beautiful family, their children, grandchildren and great grandchildren. My blessings to them for all they do for me and others.

Menucha's Words to Leah

My Dearest Best Friend Leah,

Your suffering breaks my heart. There is no way I can know it to the depths you've experienced. May I never need to know. I will always remember that during your most challenging times, you never said, "I can't." You never asked, "Why me?" You did everything within your ability to keep moving, living your life of dignity with gratitude. Having immersed myself in most every aspect of your life, I understand that your riveting account is not just another Holocaust story. Like every life, it is a living memory of hope, healing, and friendship; a testimony we recorded for eternity, a story that must be told and retold. As your "other daughter," I commit to endorse your story of faith, valor, and wisdom as long as I am able. My outrage will allow nothing less.

You are a woman who has moved beyond the atrocities of war to create the tapestry of your normal life. Not so long ago you were nearly murdered in the Holocaust that stole most of your family, yet you bravely carried your sorrow in silence for the protection of your children's innocence. Through intense and focused *Soul-Writing*, you slowly and courageously revealed secrets suppressed for decades. Without bitterness, you've lived a model life, never giving in or giving up. You rose from the cinders as a symbol of hope, an awesome human being.

Writing for you has been my privilege. Knowing you has transformed me in many ways. In examining your life, I've also explored mine. I've learned I can take bigger risks and set higher goals, attainable with clear intention and rigorous focus. That collectively, we can accomplish anything that seems insurmountable alone. You have been my teacher. You found your way to endure misery and loss. As someone who grew up without extravagance of any kind, you're satisfied with simple things and grateful for the tiniest kindness. You stand up for what's right. As you often remind, "Time goes. It doesn't come back. Use it wisely, with gratitude, everyday."

Your presence is in my heart, reminding me of the potential inner resources within us all. You've brought a new dimension to my life, a new existence overlapping mine. Writing with you has balanced our passionate, disjointed worlds. My clarity has emerged from quiet moments with the pen, the equilibrium of my wellbeing. I try to understand the depth of the dark chasm between the opposing energies of evil and sparks of loving kindness. Your ability to mend bridges between countries and people is a selfless lesson for us all. By rescuing your story for future generations, we are helping repair the world.

From you I understand the deeper meaning of our Shabbat prayer, "A Woman of Valor: 'You shall be blessed at the gates by your very own deeds.'" Surely God is proud of you.

Forever grateful,
Menuchala

Acknowledgements

For my husband, **Eddie**, who is most
familiar with Leah's lifelong saga.

You've embraced Leah as a new member of our family.
You edited for hours and assisted our late night
computer challenges with humor, bringing relief and
uproarious laughter during our most trying times.
Your calm during many storms has
carried us through to completion.
Not only did you believe in this book and
what it has to offer the world,
but most importantly,
you believed in me.

I love you Eddie!

For **Alan Freeman**, Vice President, Jerusalem Foundation in Israel:
Leah and I have the deepest gratitude to you for joining our team and our family, and inviting us to join yours. You have committed your time and resources, reassuring our confidence and working in sync with us to help move our project toward publication and dissemination through collaboration with your Foundation, and in concert with the Jerusalem Music Center, planned for April 16, 2015 on Yom Hashoah.

To **Professor Sara R. Horowitz**, York University (Toronto, Ontario, Canada).
Your Introduction to "My Eyes Looking Back at Me" has added to the far reaching magnitude of Leah's story, with challenging new insights and understanding of women's' memories from the Holocaust. Your work elevates Survivor's voices to more significant and reliable narratives. Thank you for underlining Survivor's contributions to Holocaust memory.

For **Rabbi Fredrick Klein**, my mentor for the mitzvah of bikkur cholim:
Thank you for accepting me into your life-changing program at the Federation, for mentoring me in the spiritual care of others, and for encouraging us to complete our book. Leah and I are grateful for your insightful and encompassing foreword.

To "Aunt" **Marcia Cohen, Esq.**, dear friend and loyal confidant
Leah and I are indebted to you. You embraced our project, edited our final manuscript, and remain devoted to it and to us.

For **Randy Ladenheim-Gil,** initial editor:

Leah and I thank you for your patience, dedication, sensitive editing, and cogent advice to a newbie, always asking the right questions.

Reviews and tributes from your hearts and your lives honor Leah's memory as she testifies for the silenced voices of lost generations. Thank you for supporting our cause to remember and to educate about the Holocaust, a reminder that every single recorded memory makes a difference. We are grateful for your time commitment to read the manuscript of *"My Eyes Looking Back at Me: Insight Into A Survivor's Soul,"* and your carefully crafted reviews.

Rabbi Shabtai Alpern, Chabad, Brazil, who reminds us to learn the lessons the Holocaust teaches and to never forget; **Miriam Jaskierowicz Arman**, Vocal Pedagogue, Author, Poet and Fine Artist — an artistic soul who knows truth and trusts wisdom. **Michael Berenbaum, Ph.D.**, Sigi Zieirng Institute, Professor of Jewish Studies, American University, California — for your insightful and poignant summary of Leah's story gracing our back cover; **Jürgen Borsch**, Consulate General, Federal Republic of Germany, for Florida and Puerto Rico — your confession and contrite apology provided a turning point in Leah's life story; **Ranley Desir, M.D.**, Miami — you've kept our hearts beating strong, steady, and clear, reminding that we must "stand, together, against the apostles of hate;" **Hindi Diamond z"l**, Latin American Foreign Correspondent — for your ongoing experience and encouragement through it all; **Alan Freeman**, Vice President, Jerusalem Foundation, Israel — a dearest friend and confidant; **Avi Hoffman**, Entertainer, child of Survivors and Director of the Dachau Album Project — for your command to "Remember Forever!!!" **Miriam Klein Kassenoff, Ph.D.**, University of Miami, Holocaust Educator — you helped us pave our way with cogent advice from your long years of Holocaust Education experience; **Angela King**, Editor, *Life After Hate*, Miami, inspirational speaker — you demonstrate that deep personal change is possible; **Joyce Klein**, Educator and Playwright in Israel — for your technology ideas to reach young people.

Joseph Lebovic, Ph.D. (h.c.), Philanthropist — thanks for a wonderful review; **Maurice Ostro, OBE, KFO**, United Kingdom — for supporting our "powerful narrative" project; **Wendy Reiss Rothfield, MSW, LCSW** — another survivor who has a story of her own; **Roberta Shapiro, M.Ed, LCSW, NBCCH** — who commends the bond of our relationship; **Kenneth Treister**, Author, Architect and Sculptor of the Miami Holocaust Memorial — for inspiring poetry from our souls every visit; **Peter Weisz**, Publisher — a new colleague and friend who reminds us that this is a historically significant testimony, your appreciation is gratefully accepted; **The Rev. Dr. Priscilla Felisky Whitehead**, Minister Emerita, The Church by the Sea, Bal Harbor, FL — you remind us that "we are all children of God."

Leah and I have gratitude to our dear friends and classmates from Florida International University – **Rosalyn Kaplus** and **Marjorie Waterman**. As *Aventura Authors*, we've would meet weekly at my kitchen table to spend endless hours studying about minutia of writing, wordsmithing, rewriting, and rehashing our golden "masterpieces," struggling to find the best way to clarify what we really mean to say. Thank you for your loving kindness, devotion to our mission to complete an ongoing story to honor memory, and for the selfless generosity of your precious time at all hours. Writing sisters and best friends we are and will always be.

Several "readers" have volunteered as coaches, editors, researchers, and historians. You've helped research the minutia of the treacherous map of European Jewry and encouraged us write as honestly and in as much detail as Leah's memory would allow: **Dr. Roberto and Joanne Hamburger** of Ascona, Switzerland; **Dr. Marvin Klein,** St. Thomas University School of Law, Miami, FL., who spend the summer of 2013 vetting accuracy through the Hammond Atlas, editing, advising, and questioning.

Leah and I appreciate the professional and scholarly feedback from **Marylee Martin (1929-2014),** my best friend from college for the past 54 years. You worked with meticulous diligence, rendering scholarly overview and direction during the last few months of your waning health before you left us too soon. I suppress my urge to call you. Instead, I reread your careful and detailed notes for courage and guidance. May your soul be blessed with comfort and peace, earned from a gracious life well lived.

Thank you to my dear friend and writing mentor, **Hindi Diamond z"l, (1924-2014)** from the Osher Lifelong Learning Institute of Florida International University. You have changed my life by encouraging me to write my truth, guiding me to always trust my intuition and common sense. I know you are resting in peace, your reward for a lifetime of generosity to others.

Several writing professionals have been instrumental in helping us to sustain the impetus of our project. As Leah's story became longer and the book more complicated, many encouraging consultations at the Miami Dade College, Center for the Literary Arts, Writers Institute and *Books and Books* gave us the support and direction we needed to perk up our occasional flimsy confidence and to keep writing anyway.

Miriam Arman, you have been a spark of love in my life. I listened to you. "You can write, you should write, and you will write." And now I write. Blessings, dear sister.

We thank our **Rabbi Jonathan Horowitz,** *Willie and Celia Trump Synagogue,* who encouraged us to be tenacious in our efforts to give voice to Leah's story.

Without the computer expertise of **Joseph Behar** for technical editing and support, digital typesetting and formatting, this book could not have become possible. You were gentle and graceful dealing with our inexperience and utter frustration with the myriad complexities of modern technology. Thank you for your detailed map of Leah's trek though life, an important visual of her timeline.

To **Danielle Behar**, graphic artist. You beautifully translated Leah's message of friendship, hope, and healing, incorporating the meaning of Leah's favorite flower, the iris, utilizing her watercolor for the bookmark, representing her character traits of faith, valor, and wisdom.

Leah and I are grateful to our families who read the manuscript with great care, and offered astute editorial remarks and suggestions. To Leah's children, **Elia Filhart** and **Moshe Roth, OD**, we are grateful for your shared insights and support. And we appreciate my children, **Ahuva Druin, Jacob Wood, and William Wood,** for your meticulous reading, suggestions, and encouragement.

We thank the teachers who inspire their students to write heartfelt responses to their newly found awareness of the effects of hatred and genocide on individuals and societies. Menucha's grandaughters, **Riki** and **Tzivia Druin,** responded to Holocaust education with intense and profound poems. Your personal interest in Leah's story supported our journey and gave special meaning to our efforts.

Leah and I offer our warmest admiration to our mutually treasured friends **Gaby Bastida,** for keeping *Aventura Authors* well fed; **Barbara Davis,** from the Jewish Community Volunteer Services, for introducing me to Leah, "a lady who wants to write her memoir, after sixty-five years of secrecy." **Mildred Kagan**, our friend, for your constant mentoring and encouragement; **Cookie Medina,** massage therapist, for your tender gentle care of body and soul; **Mindelle Pierce**, for your snowbird presence at *Aventura Authors*; **Fran Purcell,** for your dedicated and insightful editing; and to **Sandee Simon,** for your volunteer hours, patiently transcribing barely readable handwritten narrative and rambling recorded interviews, and editing the "almost" final manuscript.

Esther Basha, you've come into our life as an angel, using skills that have enhanced our marketing and publishing efforts through editing, recording our audio book, for planning social media exposure and development.

To my **Chai Lifeline** workshop of mothers of medically fragile children who taught me to understand that survivors of trauma exhibit similar patterns of resilience and hope. Your valor and courage is echoed by Leah throughout her narrative. Thank you, **Ellen Weiss** and **Marilyn Bensinger** for this rare opportunity to coach women who have much to teach.

Reviews

Rabbi Shabsi Alpern, Chabad - San Paulo, Brazil

The Jewish Nation has sad dates built into the ebb and flow of our year-ly cycle. This is not only so we do not forget the past, but more importantly, so we can learn the lessons they provide us. Certainly, events that happened in the last century should be even more relevant.

Among the many tragedies that occurred, the Holocaust was unique in that the Nazi goal was methodically carried out by indescribable killing machines that affected six million people, including indiscriminately mur-dering one million innocent children who were targeted simply for their lineage.

There should be six million books about the Holocaust, for each per-son had their own story to tell, of their own shortened life. Yet sadly, those books will not be written. "My Eyes Looking Back at Me" is the saga of one woman's life as she encounters challenge upon challenge. The rich details of each character and the choices Leah is forced to make, mark the reader forever.

Leah Roth's story of survival and dignity are woven into the most beautiful tapestry. Menucha Meinstein's prolific writing style transforms Leah's life's journey into a work of art and a textbook on this period.

Assimilation into Western Culture did not and does not provide safety from the dangers of a Jewish birthright. To think so is a cruel joke. This is a fitting remembrance when Jews are accepted like never before. This book is a must for any age group and for our future generations. I lack the words to describe the rare contribution that Leah and Menucha have made to all of us. May the Good Lord bless them with long, healthy and happy lives.

Miriam Jaskierowicz Arman - Tiberius, Israel
Vocal Pedagogue, Author, Poet and Fine Artist

Staring into the faces of murderous death, lives ripped apart, dealing with the hunger, pain; the sorrow, loss and the overwhelming sadness, a sense of personal devastation - dehumanized, yet wholly human after all...

This is the survivor whom no one can really understand or compre-hend - except a Soul large enough to empower and put into words, deeds, thoughts and actions the incredible need of one, who lived those untold pic-tures in her life.

This is the enormous dedication, energy and the giftedness of a brilliant, soulful writer, telling the story of a woman who survived and defied all of her experiences by sharing her story, her message through the living eyes of a beautiful human. Thank you Leah and Menucha for so enriching the world.

Michael Berenbaum, Ph.D., Professor of Jewish Studies, Sigi Zieirng Institute, American Jewish University - Los Angeles, CA

Former Project Director, US Holocaust Memorial Museum

Former President and CEO Survivors of the Shoah Visual History Foundation

"My Eyes Looking Back at Me" is the powerful collaboration between two friends, both committed Jews, one a Survivor of the Holocaust. The story that is told is painful, but not only painful. The world before the Shoah is revealed, one rich with community and family, most is lost, remnants survive but memory endures. And the world afterwards is also presented, the journey back from the abyss into a life in Israel and in the United States, to a life of normalcy and ultimately to a life filled with dignity and decency as Leah Cik Roth moves from being a helpless victim to a poignant witness. Her story of the life during the Shoah is told with depth and painful honesty. She takes the reader into that darkness without glossing over the anguish and indignity. Above all, this book is a tribute to a friendship between two women, who had the courage to look back on the past together and the skill to tell of that past so compellingly.

Jürgen Borsch, Consulate General of the Federal Republic of Germany - Miami, FL

After all has been said and done, I see myself standing eye to eye with Leah. I see her past, her suffering, her resilience, her perseverance and her hope, which will never cease to dominate her amazing personality.

From her sheer endless ordeal, she asks, as many others, and I also: "Why did God let this happen?" None of us will ever have an answer.

But today, looking into Leah's eyes, I see a message for us and for coming generations. I have been given a chance to promise that we will do everything to lead our children into a world where all the atrocities she suffered will no longer be possible. I am blessed that I have met Leah and am able to share her life story. We both know that education is paramount.

Leah's perseverance to survive has one deep significance and meaning above her own fate, and if only now, after so many years of silence, inner fights, repression, and sufferings, Leah has finally taken the chance to tell her story, a chance not to remain in bitterness. Leah has come a long way, finally seeing that her story matters to history.

Ranley Desir, MD, Haitian Born Cardiologist - Aventura, FL

"My Eyes Looking Back at Me" is the moving story of my patient Leah Roth, one of several Holocaust Survivors I had the privilege to care for in my practice over the past 20 years. Leah's personal experiences as narrated by her friend Menucha opened my eyes to her courage in the face of extreme adversity, her will to survive and her resourcefulness. And all of it told without the anger one would expect after such a horrifying ordeal! She is an inspiration to the millions of human beings who are still living in totalitarian states across the globe.

This book is a "must read" for the younger generations who may not realize how much evil man is capable of, and may not understand why it is so important for all of us to stand, together, against the apostles of hate.

Hindi Diamond z"l (1924-2014),
Latin American Foreign Correspondent
TIME/Life, Newsweek, United Press, McGraw Hill, NBC;
VP South Florida International Press Club

Leah Cik Roth's life story, as passionately told by Menucha Meinstein, may be classified by some as a Holocaust book. But it definitely is NOT. The Holocaust only acts as a backdrop to what is an inspiring and awesome tale of how a cultured and elegant woman had the strength and spirit to overcome indescribable horrors and emerge a vibrant, optimistic member of society. If you're looking for inspiration in your life, this is a good lesson for us all to learn. Her eyes may be looking back, but they always revert to a future of hope. She may be a prototype of what an older, mature Anne Frank would have been, had she lived.

Together, the book's Author and the Survivor create an unbreakable bond between them, which seeps out of every page in the book and produces an awesome legacy of love.

It will impact and imprint itself on every reader's heart and prove that the impossible IS possible as Leah overcomes even the most horrific events with an undaunted spirit that emerges whole and hopeful. If your eyes are looking back at you, you MUST read this book. Because of the author's deep involvement in Leah's life, her remarkable style of understanding and empathy is heightened, and produces a meaningful story, which will appeal to readers at any level of their lives.

Leah Roth's struggle and survival interpreted by this new writer, to be watched in the future, produces a prize-winning portrait not to be missed.

Alan Freeman, Vice President, Jerusalem Foundation - Jerusalem, Israel

I was only four years old when one afternoon I asked my mother where her mommy and daddy were. Not taken aback by the question, she sat down and explained to me that they had been murdered a decade or so earlier, in what is now known as the Holocaust of European Jewry. Over the course of six decades, I had the personal privilege of engaging in an ongoing dialogue with her and my father, also a Holocaust Survivor, on multiple aspects of this trauma which always hovered around our lives.

Their stories of horror and courage gave me a unique perspective that the great histories written over the years can supplement but cannot match.

Jews around the world mark a much earlier trauma in their flight from Egypt by two essential traditions. The first commands them to read the story of the Exodus as if they themselves had experienced it. The second requires each generation to pass on the story to the next generation by repeating it year after year.

Both my parents are now dead. As the numbers of Survivors continue to dwindle, the importance of conveying the enormity of this unparalleled tragedy grows incrementally. It is vital that future generations have the evidence at their disposal, which will enable them to feel as if they had been there themselves.

Leah Roth's tale of survival against all odds so effectively and lovingly put into text by Menucha Meinstein, achieves this. It has a Bashevis Singer or even Dylan Thomas-like quality to it. Characters from a lost world, the seamstress, baker, ritual slaughterer, suitors, friends and neighbors with all their strengths, weaknesses and foibles come to life. They then disappear as the Nazi murder machine deports and disposes of them. Told in the first person, each page documents in a highly personal way the human dimensions of one Jewish woman who, through sheer tenacity and courage, kept her dignity amidst a world preparing to devour her, her family, friends and neighbors. This is an essential read to comprehend those times so that it can be passed on from generation to generation.

Avi Hoffman / Entertainer, child of Survivors and Director of the Dachau Album Project - Coral Springs, FL

As I read the moving memoir: My Eyes Looking Back at Me, I realize once again that The Holocaust, as enormously iconic as it has become over the past 70 years, is ultimately the aggregate accumulation of many millions of individual experiences, each a brilliant and unique gem; each a story of human survival in the face of unimaginable horror; each a story that must be told and retold for all of eternity. Luckily for humanity, Leah Cik Roth met Menucha Meinstein, who was able to elicit and express the extraordinary courage and perseverance in one Survivors tale, as an example to the world of the meaning of LIFE! Remember Forever!!!

**Miriam Klein Kassenoff, Ph.D., University of Miami –
Coral Gables, FL**

Director, Holocaust Studies Summer Institute/
School of Education

University/ Miami, Coral Gables, Florida

District Education Specialist/Holocaust Education

Miami-Dade County Public Schools/Holocaust Memorial

"At 19 years old my world had fallen completely apart — what is going to happen to me now?" Chapter 10 called "Train To Hell" opens when the train she is on approaches the infamous death camp Auschwitz. I have read many Holocaust Survivor memoirs, but Leah Roth's story touched my heart with such intensity, I could feel the ache and pain and love and joys as I read her incredible story of survival from the Holocaust and then the hope of rebuilding her life.

"I have gone from Victim to Victor — My story is my legacy."

In Chapter 23, "I Have Spoken," Leah proudly says this is the time for her to teach the lessons of what apathy and indifference can lead to. Each one of the students she speaks to in the younger generation can indeed make a difference in healing the world by learning to live with one another in dignity through tolerance and understanding while appreciating diversity.

"Hitler did not win — I survived."

As a child Survivor of the Holocaust myself, when I read these words in Chapter 23, all I could really hear were these very same words that were said all my life by my mother, of blessed memory, who also intoned this same phrase many times in my childhood years. Yes, I understand all

Leah is saying in just those six words: The monster did not win. Hate did not win. Hope and love and perseverance and all that is good won in the soul of Leah, who represents us all today. On a personal note, I recently met my new friend Leah for the first time, and I assure you she is the personification of all that is sweet and good.

I urge you to read this book, to savor every chapter of beautiful prose so well written by the writer/scribe, as she calls herself, Menucha Meinstein, and to learn about what it was like for Leah Roth to live a life with such perseverance, such bravery, and such hope.

I will be recommending this memoir to all students of the Nazi Holocaust of 1933-1945 as a primary resource, whether they be high school students, college students, or scholars and professors. It must be read and reread and retold for future generations.

Angela King, M.A., Former Skinhead; Editor-In-Chief,
Life After Hate - **Miami, FL**
Specialist: Violent Extremism

At the age of nineteen — the same age Leah was when she fought for her life in Auschwitz — I was denouncing the atrocities of the Holocaust. I denied that Survivors like Leah existed.

My parents unknowingly planted a ticking time bomb in me during my developmental years. Years during which I learned to dehumanize other human beings with words, actions, and attitudes in the form of racial slurs, tasteless jokes, and ignorant stereotypes. As an adolescent suffering an acute identity crisis, I stripped away pieces of my own humanity to such a degree that I spent nearly a decade doing the same to others. From the time I was an adolescent and into my early twenties, I was a violent far-right extremist — a neo-Nazi skinhead.

At the age of twenty-three, I found myself sitting in a Federal prison for my part in an armed robbery of a Jewish-owned store, a hate crime. It was during my time in prison that my life and mind changed completely. Ironically, the very same women I would have hated because of the color of their skin or the religion they practiced, disarmed me with kindness and compassion. The kindness and compassion they showed me changed the very fabric of who I was. I was released from prison in May of 2001, but not before I learned to take responsibility for my actions and to value myself as a human being.

I have been a peace educator and motivational speaker for nearly thirteen years now, traveling the US and sharing my experiences. It was in this capacity that Leah and I met. We were both present at a Student Awareness

Day event in South Florida, Leah an honored guest speaking as an activist and Holocaust Survivor, and me sharing my most shameful decisions and acts of redemption. I had the privilege of not only meeting Leah that day, but the gift of knowing that she supports what I do now to make amends for my past. It is beyond humbling to share space with her and the other Survivors, and to have her blessing is a gift I will cherish for the rest of my life.

"My Eyes Looking Back at Me," Leah's memoir detailing her triumph over hatred and the unspeakable acts of inhumanity leveled against her and others moved me beyond myself. I wanted to reach into the pages that detail Leah's experiences and console her, hold her hand, and let her know that she is not alone, that she is dearly loved and respected. I am grateful that I have had the opportunity to take Leah's small hand in my own for a brief few seconds, and to hug her in my arms when she first told me about her endeavor to finish her memoir. Menucha's beautiful prose combined with Leah's raw account of being a Holocaust Survivor make this work a compelling personal narrative that embodies strength and teaches imperative lessons to future generations. These are lessons that must be shared over and over again — lessons we must never forget, lest these horrific acts be repeated.

Today, I work as a Violent Extremism Specialist, as a peace educator, and Editor-In-Chief for a non-profit organization called Life After Hate (lifeafterhate.org). Started by former far-right extremists like myself, Life After Hate is a consultancy and speaker's bureau dedicated to helping communities and organizations gain the knowledge necessary to implement long-term solutions that counter all types of violent extremism. We do this work because we have a responsibility to the world and to humanity and, for me personally, to Survivors like Leah. This work makes me feel closer to Leah, and akin to how she felt when she realized she can share her past experiences and move on: It has freed me from the prison in my soul.

Joyce Klein, Educator, Storyteller, & Playwright - Jerusalem, Israel

"My Eyes Looking Back at Me," Leah Roth's amazing life story as told beautifully and with great compassion by Menucha Meinstein, is unique in the galaxy of holocaust memoirs.

The memoirs written by Survivors of Hitler's Holocaust are increasingly more important as the years pass. They put an individual face on this terrible and frightening chapter of Jewish and world history and make it accessible. As the Survivors dwindle in number, and we contemplate a future without eyewitnesses to describe what they experienced, we will grow to rely more and more on these personal stories to help us understand the past and feel its truth.

"My Eyes Looking Back at Me" goes further. Out of 304 pages, only 42 are devoted to Leah Roth's experiences during the Holocaust, from Kristallnacht to liberation. The book, instead, presents us with a full life story; the Holocaust is an important and pivotal component, but we encounter it in the context of Leah's whole biography. Here are the details of her childhood between the wars, a portrait of Jewish living in Europe in the 20s and 30s; her apprenticeship to a wigmaker at the age of 14, to learn a trade that would save her life more than once. Here, too, are post-war stories of Leah's twelve month journey across seven countries, as she travels toward passage to Palestine; her years in Israel before and after the state was declared; her reality as a Survivor in a society that does not want to acknowledge her past; her immigration to the United States and her transition to bearing witness.

Many of these periods and stories are too often neglected and untold. And yet – when we read the horrendous and painful episodes from Leah's personal experiences during the Holocaust as part of the entire spectrum of her life, we are able to understand Leah, and the millions of others who perished and who survived, in a much more complete and insightful manner. The intricate tapestry that Menucha Meinstein has woven out of Leah Roth's life story enlightens the reader with historical perspective and opens a door to the beginning of deeper understanding.

We have entered a new era in education about the Holocaust. As important as it is to learn about the suffering and the deaths of the 6 million Jews who were killed during World War II, it is time that we also begin to learn more about their lives before that war. What we are really mourning on Holocaust Remembrance Day is the loss of a large and vibrant community of Jews who enriched European life for 1,000 years and created a legacy that informs Jewish life to this day.

"My Eyes Looking Back at Me" is the portrait of an era; it is the story of one woman, strong and wise, whose spirit will touch and inspire every reader. This book has the potential to be an invaluable tool in a renewed approach to education for our time.

**Joseph Lebovic, Ph.D. (h.c.) Humanitarian and Philanthropist -
Toronto, Canada**
President, Lebovic Enterprises, Ltd.

BILD Lifetime Achievement Award; Joseph and
Wolf Lebovic Jewish Community Campus

*Anyone who wants to know anything about the Holocaust should read
Menucha Meinstein's "My Eyes Looking Back at Me," a page-turner, a tear
jerker; a true Kafka-like story so true that it couldn't be written as fiction.
It's so good you can't make one part better than another.*

*I am Leah Cik Roth's first cousin and the second oldest Survivor of the
Adler-Lebovic family. I was there. I grew up in the same pre-war town of
Brustury, Czechoslovakia as Leah, and I also survived the Holocaust. This
book contains genuine, firsthand information.*

*Poverty was even more severe than Leah remembers. Though the third
most influential family of Brustury, we were able to have meat only once
a week. We ate regular bread only two or three times a week; otherwise we
were lucky if we had cornbread. Jews went barefoot to beg for food in nearby towns. Poverty was so severe that the Cheder (boy's religious school),
could not afford to rent a room for classes, so we moved the class from
house to house: We had to bring our own firewood to the homes for heat.*

*Now I am grateful to be a successful businessman in Toronto, support-
ing a broad spectrum of Jewish humanitarian causes.*

**Arnold Mittelman, National Jewish Theater Foundation,
Coral Gables, FL**
President & Producing Artistic Director |
Holocaust Theater International Initiative

November 4, 2014

To those who care and those who need to care.

*I write in praise of "My Eyes Looking Back at Me, Insight Into a Survi-
vor's Soul", Lived by Survivor Leah Cik Roth and Told by Menucha Meinstein. Caring people of all ages will benefit anew by reading this remarkable
story of Leah Roth's courage, will, tenacity and hope told inspirationally by
Menucha Meinstein. Together they have created a manuscript that is truly
Theater of the Mind. It is impossible not to comprehend the images and moments in this survivor journey that portrays why we all must never under-
estimate the power of the human spirit and its capacity for hope.*

*I urge all to read its pages and learn its timeless lessons. Thank you
wonderful Leah for trusting Menucha and us with your humanity.*

Maurice Ostro, OBE, KFO, Prime Minister's Holocaust Commission
Vice-Chairman, Council of Christians and Jews - UK

London, England, January 27th, 2014

Today is Holocaust Memorial Day in the UK, the date which commemorates the anniversary of the liberation of Jews from the Nazis' biggest concentration camp at Auschwitz, from which Leah is amongst a very small number of Survivors.

I sit to write these comments after returning from an event in 10 Downing Street that our Prime Minister David Cameron hosted to announce the establishment of a Holocaust Commission to which I hope I can contribute as the son and son-in-law of Survivors. In our meeting, the Chief Rabbi touchingly explained to the Prime Minister why in the Torah there is both an injunction to 'remember' (Zachor) Amalek- the tribe who wished to kill the young Jewish nation escaping Egypt, and also an injunction 'not to forget' (Al Tishkach) what Amalek did. This seems superfluous but they express two critical messages. 'Never forget' can be accomplished by reading a history book about the Holocaust. To 'remember' one must engage in some positive action that is more than just an intellectual understanding. The Chief Rabbi's message was that we must also ensure that future generations must be motivated to make this a better world, one where the ugly spectre of hatred and persecution must be banished. This is why reading Leah's story is a must-read, for to be moved to action one needs to be moved emotionally.

Although not a historian, living amongst Survivors has educated me in many of the facts about WWII and the Holocaust. In spite of this, reading Leah's story has been eye opening, sometimes heartbreaking and other times inspiring. Leah's memories and Menucha's narrative enable the reader to make a personal connection that could otherwise be tragic but dry and brings them alive with the colour of emotion. It is this potent mix of personal perspective and historical detail that makes this such a powerful narrative.

Having spent the last days reading her incredible story, and then speaking tonight to Survivors of the Holocaust and also to Survivors of genocides from Rwanda and Cambodia, I am struck by the similarities in their experiences as they are from different times, continents and cultures. In their outlook, I heard the same comment made in different ways and in widely differing accents but all with the same message. They shared in common the determination to look forward, to be positive and to hope for a better day. It is inspirational to hear how despite all their adversities and against all odds, they never gave up and never gave in. The power of such personal testimonies cannot be underestimated and can serve to inspire coming generations with the message of hope and the importance of understanding and tolerance.

Technology, transport and the increasingly interconnected world that we live in requires people of all faiths, cultures, races and nationalities to be able to live together in peace and harmony. The more people who read "My Eyes Looking Back at Me," the better chance we have of avoiding horrible conflicts and of sensitizing people to the importance of accepting people with all their differences. Perhaps more importantly, it will serve to show those who feel overwhelmed in their personal issues, the power of positivity. If Leah and her fellow Survivors could move on to productive lives despite all their terrible adversities, how can we not do the same when challenged by life's misfortunes?

Wendy Reiss Rothfield, MSW, LCSW - Aventura, FL

I have read "My Eyes Looking Back at Me", a harrowing story of Leah Roth's odyssey; an engaging historical testimony of an innocent child has brilliantly captured the essence of Leah's young life from childhood to womanhood into maturity.

I was impressed with Leah's innate, intrinsic intelligence and courage against horrific odds. She was a child who had to make decisions quickly, and somehow manages to overcome monumental obstacles and barriers and manages to survive the inferno, the Holocaust.

Once in Palestine she begins a new real life. Leah emerges into a viable caring human being. She makes friends, feels the joy of freedom and close relationships, and marries. Her natural tendencies to be kind, empathic and genuine emerge and life begins anew in spite of all the atrocities she endured.

Leah and her progeny are the victors, not the vanquished. She and her husband had two children who are the progeny of Leah and her beloved, deceased husband. Hitler and his Reich are dead and the shame and stain of his insanity will live on forever.

This story is a testimony of historical and personal endurance that must be told again and again.

Roberta Shapiro, M.ED., LCSW, NBCCH, Author - Miami Beach, FL
Creator and author, "The Calming Collection"

"My Eyes Looking Back at Me" is a truly amazing work, an act of love, combined with exquisite writing. And the story behind the writing of this book is almost as amazing as the story contained within; the story of how

Menucha Meinstein and Leah Cik Roth met, collaborated, and how Menucha turned Leah's rough-hewn, untold story into a powerful work of art. And how, through the process, the relationship transformed into an incredibly strong bond.

Through our mutual love of writing, I had long shared a relationship with Menucha, but the first time I met Menucha and Leah together, I was struck by the level of connection between the two. They were like a mother/ daughter, or maybe a mother and daughter who were also the closest of friends. Such a strong bond was forged between them during the writing of this book, as if they had been brought together by a Divine hand for the telling of this tragic, powerful story.

The writing in this book is incredible. At times it reminds me of Isaac Bashevis Singer, the Yiddish Nobel Prize winner, at times of the beautiful prose of Elie Wiesel. The immediacy of the writing really pulls you into Leah's tragic but ultimately uplifting story right from the start, as you take this harrowing journey and face her pain, her struggles, her sorrow. This is a very important book, for adolescents as well as adults. In the vast amount of Holocaust books written, "My Eyes Looking Back at Me" stands out, not only for the beauty and clarity of the writing, but for how it finds an indelible mark on the reader's heart.

Kenneth Treister, Architect, Sculptor, and Author - Winterhaven, FL
"A Sculpture of Love and Anguish," The Holocaust Memorial;
Miami Beach, Florida, S.p.i. Books, Copyright ©1993

"My Eyes Looking Back at Me" is a moving and poignant story of an unbelievable and horrific event in human history, one that has to be told and retold by Survivors like Leah, so that the world will know and never forget.

The Holocaust that Leah witnessed was a unique event in the long and perilous history of mankind. There have been many wars rife with the tragedy of death and mass extermination but never before has a single race, group, religion or civilization been marked for total extermination.

I hope that the slogan..."never again" will not be an empty slogan as Israel seems alone as it faces an evil Iran.

Your visit to the Memorial, described in Chapter 26, "Activism," is well written, moving, poignant and sad. I will remember it, for it reinforces my original commitment to make the Memorial a sacred place.

Peter Weisz , Peter Weisz Publishing - Boca Raton, FL

I spent the past few days engrossed in the pages of your very powerful and well-crafted manuscript, "My Eyes Looking Back at Me; Insight into a Survivor's Soul." Since my own family — including my grandmother and 70+ other relatives, arrived to Auschwitz from Hungary at the same time as Leah — where they all perished (z"l) — Leah's story resonated very deeply in my heart. While reading your words, I felt as if I were, in some ways, re-reading the Gerda Klein masterpiece: "All But My Life."

Permit me to express my words of appreciation for the "mitzvah" you have performed by producing this manuscript. As Rabbi Klein writes in his eloquent introduction, so many survivors will soon disappear without having left their stories recorded. You have made sure that Leah is not among them. For that, I feel that I, and the Jewish people, owe you a debt of gratitude. "Yasher Koach."

The Reverend Dr. Priscilla Felisky Whitehead, Minister Emerita - Bal Harbour, FL
The Church by the Sea (United Church of Christ)

Leah Cik Roth's remarkable story in "My Eyes Looking Back at Me" is a welcome addition to the efforts to personalize the overwhelming magnitude of an evil that resulted in the loss of some six million lives. By now, most have heard of the world's promises to "never forget." By committing ourselves to remember, we all become guardians of those memories of suffering and death because they become shared memories. But it is hard for most of us who were not touched personally by the evils of the Holocaust to grasp how it penetrated everyday life for both those whose lives were taken and those who survived. All of the victims were (or are) real human beings filled with very human hopes, dreams, and loves. Leah's willingness to draw deeply and honestly from the well of her life, offering details including its joys and its pain, helps to put a face on impersonal statistics. By finally sharing her own story from the wisdom gained over almost nine decades of life, she enables others to enter into the pain and ongoing history of her family during the Holocaust within the wider context of the world and a unique biblical people going back millennia.

I say that as a Christian because for us, and other non-Jews, Leah's life serves as a sober reminder that the horrors of the Holocaust happened before our eyes, as well, even if not in our families. Although many were unaware of Hitler's determination to eradicate a people, others chose to avert their eyes; sadly, at times those others, along with even some of the perpetra-

tors, were people who claimed to follow a faith we share, but whose behavior violated even the most basic Christian tenets and the example of Jesus Himself.

So the Holocaust is - or should be - our story, too. Leah's very personal recollections that have had a lifetime of impact upon her and others can now help to provoke our reflection about how seemingly good people can remain silent in the face of such unspeakable treatment of fellow human beings.

Leah's courage reminded me that many who suffered found solace in their faith and in the words of the fourth verse of the 23rd psalm we all revere: Yea, though I walk through the valley of the shadow of death, I will fear no evil: for thou art with me. Now I pray that those same words, along with the inspiration of Leah's life, will provide strength and courage to many in the future who will be willing to stand up and speak out for what is right so that Leah's story need never be another young woman's experience, ever. In this way we honor and value Leah's having survived to share with us her life, as well as to assure those who were not so fortunate that their deaths have, indeed, helped teach the world a lesson about what can happen when we do not remain vigilant and true to our highest and best selves as all children of God.

About the Author

Drawn to working with the elderly since she was a teen in Seattle, Menucha Meinstein volunteered at hospitals and old age homes. After retiring to Miami, armed with an M.A. in Psychology from Antioch University, she developed a technique of self-guided therapeutic journaling, *Soul-Writing,* to nurture optimism and resilience. She used the technique in a Chai Lifeline class for mothers of medically fragile children.

Photo credit: Mark Diamond (mark@diamondimages.com)

Menucha participates in the Para-Chaplaincy Volunteer Program of the Greater Miami Jewish Federation (GMJF) in collaboration with Jewish Community Services, and utilized her *Soul-Writing* skills to work with a Holocaust survivor wishing to write a memoir. Menucha, paired with Leah Czik Roth, began working on fashioning Leah's compelling history.

Through the writing experience over these last four years of storytelling, recording and crafting, all done in the Aventura, Florida home of Menucha and her husband, Eddie, Leah became such a constant and beloved presence, they invited her to move in with them.

As Leah's biographer, Menucha is the driving force for the publication and promotion of *My Eyes Looking Back at Me: Insight Into a Survivor's Soul.* Together they are deeply involved in cultivating Holocaust awareness to students and adults through educational programs in the Miami area.

Menucha has participated in a myriad of programs that provide support to the elderly, the sick and the bereaved. She volunteers with Bikur Cholim and Chevra Kadisha Societies, and participates on the (GMJF) Mishkan Miami Leadership Council. She is a member of the South Florida International Press Club, and a founding member of Aventura Authors.

Notes

Notes

Notes